A Word for the Day: Reflections

Don Talafous, O.S.B.

A Liturgical Press Book

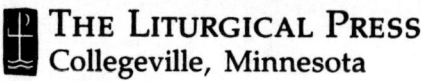

Cover design by David Manahan, O.S.B.

Copyright © 1992 by The Order of St. Benedict, Inc., Collegeville, Minnesota. All rights reserved. No part of this book may be reproduced in any form or by any means, electronic or mechanical, including photocopying, recording, taping, or any retrieval system, without the written permission of The Liturgical Press, Collegeville, Minnesota 56321. Printed in the United States of America.

2   3   4   5   6   7   8   9

Library of Congress Cataloging-in-Publication Data

Talafous, Don, 1926–
   A word for the day : reflections / Don Talafous.
     p. cm.
   ISBN 0-8146-2096-5
   1. Devotional calendars—Catholic Church. 2. Catholic Church-
-Prayer-books and devotions—English. I. Title.
BX2182.2.T35 1992
242'.2—dc20   92-19449
                                                                                        CIP

Contents

Preface 5

Daily Reflections

January	7
February	37
March	66
April	96
May	126
June	156
July	186
August	218
September	250
October	281
November	313
December	344

Preface

The chameleon, according to the story, went crazy trying to adjust to a Scotch plaid. And the person who tries to be everything to everyone easily ends up being nothing to anyone. This book of reflections must have its limitations, no matter what broad appeal I have tried to give it. I cannot expect it to appeal to everyone.

But I do hope it will be of some interest to young men and women, college age and beyond. Too, I hope it will have some appeal for lay people in general, married or single. Much of my academic and monastic life has been spent living among college age students and attempting to address them in class and in pastoral ways. My hope is that this experience has left some worthwhile effects.

These daily reflections are meant to be hopeful and encouraging. While what I have to say is firmly rooted in the Christian faith, I have tried to avoid simple repetition of traditional language with the hope of gaining more attention for what are basically some old insights.

Those who are willing to read this book should be willing to share the author's belief—in the words of an ancient saying—that those who live near the gods (the Church, religion) feel free to joke about them. Or put another way, confidence in the Christian message means that one does not think it is so fragile that it cannot endure some joshing or a light touch, let alone criticism. "It is the heart that is not yet sure of its God that is afraid to laugh in His presence" (George MacDonald).

These reflections follow in a loose way the seasons of the year and those of the Christian year. Each day's words try to provide one thought or attitude developed to a limited degree with the hope that it will serve as a springboard for further thought and a helpful motif for the day.

I have no illusions that this book will be read under big city bridges by homeless people huddled around an oilcan fire or by the kind of people who fly across the continent for lunch. My readers, I suspect, will be comfortable, middle-class people, not personally very experienced in persistent hardship or close to constant suffering and deprivation. I do expect that they will have, at some time, brushes with pain, illness, even terminal illness and tragedy, but generally they are among the happier and materially blessed of this world.

Most of what I write, I hope, will be of interest or value to a variety of Christians. A full appreciation of the life and message of Jesus Christ depends on and profits from the insights and experience of all sorts of Christians.

My thanks to Sr. Dolores Schuh C.H.M. for very helpful suggestions and editing.

January 1

All of us are a bit like our favorite team in a losing streak. We have to hope and be willing to begin again, often many times, despite a disappointing record in some area or other of our life. Hermann Hesse writes in a poem: "At life's each call the heart must be prepared to take its leave and to commence afresh courageously / and with no hint of grief submit itself to other and newer ties. / A magic dwells in each beginning / and protecting us it tells us how to live." What has been, the old and routine, Jesus and his Spirit tell us, need not be; the Holy Spirit can blow up a surprise.

With age and experience we tend not to look for surprises, rather to accept ourselves as we are with all our quirks, no matter how uneasily others may accept all this in us. And it's true, there are some pretty set and granite-like structures in all of us that seem unlikely to change significantly. There are elements to accept. But more important as we begin a new year is that we be open to the possibility of something new, to the likelihood that the Spirit can improve and change us where it counts in our hearts, in our loves, in our faith and hope.

Dwelling on the past and its failures serves no purpose. A despair weighed down by past disappointments only cripples, blocks all hope, all change. It closes us to any progress or improvement; it excludes grace because it expects nothing. We've all failed and had to begin again in many things. We probably sank or came close to it the first time we tried to swim. I read somewhere that the famous Babe Ruth, though he ultimately hit 714 home runs, struck out 1,330 times.

Who are we to give up because the first twenty, the first thirty, the first sixty years have had their unsatisfying and disappointing aspects? Success itself for the follower of Christ consists in never giving up, in always hoping and trusting.

January 2

Often the interest in the miraculous seems to be motivated by a desire to find Christ somewhere so dramatically (on the side of an oil tank, on a refrigerator door, in a weeping statue) that we forget about finding him in the less exceptional spots, in other words, in human beings who are poor, sick, abandoned, shelved. When we localize Christ this way, it often seems to be an excuse for no longer searching for him elsewhere. Instead, we sit or even kneel at this spot, lighting some candles and feeling that we have him cornered, in a sense. This is all easier than visiting the hospital, changing the bed for the sick person, taking time from our aerobics or tennis to push a wheelchair.

There is probably some of the same danger, even, in attention to the presence of Christ in the Eucharist. Historically it has happened that Christians very devoted to his presence in the bread were capable of being quite forgetful about his presence in the suffering and oppressed around them. They could genuflect and kneel before the Eucharist and not be unsettled about their slaves or the torture of fellow human beings.

But there is also a built-in protection against this in the Eucharist—if we pay attention to it. In this sacrament (as in all the others) Christ is present in something very ordinary, everyday bread. He is before us there, not in the clouds or a blinding bit of fireworks in the sky or in some awesome voice from outer space. The point of Jesus becoming present in something so ordinary as bread is to remind us that he is present in all of this routine and undramatic daily life that we so often wish to escape. Part of our happiness is tightly bound up with recognizing and learning to love his presence in the ordinary, the daily responsibilities we can't escape. That is were Jesus is.

January 3

The wandering artist-poet Goldmund in a novel by Hermann Hesse entitled *Narcissus and Goldmund* is frightened away from settling down by what he sees as a drying up of people who have done that. Although he is interested in art and woodcarving, he finds the settled, proper life of the master woodcarver for whom he works to be stuffy and deadening; he feels the master has become a machine, a timid, unadventuresome "nerd." He sees the master's commitment resulting in a life of cautious security, predictability, and dullness. He may have a point. Possibly too many of us take all the juice out of life by making sure that we always know what's going to happen next and that everything is provided for and in its place.

But to do anything lasting with our talent, our passions, our fire, our imagination, requires that we join them to some very everyday elements. The imagination of an artist or a musician has to have some truck with, in the one case, notes, staff, sharps and flats, and in the other, with paints, materials, light, and so forth, in order to put into a communicable form the vision that has seized it. The limits imposed by a poetic form, the fourteen lines of a sonnet for instance, have helped people like Shakespeare produce unforgettable lines. Happiness, productivity, accomplishment, all depend, to some extent, on accepting and using the everyday material of our craft. The seeming limits of commitment turn the raw, random energy of our life into a recognizable and memorable melody.

Our Lord did not become a generic human; he committed himself voluntarily to a particular, little-known people, to a carpenter's family, in a land measuring fifty by one hundred miles. He accepted the devotion of some and the ill will of others even to death at their hands, trusting the will and love of his Father. Faithfulness and commitment—to this place, these people, this job, these responsibilities—can lead us, too, to a more intense, larger life, can bring us something unimagined and more gratifying than we could ever receive if we remained uncommitted.

January 4

There is much more to appreciate in God's world than we ever get around to. But, why shouldn't we at least appreciate and praise more? For one thing we could broaden our range of interests to include more than sports, suds, self; to be willing to see and hear more than the Simpsons and the NFL. Instead of wasting "the days of our lives" before a TV set, why not, as long as health and energy allow, expose our minds, hearts, and bodies to some of the untried and more demanding possibilities around us? Help those who are physically limited, go to a dance concert, a play, a talk, take a reflective walk, learn some new skill, look at nature more closely.

At every Mass the bread and wine are referred to as "what earth has given and human hands have made." A description of all there is to love and appreciate: nature, the world, and what wonderful things human beings have done with them. Way beyond just avoiding the abuse of creation is trying to use it well with genuine respect and honesty, with appreciation. This is an area where many of us need to push, to step on the accelerator. We don't lose or imperil our youth, our energy, our life, but only enhance it by using it generously. Even our daily work can be a profound source of satisfaction if done with care and self-respect. As the old saw has it, if your work bores you, try doing it well. It isn't just that some have all the luck, but so often it's just that they take more initiative. We postpone not just responsibility but life itself by vegetating.

Our gifts only blossom, become worthy of God who gave them their potential when we develop and use them. Putting that off should scare us. What are we waiting for? Many of the great accomplishments of human beings have been done by comparatively young people. The great composer Franz Schubert left over one thousand pieces of music and died at thirty-one; the artist Rafael was dead at thirty-seven; Mozart at thirty-five; Therese of Lisieux at twenty-four; poets Byron at thirty-six, Shelly at thirty, and Keats at twenty-six. We all know other unsung examples.

The point is not to terrorize ourselves with the thought of early death, but to realize how much can be done—now—

during the years of our vigor and health. Nor does it mean we should put our nose so close to the grindstone that we leave no place for friends and fun. It does suggest that we demand more quality of ourselves, put more pride and energy into our work and recreation.

We should feel propelled by health, energy, talent, time, to go beyond mediocre limits, to do more and be more with the gifts we have. Give to God what is God's, our talent and time.

January 5

The readings and prayers of Epiphany circle around the theme that in Jesus the light has come into the world. One prayer asks that the saving light of Jesus arise anew each day in our own hearts, that our lives be brightened by that same light daily. For the believer, Jesus is the light of the world, "my light and my salvation," the sun that brightens my existence, that sheds light on the misery and mystery of human life.

Part of the mission of Christians is to spread further that light, to reflect it in a sense, to mirror it so that more of human life is touched by its illuminating and encouraging power. All this can be done by those who apply Christian thought to government, to human society, to education, who work to incorporate Christian sensitivity into the complexities of human social life. A very important and difficult task.

But we also do it by bringing that light to the lives of family, friends, relatives, associates, or fellow workers who are often, to varying degrees, lost in the darkness of our world. They may lack hope or courage or insight and purpose, often simply the nerve to live generously and joyfully. Our belief and hope in Jesus should bring with it the willingness and the desire to share it with others, ordinarily not by preaching or condescending advice but by the simply human acts of kindness and concern.

Let's write that letter or, more likely, those letters today; make that call; at least plan or, better yet, make that visit today, now. Send that surprise; do that unexpected but helpful deed for the sick relative, the aging friend, the devastated widow or spouse.

Let that saving light not just arise in my heart each day to warm and brighten my own life but to warm and brighten the lives of all around me.

January 6

"Tears, idle tears, I know not what they mean." These lines taken from a poem and out of context, I'm sure, express what many in our society and stiff-upper-lip civilization think. We read of the tears of Scriptural figures or even the advice of the saints to pray for the "gift" of tears. St. Benedict counsels praying to God with tears of sorrow. And it all strikes us as overdone, maybe just another example of that Latin or Mediterranean piety. We seem more likely to be impressed by stolid immobility than by ready tears.

Yet the ability to shed some tears, to be moved so much, testifies to something good. For example, a friend in his twenties writes, "I spent four weeks at home during December and January. The time was good for Mom and me, as we found each other most comforting in talking about Dad (who died some months earlier). Being home at Christmas brought out new tears which I feel were helpful for me." Tears mean that we are letting our hearts be softened, that we are remaining sensitive to pain and sorrow in ourselves and in others, maybe even to beauty, that we prize tenderness. Maybe we should be more worried about becoming too hard than about too many tears. Be comforted, all you who weep at the movies.

Since we seem to be so remote from tears over sin—a common theme in earlier spirituality—shouldn't we at least let the phenomenon of tears awaken in us more appreciation for the passion, sorrow, and pain that produce them, for the sensitivity that allows them to flow? We so often tell others in trouble, a real cry will do you good. Maybe we should be a bit more concerned not to let this same sign of feeling dry up in our lives. If we're ashamed of doing it at the office or at the cocktail party or in the locker room, maybe we should at least allow it in the privacy of our own home or at the movies. Maybe every home or apartment needs a crying room.

January 7

We may not be hunted down by an envious king or be fleeing from an army of enemies, but the psalms (in which all of this and much more is verified) are prayers with which we Christians should be familiar. "Psalm" is another name for a piece of literature usually not much more than a page or two in length, often less, that combines the features of prayer, hymn, and poem. The Book of Psalms is shared by Jews and Christians. It has been for almost two thousand years the official prayer book of the Church, used by religious orders and priests every day. The psalms are prayers of people in distress, illness, near death; people brimming over with thanksgiving, trust, joy; people sorry for failures and people trusting in God. Occasionally the context of the psalm is something very remote from our lives, but ordinarily the writers felt the same things that we do in relation to God, the world, our neighbors. Occasionally there will be sentiments that Christ has taught us to go beyond, sentiments of vengeance, cursing, and the like. But amid even these strange and uncongenial verses there are gems expressing trust in God, confidence, joy, faith. We should be familiar enough with them to choose a few we can comfortably pray and use ourselves. And in them we find phrases that can serve as themes, refrains for our daily life.

For example, Psalm 31:25 is a strong, confident verse that could give us a bracing and hopeful approach to our daily life, its responsibilities, and even its problems. "Take courage and be stouthearted, all you who hope in the Lord." Presuming we have some faith and trust in God, weak and changeable as it may be, it would help to put it into such a formulation and to repeat it throughout the day, to let it sing and soar in our heart. "Take courage and be stouthearted, all you who hope in the Lord." I am strong and full of courage—as I face that difficult person in the office, that painful confrontation with son or mother, that onerous job or task, the weight of feelings of depression and sadness brought on by the sufferings of friends and family—I am strong and full of courage, because I hope in you, Lord; I know you are with me.

January 8

Jesus directs some of his harshest words at people of his time for the importance they gave to various human traditions or practices that had been added to the demands of their religion. Jesus was careful to observe the faith of his ancestors, but he had no time for man-made rules that were like bricks or stones added to our backpacks. These human practices, traditions, were often mechanical ways of fulfilling the law that actually missed the point of the law.

When traditions come between us and love of God or neighbor, there is something seriously wrong. While traditions are important and even necessary, there are limitations to their value. Some belong to ancient Palestine or sixth-century Rome and make no sense in Minneapolis or Newcastle. Accordingly, some traditions disappear or are abandoned. Some are finally seen as positively unacceptable. Serious criticisms by outsiders, for instance, made Hindus drop the custom that a widow should be burned on her husband's funeral pyre. The separation of men and women at Mass—women on one side, men on the other—prevalent in many places into this century, has faded from the scene, deservedly, most would say.

Some traditions or collections of them can become simply oppressive and time consuming. Who would accept as a good tradition that women must always wash the dishes? A tradition of absolute silence in the church might well give way to some conversation and greeting, some expression of the loving community that supposedly gathers around the altar. Our needs and understanding change, why not our practices?

We should look at the traditions and practices, even merely personal ones of long standing, in our daily life. Do they help? Do they not only aid convenience but also forward concern for others? Or are they like walls and barriers that fortify us against others, against the unexpected, the new, the opportunity to be more generous? Even an accustomed time for prayer (a kind of tradition) could be an excuse for avoiding serious responsibilities to others. Somewhere between idolizing every tradition and rejecting every tradition is an attitude that rejoices in traditions that help us serve God and love others.

January 9

A cold or the flu, a spell of rainy weather, all slow us down, may make us abandon some of our customary practices (jogging, exercise of any kind, our hectic schedules, even our work), and what are we left with but the necessity of sitting, resting, doing nothing, as we say often so abjectly.

At least the workaholics and the very energetic among us will say this. Others may see it as a wonderful opportunity. These latter would agree with the fellow who wrote me that he had a good job with a large firm and for the most part enjoyed it. "However, I still feel best suited for a life of leisure."

Sickness or enforced leisure provides us with an unavoidable opportunity for thinking, reflecting, and for doing this in a different state of mind than our usual one. Without asking for it, we have given to us the advantage of a perspective we would not otherwise discover or be able to imagine. Instead of looking at everything from the viewpoint of power, health, vigor, and vitality, we can look—indeed we must look—at it more as much of the world does: from the standpoint of weakness, powerlessness, unasked-for idleness. We can see what life must be like for the unemployed, the incapacitated. And it certainly should make us appreciate more our usual state with all its advantages.

Illness or some such inhibiting situation gives us a slower and wider way of looking at things. Just to view the world without being in a rush is itself a favor. It can make us question the value of some of our ordinary activity, to see it at least as of more limited value than we do when the world's progress seems to depend on us staying in there. We may be led to see how relative is our contribution, is anyone's, how the world can even go on without us being there every moment. A humbling and realistic thought.

January 10

Prayer certainly means asking for help in our needs and concerns. All of us, even if only in the most desperate situations, have prayed for help or "been driven" to pray for it. And prayer is for asking, is the cry of a child, really, who knows that someone capable and more powerful can help. But there must be other types of prayer in our life, too. In the Our Father, given us in the Gospels (Matt 6:9-13; Luke 11:2-4), Jesus models for us the priorities of prayer. First we praise God (hallowed be thy name); secondly, we ask that God's will be done; thirdly, we ask for our own needs, our "daily bread"; fourthly, we ask forgiveness of our sins.

When we don't have needs pressing on us or are not aware of them, we easily tend not to pray. We're contented, things are going well. We really don't feel any need for prayer. But as the first two kinds of prayer indicate, prayer is more than just requesting; it is praise (include thanksgiving), and it is an acceptance of God's will, a recognition of God's loving concern and kind foresight.

If we think for a moment of our relation to God on the model of our relation to another person, we can see praise and acceptance as vital elements in that the relationship must be kept alive by the ordinary courtesy of communication, by words of praise, consolation, encouragement, love, interest, and also by signs of respect and love. Mass or worship on Sunday is in many ways primarily this. It is the basic minimum in maintaining relations with God. Prayer of any type, no matter how personal or private, is the same: a recognition of the existence and closeness of a friend, father, mother, one who loves us. We don't just speak to friends or call them or see them when we need a loan or to use their Toro for the afternoon. So, too, with God; we need to speak to, praise, to remember the Lord, even when we don't sense an awful need. We keep open communication and allow for God's intervention and influence on our thought and feelings.

January 11

Christianity is occasionally, I think, sold under false pretenses; some of the salespersons are guilty of deceptive advertising. They promise more than they or it can deliver. They promise health, success, financial security, and so on, all in exchange for trust in the Lord. Never mind that the Lord himself promised a share in his cross. They seem to prefer the attitude of some of the Old Testament writers, long before Christ, who believed (till experience showed them how wrong it was) that God always rewarded the good and faithful.

I think we need to remind ourselves more realistically that the following of Christ does not exempt us from ordinary human difficulty and suffering but gives us the strength and the vision to handle it. Following Christ is not some sort of brainwashing or drug that enables us to float above drudgery, weariness, misunderstanding, difficulty. It is a belief and teaching but, even more, a gift of strength through our union with Christ that enables us to share in his suffering, to endure and grow through the hardships of daily life. "It does not make life easy; rather it tries to make us great enough for life. It does not give us escape from life's burdens, but strength for meeting them when they come" (J. Christensen).

The following of Christ involves no instant cure or overnight transformation but the usually slow and discouraging path up the hill. In the example of the Lord himself falling beneath the weight of his cross we receive the hope and certainty that we, too, can get up each time and begin anew. And when the failure is something clearly our fault, it invites us to ask forgiveness and to begin again, assured that it has been given.

January 12

"It's the heart afraid of breaking that never learns to dance, / It's the dream afraid of waking that never takes the chance. / It's the one who won't be taken who cannot seem to give; / And the soul afraid of dying that never learns to live." The Gospel says that those who clutch their lives tightly, who wish to live in and for themselves will lose their lives, while those who use their lives for others and for God, who give them away with generosity, these will preserve and enhance them. This teaching seems so hostile to all that is important to us: discovering and developing ourselves, finding a good or better career or future, making money. Our efforts are all aimed at enriching ourselves by work, possessions, experience. But it is the paradox of life out of death that Jesus teaches. Only after his death, after the grain of wheat had died did the harvest come, did he begin to draw all things to himself. The mystery is at the heart of following him, yet nothing sounds crazier when put alongside all that the world and our education and culture say and demand.

We've heard other expressions of the same message and maybe nodded in agreement at "It is in giving that we receive." And we may see in some exceptional person how true it is that no life is so full as one that is empty of all self-seeking. It sounds beautiful; it's awesome to see; we're impressed. "It's the soul afraid of dying," we sing, "that never learns to live." And yet—can we live those words? We accept all this, I think, only off and on or maybe only after some rough experiences.

While we are working and praying to make this truth our own, there is one approach that might help ease us into it: trying to take ourselves lightly, with some humor. Some of the examples we see of self-important, deathly sober individuals should be enough to make us want to avoid that kind of seriousness. Mark Twain once described the type: "He was a solemn, unsmiling sanctimonious old iceberg that looked like he was waiting for a vacancy in the Trinity."

Doesn't losing one's self mean to take oneself, one's ego, this me, less ponderously? It means laughing at the self more often; not regarding every little problem or raw deal as cause for tears, anger, or litigation. Not all the events of life are material for grand opera or Greek tragedy; some of it may deserve to stay on the level of a light-headed sitcom. Why take everything so seriously? Is every effort of ours the greatest project to hit the planet since aspirin or the zipper? If we make ourselves, our feelings, our work, all of such importance that they cannot be questioned, criticized, or forgotten, isn't that close to saying that they are gods? What more do we give to God? We are sometimes so concerned not to be thought airheads that we end up being blockheads. "Lighten up," as students so easily tell their elders.

January 13

Part of the initiation of some young Hindus into their religion consists in having a religious guide or guru whisper in their ear a mantra. A mantra, as the Beatles and the Maharishi have taught much of the Western world, is a sacred formula, a word or phrase used for meditation. In Hinduism and Buddhism the practice persists to varying degrees. American rock stars of the 60s and 70s, following after various Eastern spiritual imports, have possibly helped some Christians to rediscover something similar that is very old in Christian tradition. Christian teaching has long had the notion of using a phrase or line, possibly from the psalms, as a theme, a focus for meditation and reflection. We take a phrase or word and come back to it repeatedly throughout the day because it helps focus our hearts, our spirits; it reminds us of a belief or conviction helpful to daily life.

Always an inspiring one to me, and possibly to some of you also, is this from Psalm 118:14: "My strength and courage is the Lord, and he has been my savior." For the sake of easy and prayerful repetition I would adapt the phrase, "The Lord is my strength, my courage, my Savior." I not only repeat it throughout the day within my heart but reflect on the implications, the meaning, the power, of these words. The Lord is my strength: in my weakness and fear, I rely on the Lord, I am confident. The Lord is my Savior—from all that threatens now or in the future, from much in the past. The Lord is and has been my Savior, has saved me, delivered me, will save and deliver me from all that is frightening and fearful today and all days. "My strength, my courage, my Savior." Alleluia.

January 14

Following Christ's teaching, one of the primary requests we Christians make is that God "deliver us from evil." Not from matter, the earth, this world, sex, or the body, but from evil, from what is bad. Yet there has been a strong tendency even among Christians to blame the body for all the evil that happens. We call it our lower nature. Over the centuries Catholics and other Christians have given the "sins of the flesh," of the body, great importance. That part of Christian theology that deals with sexual behavior has gone into great detail about such issues as adultery, premarital sex, homosexuality, impure thoughts and actions, pornography, and birth control. Reflecting the Catholicism of fairly recent times, someone has written: "There were moments in my education . . . when I had the distinct impression that the entire point of the creation of the sun, the moon, and stars, the journeys of the patriarchs, the pageant of the popes, etc., was to stamp out smooching." Along with this has gone very often a slighting of sins that could rightly be thought of as coming from much deeper within us: hatred, greed, aggression. As a result, Christian thought has often been far behind on such matters as war and violence, world poverty, starvation, injustice, and slavery.

To correct that imbalance, we need only read the Gospels with an open mind to discover that it is not the "flesh" that is the main concern of the writers or of Christ, whose teaching they report. There we find something else. The greater part of Christ's moral teaching (teaching about the rightness or wrongness of behavior) in the Gospels is about the abuse of power, self-exaltation, trust in self, and the misuse of or dangers of wealth. Putting our security or hope in these, in self, power, and wealth is the object of the most frequent denunciations in the sacred books. Any words of the Lord about sexual morality are few and far between.

There is no way we can honestly read the Gospels without being struck by how the whole life of Christ was an overturning of the values that dominated his society and still dominate ours: power and wealth.

Lord, in my own way I put my trust in self, power, and wealth only too often. Help me trust in the powerlessness that led you to the cross—and beyond, to resurrection.

January 15

Near the beginning of the film *Butch Cassidy and the Sundance Kid*, the latter is whipping an opponent at cards. The opponent, itching for the first gun draw, asks Sundance: "To what do you attribute your great success at cards?" With a poker face, the Kid replies reverently, "Prayer."

While the words are obviously said tongue-in-cheek, they can typify one way in which we are tempted to turn God's order around or upside down. Instead of praying to God because God is God and because we owe God everything, are thankful, have needs to plead for, want to express our trust and confidence—instead of all that, the typically human temptation is to use God for our purposes. Instead of God being our end, our final purpose, we want to use God, prayer, religion, to forward our projects, our greed, our desires, here and now.

TV preachers, thousand-dollar weekend seminars all promise that believing in Jesus or religion or faith or prayer will bring a killing on the market, a reduction of tension, a win on the hockey rink, or even something so religious sounding as peace of mind. Worship, prayer, God, are valued either for their tranquilizing effect, a sort of nonchemical Valium, or for the motivational push they give us, a spiritual Benzedrine. Success through God, through prayer, through faith.

While many of the effects sought from worship, from God and faith, are good in themselves, it is the matter of using God or thinking we can use God to get them that turns everything upside down. God is not for our convenience, at our disposal, but meant to be the one in whom we trust, whom we are bound to love and honor for all we have received, from whom we expect ultimately our fulfillment. In the meantime we need more trust, more confidence, more determination to put all into God's hands with less detailed prescription on our part about what *must* be done for us. The love of God creates happiness—true—but only if it does not seek its own happiness.

January 16

What is important? What is really vital, of lasting significance to me, for me, in my life? That may all sound like a "heavy trip," but it can be a liberating question. We can fruitfully come back to that kind of question every day, or maybe once a week, once a month.

Asked repeatedly and, therefore, in differing circumstances, the question can help us remove the stuff that isn't that important, at least see that it isn't worth our worry and anger. Such thinking can help us see particular pains and problems as less than life threatening, not worth turning all of our life and relationships sour.

One day we'll ask the question about our work in general or aspects of it. Another day, about the irritations or difficulties we think are caused by others in our lives. Or by the problems that haunt and punctuate any family or home, any existence. Once we put them in the spotlight for a while, some of these matters on which we spend so much energy and spirit will fade away, as they should. Seeing them this way does not necessarily mean just rejecting them. It means putting them in their proper place amid the realities of our life. Sometimes it will mean there is no place.

Life in any institution or organization, any society, whether it be a corporation, a church, a necessary committee, is never custom designed for me or you but for some general kind of human being who will belong to that group. Some aspects of it are undoubtedly and inevitably going to rub us the wrong way. Maybe it's simply a matter of recognizing that everything that happens in our life in these situations is not of the same importance, the same relevance. Why not use our reason to help us over time to evaluate matters accordingly and even bring our feelings and emotions to react accordingly, too? That may not be so easy but there is something that the mind, the reason, can usually do to help clear our perspective. Doing it often enough can give us a kind of freedom, a sense that we should have some control over these lesser and inconvenient elements. Our energies and spirit should be spent on the more important matters: God, my neighbor, love, faith.

January 17

Faith is one of those many-sided terms that come up again and again. Depending on our stance, it can be defined acceptably in a number of ways. In its most basic sense, it seems to be simply a willingness to be open to God's gift, God's word or message. Just a willingness to accept something from outside ourselves, a childlike attitude in many ways. Hence Jesus' commendation of the attitude of little children. Living as I write this in one of the world's largest cities and with some experience of several others, I am struck by how—at least in terms of our relation to others—big cities seem to produce in many people a sort of closed attitude. At least that is what one encounters on the street. It is a defensiveness, I think, that tells them to make sure that their faces and eyes leave no opening for others around them who may be a danger or who, in any case, are very hard to trust. Many put on an expressionless, unfocused look, which cannot be taken in any case as an invitation to a beggar, a confused person, or, above all, to someone who might use an opening to do you harm.

This is confirmed when one runs into or meets people from an entirely different background, set down in this city milieu. He or she tends to be very open-faced, smiling, inviting conversation and contact, even, of course, inviting abuse of this openness and friendliness. Others speak to them, ask them directions, start conversations, because it is obvious that it would be welcomed.

At its most minimal, our faith must be similar openness to what God has to say or ask. (I don't know whether it makes any difference whether you live in a town of thirty-five people or in Tokyo.) What counts is receptivity, willingness to receive, to learn, to be touched, moved, acted upon. Open us to your word, O Lord, to your presence around us.

January 18

One of the worst results of the strong separation of body and spirit, of dividing the human being into two such parts, has been the idea that there are two kinds (at least) of love. A spiritual (usually that means also unselfish, self-forgetting love that doesn't require expression in the body) and a bodily or carnal love (selfish, pleasure seeking, concerned only with what can be seen or touched). This is so familiar that many of us, I'm sure, would regard this as good, decent Christian teaching. But it really undervalues the body, this physical part of our existence, and is contrary to what Scripture teaches.

And how realistic is it? Can we really separate the two so easily and neatly? Doesn't what we call "spirit" enter into all of our loves and what we call "physical" or "body" also? Their interrelation is something science more and more confirms and that the Bible itself demands. The ancient Hebrews from whom the Old Testament comes and who form the background and family of Jesus himself had only one word for love: *ahava*. There was no effort to divide love into spiritual and physical, superior and inferior. Love was love. We'd do a lot for our following of Jesus if we didn't bother with distinguishing them either. Why not, as Jesus says, love God and neighbor with our whole strength, our whole self, our whole body, and skip trying to make these impossible distinctions, which only end up regarding some kinds of love as inferior. Love is love.

January 19

If you ever had to memorize the Ten Commandments you probably were a bit confused as to why the first one was about idolatry. As a kid you may have pictured people prostrate before idols like you see in the movies, some huge statue with a glowing gem in the forehead and fires burning before it. It never seemed a very relevant commandment. None of the neighbors seemed to be doing that; it certainly wasn't done in your house.

Nevertheless, throughout much of the Jewish Scriptures it is the first and most important commandment, and our Lord confirms that spot in the New Testament. In the Gospel of St. Luke, worship of wealth and possessions above all is fingered as the most devastating kind of idolatry. The rich man who builds more and more barns to store more grain and thereby increase his own security is censured for putting his trust in these things, for putting another god—security—in place of the true God. His sin is not that foreign to any of us who must, by necessity, have some concern about our future security. To avoid being reminded too much of this almost universal temptation, Christians have often preferred to make a lot of noise about the dangers of communism and pornography, crimes from which we believe we can more easily distance ourselves (or blame others).

And the Gospel, once we face its criticism of the worship of money, does not leave alone those of us who are in no danger of being millionaires. It isn't just the drive to increase wealth and the obsession with keeping it that is condemned. Wealth can obsess or taint the poorest among us, too, if, instead of tossing and turning all night worrying about losing our wealth, we toss and turn wondering how we can get more of it. Either way, it is a concern that comes between us and the first place owed to God.

Lord, despite the bills and my real needs (or imagined—I have a hard time distinguishing them), help me to keep money and wealth in perspective, to know as some of my friends say so well that "it's only money."

January 20

Idolatry in our days does not often seem to take the more picturesque forms we think of, such as worshiping golden calves, bulls, huge stone slabs, and the like. More often it is an unavowed but total devotion to money, success, prestige, self, or to some guru or evangelist promising instant and painless renovation. In the heyday of the cult of Chairman Mao in China, devotion to him took on all the features of idolatry. As one devotee put it: "We must study the works of President Mao each day. If we miss only one day the problems pile up. If we miss two days we fall back. If we miss three days we can no longer live" (Leech).

Since such cults obviously imitate or parody religion, maybe it is not out of the question for us to turn the tables and learn from them. Couldn't most of us take a page from the book of Mao and give Sacred Scripture, something we call the Word of God, some comparable attention and trust? St. Paul and the New Testament do speak of its transforming power.

While we may find the language of Mao's disciple exaggerated, we Christians need to do much more than we do to profit from the word of life, the Bible. Not every part of it is equally valuable and profitable for us (learning how David slaughtered his enemies may be of minimal help), but there is much that can provide the inspiration we need, help to transform mind and heart, to keep before us more continually the great goodness of God, who has loved us. Some reading and reflection of this nature every day should become a habit with us and a complementary nourishment to the Body and Blood of Christ we receive in the Eucharist.

January 21

The scene after Sunday Mass in some large parishes is a sad commentary on how we regard our worship. In some cases, the exit reminds one of the crowd entering a long-awaited concert by this month's top rock group; people are in danger of being trampled or, at the very least, facing severe competition in the parking lot. But bad as this may be, it may have its humorous side—if we can see it. Even more discouraging is the tendency to think that our obligation to worship God, to attend Mass, is over and we can return to ordinary life and forget it for another week.

There is a Quaker saying that goes: "When the worship is over, the service begins." When we have come together to thank God, to pray through Jesus Christ, to be united in Jesus to God and to each other, there still remains that we should demonstrate that ideal celebrated at Mass in the way we live and act. The test is how we treat our neighbors, how we conduct our daily affairs, how we face the problems and challenges of the world around us.

As the saying puts it, what should follow is "service." Like the Son of Man who came to serve, we, too, must see service as the implication of our worship. Now that I have spent this time, set aside this time, to worship God, I must show that it is real by my willingness to honor and serve the needs of all the members of this family, those with whom Jesus, in fact, has told us he identifies himself (Matt 25). As long we visit the sick, the elderly, care for the weak and the children, work for peace and harmony, help the naked and hungry—as long as we do any of these, we are continuing our worship. Worship may be over in the strict sense of the word, but it continues in service of all the others beloved of God.

January 22

Many very sentimental paintings and words have been inspired, if that's the word, by the story of Jesus and the children. "Unless you turn around and become like children, you will never enter the kingdom of Heaven" (Matt 18:1-5, 10). Yet the story itself, far from being sentimental, is the wrapping for a tough teaching that is contrary to all our usual instincts. It knocks some of our favorite words and concepts: achievement, getting ahead, advancement, self-reliance, and the like. Like the questioners in the Gospel who got the answer quoted above, our equally irrelevant question often is, Who is greatest? How do I get recognition, position, prestige? How do I get ahead of Jim or the rest of the people in the firm?

The most convincing commentators say that to be like little children means to recognize that the kingdom, God's reign in us, must come as a gift, that we have no right to it. We must relate to God as children to parents, as to the one who gives us what we need. The implication of this is the tougher aspect: we do not by ourselves achieve holiness. It doesn't come because we are such masterful take-charge types, such know-it-alls. Certainly at our job there is a place, a need, for competition and achievement, but this teaching reminds us that even something so necessary should not become a god, something for which we will sacrifice anything and anybody.

The whole point is to be more yielding, open, receptive, trusting, maybe even at times—forgive the word—passive. A blast like this against our self-sufficiency, our pride, our self-assertiveness, is something we should be able to endure at least for a few minutes today. After all, we probably spend most of our day, much of our week, trying to be achievers, assertive, take-charge types. There is little danger that most of us are going to lose the attitudes that inspire much of our activity. An invitation to be like "little children" is not all that threatening, is it?

January 23

Some preachers and religious writers today are, I suspect, a bit afraid of pushing prayer too much. I think the reason is that prayer can easily be taken by some as an excuse for doing nothing about bad conditions, just accepting what is or enduring what is unjust. By prayer we simply leave it all up to God and don't exert ourselves to better the situation. There is the belief and some evidence, too, that the poor and persecuted have been told at times to pray and accept unjust circumstances, with both the advice and the unjust circumstances coming from the same people.

The lesson of such famous stories in the New Testament as that of the Good Samaritan is that we are expected to do what we can to alleviate human misery. The lesson in Christ's many cures is the same. He doesn't simply tell the hurting and diseased to go away and pray, trust in God; he heals all who come to him. It can be presumed from his example and from his teaching that his followers are called to do the same.

But we are expected all the while to continue praying. Jesus himself is our great example. In Luke's Gospel he is pictured as praying before every new move, every important decision, and persevering in prayer even when things look hopeless. At the most desperate moment of his life, before his crucifixion, he prays in the garden to his Father asking that, if possible, he be spared this awful death. The answer, of course, is really no. Prayer must entail not just asking and hoping but a final trust in God.

Our immediate request for a change in the behavior of a daughter or a husband, a better job, a mini-van, whatever, may not get any obvious response. Our confidence must tell us that God who wants us to pray also knows finally what we need. Jesus did not receive freedom from death on the cross but he did receive resurrection, something unimaginably greater. In ways that theology and human thinking will probably never figure out, God hears and acts in response to prayer. The example of our Lord should keep us praying with trust and confidence.

January 24

Christian hope is rooted in what God is, who God is, not in what we have done or who we are. In order to hope, in other words, we do not need an impressive résumé in terms of our following of Christ: that is, I have not committed adultery, never robbed anyone, lied, cheated. Even if we do have a pretty clean record, in all honesty most of us would have to list a few redeeming faults. But the very central point in the teaching of Jesus, something dramatically highlighted once again for the Christian world by Martin Luther, is that we have every reason to hope. We hope not because we have done so splendidly but because God's love for us is there before we've done *anything*, and persists throughout, whatever we do.

It's not because we're okay that we have reason to hope for all good things but because God is loving in such an unlimited way. This central Christian belief supports the other notion of which we think all too rarely: that our salvation, any following of Christ on our part, depends less on gritting our teeth, hardening our jaw, and having a little backbone than it does on letting God's love come in and act. No matter how empty of meaning our life may seem, no matter how little others may esteem it or what we have done, no matter how little there is for us to show God (if God ever asked for that), God loves us and accepts us.

This is part of the really radical selflessness that Christianity requires: not that we by some extraordinary effort become selfless, models of selflessness, but that our attention and trust are so completely on God that self more and more ceases to be a concern.

Christian hope is rooted in what and who God is rather than in something so shaky and untrustworthy as who or what we are. That changes from hot to cold, from firm to feeble, from resolute to lazy as easily as we change clothes. Hope is there because God is a rock, a fortress, a stronghold, an ever-loving Father.

January 25

It hurts! To read the words that follow from someone who apparently is quite intelligent. Speaking with Billy Graham in a TV interview about conversion, Woody Allen says, "I'm open to it, and I'd be glad to have a go at it (with him). Sure, I'd love to be converted. Life, it seems to me, is much easier if you're a believer. You can always come up with easy answers."

Yet I suppose the serious misconception in his remarks may come less from any problem with Allen's intelligence than from what he sees and hears of religion, let us say, Christianity. It is presented often enough as a simple package for the sake of winning and keeping people, as providing all the answers: You must do this to be saved (baptism, some special formula like "I accept the Lord Jesus"); the world will end on December 31 at 11:59 P.M., 1999; you must believe what this authority has said on a particular issue (the person providing the answers has it down cold and clear). When it is presented in such a manner, oversimplifying our complex and difficult world, then it deserves suspicion and merits Allen's answer.

But the reality is that the Christian does not have all these simple, clear answers. The valley that Christians walk through is as dark as anyone else's (Ps. 23). But I have confidence in one who has loved us, *not* knowledge or certitude about the details. I must keep at my daily, boring, and difficult tasks sustained by that hope and trust but not accompanied by all sorts of tangible consolations and assurances. I believe and trust because of witnesses of the risen Christ, not because I have seen him risen.

To be a follower of Christ is not to follow some set of propositions that clarify all of life's problems but to allow oneself to be led by Christ through a life that is varied and overwhelming in its complexity and that remains obscure and incomprehensible. We believe that our leader lived through the same life—without any of the simple assurances that Allen speaks of—and rose again. We hope and trust in the same.

January 26

Is he a nice person or is he a Christian? That may be putting it in extreme form, but it is important to realize that while all Christians probably should be "nice" in our usual use of the word, still the two words are not the same. Acts 11:19-26 tells us that "it was in Antioch that the disciples were first called

Christians." (This Antioch is not in Ohio but in the southern part of present-day Turkey.) The "disciples," that is, those who learn from a teacher, came to be called Christians after the Christ they were learning from, the person they were following. The word "Christian" suffers a lot in its use today. For some in our part of the world it is almost synonymous with that bland and overused adjective "nice." And we use *that* for everything from bagels to baseball games, bathrooms, and boats. She's a nice person, I had a nice time, and it was nice to see you. Christian is used with similar abandon very often and with as little specific meaning. Some years ago an American politician urged the Jewish and Muslim leaders in the Middle East to get together like good Christians.

Historically, we've used Christian to identify people who believe certain things (that Mary was a virgin, the pope is infallible, or that there are three persons in one God); it has been used to describe one who is baptized, or who goes to church, or even one who doesn't smoke or drink.

But shouldn't we save it for people who are disciples of Jesus Christ? If we use it that way, then it reminds us that we have an ideal made flesh in a particular person whom we try to follow. And follow is the best word, since we never seem to quite catch up with him. A Christian is one who follows the person Jesus Christ, not a doctrine or set of laws or even a Church, no matter how helpful these can be.

Let's save the word "Christian" to describe all who follow Christ no matter at what distance and remind ourselves that in a very real sense we are always on the way to giving the word more meaning, toward becoming better followers, disciples.

January 27

When Catholic students attend a worship service in another Church they often report back their surprise at hearing the words "We believe in one holy, catholic, and apostolic church," in the Creed. One, holy, and apostolic don't really surprise them but "catholic" does. The word has a long history, which may be one reason many Churches retain it. But even more, it has a basic meaning that should appeal to all Christians. In the dictionary sense, catholic means "of broad or general scope; universal; all inclusive; broad and comprehensive in interest, sympathies, or the like, liberal." We should hope, as we put more and more centuries between ourselves and the days when Christians routinely silenced, tortured, jailed, and killed others who differed with them on points of Christian teaching, that catholic becomes more and more descriptive of any Christian Church.

We should be happy with the term and work to give it more reality in our thought, talk, and action. It means an openness to many types of people; a recognition that there are many ways of speaking of such a mystery as God and of religion itself; that God and religion should not, cannot, be boxed into a few small and neat formulas thought up by one group at one time in human history.

The name "catholic" is not enough to guarantee this wide, friendly all-embracing spirit. It is often more a hope than a reality. Everyone who likes and uses the word—Lutherans, Episcopalians, Catholics—needs to work at giving it more substance. Christ's words in the Gospel are catholic: ". . . for any man who is not against you is on your side" (Luke 9:50).

All of us need to claim proudly the word "catholic" and even more proudly make the effort to take it seriously, to welcome whatever points to Christ and forwards trust and confidence in him. Even while we seem to be waiting for the Churches themselves to take the term seriously enough, we can do that in our own relations with other Christians and in our parish communities.

January 28

"I keep busy. I don't have time to think about my problems." The words come from an interview with a forty-two-year-old tycoon famous for arrogance and the ability to make money. He probably exemplifies in a blockbuster manner the more common practice, an absorption in work, career, day-by-day responsibilities, that seems to leave little time for self-examination. That may push problems out of view rather than allow us to face them. One certainly can avoid unpleasant realities by enough movement and distraction, whether in work or pleasure.

But while the tendency may be common to many of us, we should make a distinction between good honest work, necessary to make a living, and a more total, frenetic devotion to making money, to acquisition at the expense of any real interior life. Most of us need a certain amount of regular employment to avoid spending time magnifying our problems or manufacturing new ones. Often we are saved from the devastation of a grief or serious disappointment or failure by having the unavoidable responsibility of some work on which others depend. The necessity of taking our minds off the self and devoting some energy and time to others, to something outside ourselves, can maintain a certain amount of proportion regarding ourselves and our problems.

The really harmful thing is to use work or activity as a way to stifle all the cries from within for love, integrity, satisfaction, peace, purity of intention. How you or I individually balance these conflicting needs (work and reflection) is somewhat a personal matter. But in any case, it is one that needs thought. The realistic balance of the two is finally up to me and you, not to be decided in advance by someone else. Both must be done: honest (even satisfying, if possible) work and some self-examination, an examination of the direction and purpose of our life itself, including that work.

January 29

"They will know we are Christians by our love." So goes a popular hymn, and early Christian history tells us that the pagans were impressed by how the Christians loved one another. And no one is going to object to more evidence of that, evidence given by concern about famine-stricken peoples, flood-ravaged countries, the cripple person next door or the aging parent. There can hardly be too much of that. But one can also point to atheists and other nonbelievers who demonstrate kindness, concern for others, commitment to better human life. Often they have been way ahead of Christians in some of these matters. We only need to read the papers to see, between the wars and the murders, great examples of people doing brave, fine things, people with no belief in Christ.

Someone has gone so far as to say that Christ does *not* manifest himself to the world through the good example of Christians, through their love. To our ordinary way of thinking that certainly sounds questionable or extreme. But the writer goes on to point out that the true sign of Christ's presence is something even deeper; it is the faith, the trust with which Christians cling to God—even when *they have failed miserably to show love*. After all, to varying degrees, we all at times fail to demonstrate love; we end up being peevish, small, unkind, vindictive. The writer means that trust and faith can and must continue even though there is moral failure, even though, even when, through laziness and selfishness, we don't love. That faith and trust enable us at some moment to repent our lovelessness, to ask and receive forgiveness and start anew.

The more basic thing, then, is the faith and trust we have in God, our belief and confidence that God can do more in us, even forgive our lack of love; that no matter what happens, we can trust in God. Nothing can separate us from God's love for us even when our lack of love puts up a wall between us, God, and others. Even if our love wilts and limps, God's continuing love for us gives us hope that our love can get back on its feet and run in the path of Jesus, who has the copyright on love.

January 30

"One hour's misery wipes out all memory of delight" (Sir 11:27). Who remembers, in other words, the joy of that first love for Ed or Lucy, the thrill of winning the marathon, or the last payment on the house when pain makes you incoherent or grief takes away all appetite and zest for living? But isn't the opposite also true? That one hour's happiness or joy wipes out all thought of past misery? We experience the same forgetfulness when we're intensely absorbed in anything satisfying. The past, the future, and even the present seem to dissolve while we play a fast game of basketball, are intent on a gripping hockey game, or are carried away or lost in music, dance, a movie. In all these we slip away from time for a while. There we are in a moment that seems to hold something of eternity.

All this points up the merit and charm of living more in the present, something urged fairly often in these pages, but also the limitations of that approach. As expressed in that opening proverb from the Book of Sirach, our absorption in the present can have its dark side. Most of us would not object to prolonging present delights that blot out the past and its miseries and disappointments. But when present misery and sadness blot out all memory of past delight or the good things of other days, the present seems a questionable good.

Cannot the memory of the good, of what amount to God's graces in the past—all the people, places, and pleasures that have brightened our life—be kept before us and with us more often? After we have allowed our grief or pain to run its course or even during it, we do right to recall that we have experienced the love and care of God, of God's messengers: our friends and family. That there have been and can be yet more all-absorbing moments to both enjoy—and remember.

January 31

The presumption behind every page of the New Testament, one that we so easily take for granted, is that the Jesus of whom it speaks is *alive,* here and now. The New Testament writers were not sitting at their desks, eyes misting over with tears for someone no longer present, but wrote of someone living in whom they believed and in whom they hoped you would believe also.

They believed him to be alive because they believed that unlike other human beings, he had risen from the dead and appeared to his disciples and some faithful followers. They know he lives forever as the first of many to follow him, as the assurance that being beaten by life or suffering or by death, is not the last word. That is why the four Gospels are by no means simple biographies meant to recall the details of the life of one now gone, but are stories selected from his life and words to encourage belief in the reader. "There were indeed many other signs that Jesus performed in the presence of his disciples which are not recorded in this book. These here written have been recorded in order that you may hold the faith that Jesus is the Christ, the Son of God, and that through this faith you may possess life by his name" (John 20:30-31).

When we read or hear those stories we hear about one who lives and now speaks to us. We hear one who lives in a new existence and calls us to it also—beginning now—and promises that our present life in him is leading us to fulfilled life with him. Part of the lesson we all need as we face life's difficulties and even terrors and as we try to do more than just bear them is that we needn't be afraid. "Do not be afraid. I am the first and the last, and I am the living one: for I was dead and now I am alive for evermore" (Rev 1:17-18).

February 1

"You can't go home again." On many levels that seems true. Most likely your parents have moved, or the house no longer exists, or you have lived in so many, which would you call home? Statistics say that at least one out of five Americans changes addresses each year, and that more than half of the listings in a large metropolitan phone book can be changed from one year to another. And even if some of the neighbors are still there, divorce, separation, and remarriage have often changed the scene. Try to track a recent college graduate and you have an almost full-time task on your hands, from job to job, city to city, within months.

But family and friends remain one of the most satisfying elements in human life. We need to continue our relations with those we love, assure them of our care and be assured, too, of their abiding love. As has been said often in these pages, the love of God for us, for anyone, becomes real in the love given us by others, by husband or wife or parents, to be sure. But even beyond that, all of us need other loves and have a capacity that isn't exhausted within the family. The greatness and varied possibilities of God's love come more clearly to us through a variety of friends. The instability and changes of our time and place should not kill or prevent this love from continuing. The same fast and highly technical society that often separates us also makes possible the means for keeping each other in mind and heart. Letters, of course, but probably even more for many, the phone.

The effort to think of the other, to ask about him or her, is part of sustaining any friendship. People of another time may have had more stability but even more insurmountable obstacles in keeping in touch with absent friends. Getting around and communicating was extremely difficult. We have both the disadvantages and the advantages of swift and easy mobility. We can use the advantages to maintain some essential and stable points in our lives: our friends.

February 2

"There is no use trying to be more spiritual than God. God never meant man to be a purely spiritual creature. That is why God uses material things like bread and wine to put the new life into us. We may think this rather crude and unspiritual. God does not: he invented eating" (C. S. Lewis, quoted in Stephen Longstreet, *We All Went to Paris* [Macmillan, 1972]).

One of the most difficult things in writing this book is to avoid the traditional word "spiritual" in speaking of our life in Christ. For one raised in Catholicism in the last half-century or so, it comes naturally to the lips. We've used this most inadequate term for years. Inadequate because it suggests to many something invisible, without body or weight or appearance, something unlike the world we live in, even and maybe especially the world we worship in. Our life is lived amid words, sounds, sights, touches, temperatures and substances, tastes and weights. Our worship, too, thank God, is with words, sounds, smells, tastes, and bodily movements. We approach God through people, things, music, furniture, words, gestures, visible and tangible beauty and expressiveness, and God comes to us in bread and wine, oil, water, words, above all in flesh-and-blood people. There may be something spiritual about this, but it is certainly not disembodied as the word usually suggests.

"Spiritual" can have a more Christian meaning if by it we mean a life lived under the influence and guidance of the Holy Spirit. St. Paul uses the term that way, and that would be a good understanding of the term. But in our society it so often means that which is not open to our senses or, worse yet, that which has no contact with or relation to our material world. That has served often to excuse Christians from involvement in the world around them—they're too spiritual. Or it has given those who do not want to be disturbed by Christian ideals a handle for telling Christians to stick to their business, to what is "spiritual," that is, irrelevant, of no importance to suffering, poverty, and oppression here and now. Christians have every reason to rejoice more in the material world, the world of matter that is part of our composition. Through it we honor God and God comes to us. Further, the teachings of Jesus are meant to have an impact on it. Let us always test our religion by what it does in the world around us, how it affects others, our society, our neighborhood.

February 3

In a famous piece of poetry, the poet asks: "How do I love thee? Let me count the ways." But when it's not the love of Kathy Malone or Jim Schmidt but the love of God, we are more apt to ask: *"How can I love thee?"* Diana Ross, Elton John, and all the rest may sing of love without end, but can we even think of a beginning for something as distant sounding as love of God? We must admit that the love of God seldom makes the pavement dance beneath our feet. We'd be happy if it ever got near such a concrete level.

The solution that tempts us is to equate the love of God with the love of neighbor. We tend to think of it that way—not that we go overboard in loving the neighbor. But if loving God is exclusively a matter of loving each other, our Lord could have been more pithy and just said, "There is only one commandment: you shall love your neighbor as yourself." And Jesus does insist, of course, that what we do about the neglected children, widows, strangers, the poor, is the test of our love for God. How we love those who fascinate and charm us is a minor problem by comparison.

That it is possible to love God, Jesus himself demonstrates by spending whole nights in prayer, even though he, of course, spent a lot of time working cures. His prayer is evidence that God can be loved and honored in himself; if this were not so, our personal prayer would be just a type of daydreaming and public worship, just another brand of group therapy.

Behind and before all our efforts to love God by serving others, there must be some time, attention, and energy given to God in reflection on the Gospels, his Word, in a kind of daily prayer that will consist primarily of being open to God's influence, of waiting to know what is desired of us. This is the basic, maybe first, function of prayer: to open ourselves to God's rule; not to make requests of God (that comes later) but to learn what God requests of us.

February 4

Someone has said we should take our responsibilities, not ourselves, seriously. Clearly, we *cannot* laugh off the pains and sorrows of others. Or our obligations to them. We're safer taking our own problems lightly than trying to tell Joe or Ann to forget that painful breakup or loss of a job. Humor does not, cannot, replace compassion or sympathy. By no means is it a universal principle, a way of facing everything from a poor test to a red alert. There are very few such principles. (Probably the closest thing to an absolute principle is the advice of the doctor who said: "If it tastes good, spit it out.")

What I'm talking about here are all the lesser moments in daily life when we do better to forget some irritation rather than treating it like the last game of a tight World Series or a Greek tragedy. "Wisdom," someone has said, "consists in knowing what to overlook." Aren't many of the events of ordinary life better off left at the level of The Addams Family or the comics? One way of doing this is to set our imagined ills or crosses alongside the problems of others. Even our midwinter blues are reduced in size when compared with the grief of a friend who lost a parent in the last month or with the deadening routine of another's job. Our anger over a supervisor's insensitivity becomes negligible when put alongside the financial collapse of a neighbor. Our concern about getting to San Diego for a vacation or Colorado for skiing seems less world shaking beside the lot of a relative with AIDS or an abused child.

Time and distance, too, help take the bite out of even serious problems by giving us a new perspective. We can look back on a broken relationship and even sigh with relief when we see dear old Harry or Beth having a spat with his or her new flame. Many of the ordinary irritations of life are better treated the same way: with humor or lightness, as small beer compared to the cup of sorrow that many must drink.

February 5

"Some day my prince will come." Commitment is by no means simply a matter of finding the right place, situation, or person, "my prince." That can be a basically irresponsible and silly search for some incredible blend of Brooke Shields and Mother Teresa or of Wayne Gretzky and Mario Cuomo. All that picky searching can be a way of excusing ourselves for not being what *we* should be. Instead of looking for the perfect person, the perfect experience, the perfect spot, we need to look for a more perfect me. What we see as the shortcoming of others may be an excuse for delayed maturity on our part.

Before we expect perfection in others and in everything around us, we'd do well to ask more of ourselves. When we share the bread and cup of the Lord, we share in his basic commitment to both the pain and joy of his human life. We also share the strength with which he himself lived it. That strength can make us capable of lasting love, of dependability and fidelity. We become individuals who realize that happiness and growth will come from pinning ourselves down. Eventually we must understand that commitment is the way to happiness and accomplishment, not a barrier.

As long as we feel that happiness is tied up with being free and backpacking in Lapland (and maybe there must be time for that in our lives), there's no point in promising another or an enterprise that we'll be there. Certainly there is a kind of freedom in wandering around the world with no watch or calendar or deadlines. But there is a deeper and more ultimately satisfying freedom, freedom from small selfishness, that comes from giving of ourselves generously to what we believe in or to someone we trust.

February 6

An interesting story in 2 Kings tells of four lepers at the gate of an Israelite city under siege. They decide that they can go into the city and starve or go to the camp of the enemy Arameans and, at worse, be put to death. Not much choice. Going to the camp, they find the enemy has fled, frightened by some imagined or real fear; everything has been left, food and drink, silver and gold, clothing. The four enjoy the good things available and hide some of it for future use. But then they think, "What we are doing is not right. This is a day of good news and we are keeping it to ourselves. . . . We must go now and give the news to the king's household" (2 Kings 7:9).

Of course, theoretically, all of us Christians probably know that this day and any day is a day of good news, the good news that the Son of God has become a human and shown us the path through human life to final victory. "Gospel" means good news. By faith we have accepted the good news and tried to live by it. To keep it to ourselves would not be right; like the men in the story, we realize we must not keep it to ourselves.

Sometimes this kind of talk means that one is being invited to stand on street corners or buttonhole people and give them in words (often formulas) or pamphlets the news that would be so good for them. Some of us undoubtedly are called to preach the good news in words, at Mass, in talks, by raising the issues in conversation.

But I think most of us are more effective announcers of the good news when we feel impelled to live and act from our conviction that life is worthwhile, that hopefulness is the primary attitude, that there is even reason for some kind of joy, that what we have received requires that we be generous with time, resources, love, sympathy, interest in others. A kind of need to live up to what we believe should make our life and actions such that they would not be comprehensible apart from that belief. Let's not keep the good news to ourselves, but let our lives first of all, and our words, witness that we really regard it as good news.

February 7

I remember a very sensitive woman, apparently also very serious about her religion, coming up in tears one day after a weekday Mass. She had a list of disasters and horrors of our world at hand: famine in Ethiopia and the Sudan, earthquakes in Chile, the homeless people in big cities, the crash of a huge airliner, abandoned and abused children, women and children driven into prostitution, and on and on. "What can I do?" Obviously very anguished, she was literally in tears.

One gets a similar, more localized feeling walking on the streets of any large city, seeing people begging for food, money, help. One knows one cannot respond to all of them and wonders at times whether he or she should respond to any. If I do give something to someone, to which one do I give it? How do I know the request is not a con job? A lot of questions race through our minds. But do we let the crowd in the streets, the starving in the Sahara, and the homeless in some war zone just paralyze us? Who am I to do anything about it? It's too big; I can't make a dent in the problems.

Somehow, any response has to fit our own abilities, our own situation, has to fit what I can do here where I am. Better to do some little thing where we are than to sit in absolute paralysis doing nothing because we can't do everything. A prominent woman in the arts probably has the right idea. She says she began to feel overwhelmed by the problems facing the world and its future. "I felt so helpless at a certain point, and I talked to so many people who felt the same way." She says she'd rather not have to think about things like thermal inversion, global warming, pollution; she'd rather retreat and do her art. But with a daughter who will be sixteen in the year 2000, she feels she must do something to better the world. She chose to become a very active campaigner and spokesperson for safer pesticides.

Rather than fruitlessly wringing our hands over how little we can do, we must do what we can realistically in our situation. There are enough of us that there should be some competition in doing the good.

February 8

History tells us that the following of Christ was very early on called simply "the Way." Throughout the Gospels we have accounts of Jesus' travels in Palestine, and the language used makes these accounts more than simply geographical and historical detail. It suggests that the authors meant the readers to continually recall that to be a Christian means to follow Christ, to go his way, to have him leading us. "They were on the road, going up to Jerusalem, Jesus leading the way" (Mark 10:32).

Looking at the world around us, one wonders at times whether the tendency or the drive to follow someone is not the most frequently corrupted of human drives. The ease with which a good actor or persuasive speaker or charismatic type can gather a following with his or her credentials barely scanned makes one tremble. The more famous and frightening ones are always there: Hitler, Mussolini, various discredited evangelists and preachers.

The following of Jesus requires a decision in faith, requires trust. And we know it may lead with him to Jerusalem—where he was crucified. But also, of course, beyond that, to resurrection.

We make our following of Jesus, whether it's trudging, leaping, skipping, solemn or joyous, stumbling or skating, more durable if we continually make efforts to ground it in more knowledge and understanding of his word and his life. It's not meant to be a blind following: In fact, the Gospels tell of the blind man being cured, given his sight, and then following Jesus. Our faith will not give us a blueprint for the future or take away all care and worry or answer all our questions (only TV evangelists and politicians will do that), but it can and should give us a well-founded hope, even joy, as we follow behind him who leads to joy beyond Calvary.

February 9

Monotheism (belief in one God), monogamy (one wife per husband), and monotony all seem too characteristic of Christianity, judging from our world's resistance to them throughout the centuries. One demanding God has always had competition from the other gods (money, success, native country, etc.) to whom we're tempted to give our supreme loyalty. And the difficulty that human beings have with faithfulness to one man or one woman is well attested for all of us—if not among our friends and families, at least in our popular culture. (Where would films and drama be without the possibility of unfaithfulness, and where would that be without a background of monogamy?) And even when monotheism and monogamy are accepted, ordinary Christian life often seems simply synonymous with monotony: Mass or worship every Sunday, regular prayer (often with little excitement or apparent result), patience with difficult members of the family or people we must work with. The same old round year after year of Church celebrations: Advent, Christmas, Lent, Easter, for example.

But that is just the necessary and important truth to grasp: that transformation into the likeness of Christ, becoming more selfless, more habituated to giving and less inclined to grasping, takes time, effort, prayer, patience, new beginnings. We should all try farming sometime in order to understand the need for patience in regard to growth. The impatient and easily bored human looks after a while at the round of Church celebrations, even Christmas (such a thrill in childhood), as ho-hum, more of the same. In more generous moments we may see more realistically and with gratitude that it is just this opportunity to try again, to let the old truths sink in more deeply, the example of Christ to take root more firmly, that we need. Some faithfulness to the yearly recall of Christ's life is just the way to deepen our grasp, our insertion into this transforming life. As the physical-fitness devotee learns and accepts eventually, there has to be some long, steady effort in the same direction to make progress and to maintain what has been accomplished. Jesus, even while I kick against the same old plan, help me love the learning.

February 10

Renan, a famous ex-believer of the last century, said that human life was basically very dark and bitter. A strongly Catholic contemporary of his replied that such a statement was the most blasphemous statement against God and creation. His idea was that such a negative evaluation of human life was an insult to God in that it suggested the whole thing was hopeless and would not possibly have any good resolution. I share the believer's confidence that God who made all good, as Genesis tells us, will also bring all to an even greater good.

But I think we need to be more understanding in regard to such sentiments as the other one expressed. When you add them up, the circumstances of human life, the pains and problems we ourselves are aware of in our immediate milieu, let alone those of the Sahara, Pakistan, the Middle East, and Central America, are all certainly—at least on the surface—good reasons for fear, tears, doubt, some low spirits. You survey your life and that of your neighbors and friends, and there is cancer, marital breakup, children caught in drugs, a neglected senior citizen.

We can, of course, and should turn the other way and see all the wonderful hope-filled realities around us: the happy birth of a child, the joy and confidence of a young person entering a good career and/or a happy marriage, someone who has just found his or her true love, success in various endeavors. All that is helpful, and we must use and enjoy these aspects for all they are worth.

But still, we need beneath both of those lists a more profoundly anchored hope in the Lord, whom we rightly call Savior because we do see there is much to be saved from. The irreplaceable foundation has to be built on some reflection and prayer, some willingness on our part to let the grace of God, which has shone on our world, shine on my life, too, producing hope, love, and joy. I don't think we can expect it to be there or to be significant if we rarely think of it. Daily prayer, not just for this or that but for and with confidence, has to inspire our lives.

February 11

Zacchaeus, in Luke 19:1-10, models the human relation to God. Anxious to see the Lord but prevented by the crowd blocking his view—he was very short—he runs ahead and climbs up a tree, a picture of willingness to see the Lord. As one of the hated tax collectors of his country, he was undoubtedly a man of some wealth and, at least in his own eyes, some dignity. Climbing a tree to see this preacher is certainly an act of impetuosity more appropriate to a love-driven St. Francis or a teenage Romeo. Jesus, seeing his curiosity and good will, says to him: "Hurry down; I'm staying at your place." Zacchaeus joyfully acquiesces, has Jesus to dinner, and under this influence decides to make restitution for the skimming and graft that had made his profession so hated by his fellow Jews.

Human receptivity to the Lord goes all the way from hiding like Adam and Eve behind some bushes, to what someone has called a "groping discontent," to Zacchaeus' positive welcoming. In extreme cases we want nothing to do with God. In between that and positive welcome are probably a whole range of other possibilities. Often human seeking of God is hardly that explicit; it is something more unspoken. It shows itself in some dissatisfaction with life and the world rather than in anything positive, that groping discontent, an aching loneliness. Ultimately only a genuine welcome on our part can allow God a place in our lives and change them.

In Zacchaeus we see all the elements of a response and conversion: Zacchaeus' receptivity and interest, God's grace and intervention, more faith and trust from Zacchaeus, and finally an indication in changed behavior (where it hurts) that he has truly opened himself to the Lord. A growth in stature, you might say, for Zacchaeus.

St. Francis of Assisi compares God to any polite, well-bred human and says that he is always courteous and does not invade the privacy of our lives without some indication from us that he is welcome. Part of our daily prayer should be (along the lines, in fact, of the Our Father) to offer better hospitality to the Lord. Instead of a perfunctory "Nice to see you," or some worry about "How long is he staying?" we must increasingly ask for and be open to God's suggestions about all the elements of everyday life.

February 12

The strong human tendency to develop close and exclusive attachments is founded in a need or desire to have someone on whom we can depend for support, love, and encouragement when life otherwise seems so full of challenges and combat. In them we are assured, after a hard day or in the midst of problems, harassment, and disappointments, there is someone whom we can come home to, who loves us and more than anyone else understands us. "You'd be so nice to come home to," goes an old song.

The Scriptures and faith tell us that God loves us, but unless we see and recognize that in a face, in some hands, in a smile, a touch, a look, words of encouragement, it remains very abstract, as relevant to daily life as some obscure formula from astrophysics. Even when the friend, husband, wife, is absent or we are, we can and are helped by our memory, a phone call, a letter. We sit and think of the person, and the pains of the moment are lessened.

The poet W. H. Auden defined sanctity as just this quality our friends and loves have of affirming our worth, our goodness. He wrote, "I have met in my life two persons, one a man, the other a woman, who convinced me that they were persons of sanctity. Utterly different in character, upbringing and interests as they were, their effect on me was the same. In their presence I felt myself to be ten times as nice, ten times as intelligent, ten times as good-looking as I really am." We might quibble with that "I really am." But otherwise it makes the point very well.

Why the quibble? Well, who's to say that those who love me do not see the genuine me more than those who are not attached to me? Doesn't love perhaps give an insight that the more objective observer cannot have? Love is necessary for us because it confirms our God-given worth and may even uncover the hidden worth that is open only to the eyes of the lover.

February 13

Open almost any chapter of a book like Leviticus in the Hebrew Scriptures (Old Testament) and find yourself in an absolutely foreign world that seems to have no meaning for us. For example, "One who suffers from a malignant skin-disease shall wear his clothes torn, leave his hair dishevelled, conceal his upper lip, and cry, 'Unclean,' " (13:45). Or "The ram for the guilt-offering shall then be slaughtered, and the priest shall take some of the blood of the guilt-offering, and put it on the lobe of the right ear of the man to be cleansed" (14:25). So it is a bit difficult to honestly suggest that we can open the Bible, put our finger down, and inevitably find great help for the present moment. But most of us could make more of an informed attempt and actually find the Scriptures to be a source of life and refreshment.

Among the verses of Psalm 119 we may find: "I lie prostrate in the dust; give me life according to your word" (v. 25).

And: "My soul weeps for sorrow; strengthen me according to your words" (v. 28). Christians in general make poor or little use of the power of the Word of God to revive us, to raise us up from grief and low spirits. A few psalms such as I have pointed to in some of these pages could easily become for us the sort of encouragement and strength we need. Quite a few of them are accessible and suitable, as well as, of course, the Gospels of the New Testament. In a period like our own where there are so many opportunities, in parishes and through schools and colleges, to get to know more about Scripture, or else by teaching ourselves, those who do read at all should give this project some time.

Granted some such preparation, we can find in Scripture the help, the strength, we so often lack to approach our life and work with energy and zest. One other requirement is somewhat presumed but should be made more clear. We must come to the Book with faith, with belief that it does convey the power and grace of God and that we can be touched by that power. Our soul may be at its nadir, our spirit may be in a dead, despairing mood, but even our so frail-seeming faith can find some revival, some assurance that God still loves us by turning to this word.

February 14

What the heck! It is Valentine's Day. So why not a bit of poetry?

> Oh, when I was in love with you,
> Then I was clean and brave,
> And miles around the wonder grew,
> How well did I behave. (A. E. Housman)

Real change in our lives (the purpose of Lent and Easter) comes about because we love or are devoted to a person or persons. We do our best, undertake the otherwise impossible, when spurred by love. Think of how empty, pointless, and stale life seems without love or friends or after a breakup, how little point there seems to be in doing anything. But when love is in charge, everything is changed. Time flies by, the GPA in college soars, we don't notice the clouds and rain or even that grumpy neighbor.

Former students of mine now in the early years of their marriages so often say or write things like this: "Sarah Elizabeth, born Nov. 7, 7 pounds, 9 ounces. She's a handful. Our lives now revolve around her schedule. It's tiring when you have to go to work and she wants to stay awake two or three hours a night. Tough to find the hours, too, for everything. But we wouldn't be without her for anything."

Bill Cosby speaks of how that child makes you give up quiet evenings, lazy weekends with good music, "intimate meals during which you finish whole sentences," all out of love for a person.

Ideas, concepts, movements, never will move us the way a human face, a pair of eyes, or a smile can. The desire to please and live up to someone we love can bring us to a generosity that we otherwise can't pull off. "When I was in love with you, then I was clean and brave."

February 15

One of those Christmas letters we all get or send telling of the past year's activities (everything from the Boy Scouts to the latest move, a change in job, or the long-awaited anniversary trip to Hawaii) came to me from a young woman who only some six or seven years ago was one of the brightest and most alive students I had in class. We hadn't kept very close contact for a few years, and as I read the letter my eyes, I'm sure, widened with surprise as I read first of Ben, born just a month ago, and then of a doll house for Sally, Kevin and his cars and trucks, and finally of little Kelly who is called the Amazon because of her feats. I felt a bit like their neighbors: "Everyone has some reaction to *four* kids. In Middleville people have two or three children and they are two-wage earning families. I don't expect we'll ever fit the mold but we don't intend to. We keep hearing that the teenage years are the worst but I think we'll enjoy the kids as they are now. It's certainly a lot of work but fun."

This *Christmas* letter, by the way, arrived in late March. "I wish I could have gotten a letter off to you earlier, but at least this isn't a bill!" One understands the difficulty in finding time to get the letter out at all. I hope she and her husband do take and find the time to "enjoy the kids as they are now."

One of the tensions I'm conscious of throughout this book is that between our focus on the future, our hope, the impulse to work, to struggle for change, improvement, . . . *and* our need to live here and now, to not let the present slip away unloved and unappreciated while we anticipate with fear or longing the future (those teenage years). Each of us has to deal with these poles.

In any case, let's enjoy the kids as they are now. Their beauty, vitality, the softness of that infant skin, the inquisitiveness, the little stirrings of individuality, the heart-melting smiles, their need for consolation and encouragement—all that deserves wholehearted attention and love right now. Even if there aren't four kids, there are other elements in our life that shouldn't be allowed to pass unkissed, unloved, unappreciated, unenjoyed. They will never be again in quite the same way; loving them now helps make them eternal, at least for us and maybe for them, too.

February 16

A provocative movie I saw some time ago may not be well known to everyone. It did not compete at most multiple-screen movie houses with *Rambo XIII, Ghostbusters V,* or *Crocodile Dundee III.* It is set in a desolate country area of Denmark toward the end of the last century. Two sisters, probably in their twenties, live with their widowed father, the local pastor of the small community. He is a respected religious leader and well assisted by his daughters with their regular attendance and good singing voices. After his death the community continues to go to the church and, further, the daughters and a group of parishioners meet regularly for Bible study and a bit of hymn singing. The sisters pass up opportunities for love and marriage. Their quiet and regular life is interrupted by the arrival of a French woman named Babette. An unsuccessful suitor of one of the daughters has sent her to them. She has fled some serious disappointment in Paris and asks only to cook for them. Their first reaction to this is to regard it as impossible; finally their objections are overcome and they accept her offer.

In the meantime the Bible study group has been degenerating into backbiting and recrimination. After some time with the sisters, Babette wins a large sum on a lottery ticket that someone back in Paris has bought for her. The sisters presume that she will use the money to leave, but instead Babette insists on providing a feast for the sisters and their circle. The generosity and scope of this project at first provoke not just surprise but real fear among the local people. Such unabashed joy in food or a meal strikes them as excessive. But all goes ahead; Babette has the food and drink shipped in and prepares the big banquet.

The day for the feast arrives and everyone comes and enjoys this unheard-of dinner with the deceased pastor's picture looking down on it all. In the course of the meal, apologies begin to be offered for past offenses, bygones are made bygones, and love is rekindled. One ordinarily rather quiet member utters an occasional alleluia in his excitement over the feast. Finally after hours spent enjoying the dinner, the group ends up dancing in a circle in the village square.

One could see a number of strong pointers to the message of Christ here: someone coming from out of nowhere and affecting the lives of these people; their hesitant and even hostile reactions at first; the complete gift of self and her means by Babette. But for today, could we think of it in connection with the Lord's Supper, the Mass? We come to the table in order to be bound together in greater love. We do it in memory of the beloved pastor, shepherd, Jesus. The meal helps us carry out and experience the meaning of the Scriptures we hear and have discussed in the homily. The meal is meant to cause reconciliation. We come together on Sundays to celebrate the feast in memory of the Lord and pastor Jesus Christ, called the Mass, the Lord's Supper, the Eucharist. How does it affect us?

February 17

Despite some difficulty for us with events and persons lost to the memory of most of us, there are a number of the psalms that are relatively lacking in these references and that expand our hearts, lifting our sights and minds to thoughts that are not simply me-centered. One of the most positive, almost breathless in its desire to praise and thank God (bless God) for goodness and care, is Psalm (102) 103.

The opening two verses do this well and also illustrate the style of the author, where instead of rhyming verses he repeats the same thought in slightly different words:

> My soul, give thanks to the Lord
> all my being [soul and all my being are the same]
> > bless his holy name.
> My soul, give thanks to the Lord.
> And never forget all his blessings.

With the author we can join in his list of blessings for which he thanks the Lord: The Lord forgives all your guilt, heals your ills, crowns you with love and compassion, fills your life with good things.

"The Lord is compassion and love, slow to anger and rich in mercy." God's love is at least as certain and lasting as that of parents; God knows how frail we are, how fragile our life. "Our days are like grass: we flower like the flower of the field." In contrast to yesterday's irises, "the love of the Lord is everlasting."

As we pray the psalm, we could easily customize it by adding our reasons for thankfulness, for gratitude, for trusting that God is with us and cares for us: the love we have experienced, the friends and family who mean so much . . . But I'm not going to customize it for you!

And, as always, the psalmist is not content with listing all the good God has done but ends with the thanksgiving that should be a daily part of Christian living, not something limited to a day in February. Every time the Lord's Supper is celebrated, with the Lord Jesus we give thanks to the Father. There's no reason why that shouldn't enter into every day's prayer, every part of our life.

February 18

Our temptations to discouragement, to lack of hope, vary in their depth. We can be lacking in hope in a very final way if, for instance, we lack any trust that God will bring our life and our world to any good end. Woody Allen claims that as a young boy he was quite hopeless because of his understanding of the theory of the expanding universe, which left him feeling the whole thing would fizzle. We experience a fundamental lack of hope when just getting out of bed strikes us as futile. Why, why bother? Where is it all going? Or we face more immediate failures of hope: discouragement about strife in Northern Ireland or Los Angeles; a feeling that we're stuck in a job or position we consider far from ideal; or we wonder if a friend or family member will ever be pulled out of drug or alcohol abuse.

One faltering hope among many committed Christians today concerns Christian unity, the whole movement we call ecumenism. After an exciting lift given to it by Pope John XXIII and others a couple of decades ago, it seems to have ground to a halt, to say the least. One Catholic spokesman recently laid the lack of common witness by Christians to the fact that they have been unable to come to any substantial agreement on the content of their belief. That may be, but I think we're entitled to question whether this agreement at the top is as essential as officials would like to think.

Christians of all kinds should be more ready to cooperate for the world around them and also in expressing their trust and faith in Jesus Christ the Lord. One sees this so often as a strong force not identical with any particular Church or confession. If my Baptist neighbor has a strong trust in the Lord, that should encourage me. If we know our Lutheran friends are firm believers in Jesus, we should not hesitate to appeal to that in times of stress and difficulty. A good deal of unity can be achieved by ordinary sharing of our trust in the Lord and the Word, by praying together, condoling in times of sorrow with the same faith and hope in the Savior.

February 19

Often fasting and various forms of voluntary self-denial ("giving up" drink, luxuries, etc.) are themselves sort of luxury items. We often offer them in place of the more obvious and less romantic "sacrifices" we should be making, dictated by daily life and our immediate responsibilities. Before we decide to offer God some self-denial, chosen by ourselves and capable of making us feel truly martyr-like, we'd do much better to look at how we discharge the demands of our ordinary life, our family, our jobs, our position in the world or a smaller society.

First Samuel (15:22) gives us the most famous statement of this: "Does the Lord desire offering and sacrifices as much as he desires obedience? Obedience is better than sacrifice, and to listen to him more pleasing than the fat of rams [offered in sacrifice]." Obedience in such instructions is never simply a matter of listening to someone's commands, even God's (were it that simple!) but of living up to the demands put on us by our position, our place in the world, our daily life, our work, our neighborhood.

Before we choose to add more hours of prayer to our life, more assistance at Mass, more fasting, less Fanny Farmer or Chivas Regal (but not necessarily excluding these options), we must ask how well we carry out our obligations to those who depend on us and whom we serve. How do we do our job? What efforts do we make to light up the drabness of a February day with some pleasantness and understanding? How do we bolster the weakness and weariness of friends and colleagues? The "luxury items," special self-denial and the like all offer room for self-congratulation; after all, *I* choose to do them. The real sacrifices are not those we choose ourselves but those foisted on, given us by our life itself. Words of encouragement and hope to others, deeds of service and concern are much more a following of Jesus than arbitrary "sacrifices." His sacrifice was the consequence of a life of service and love.

February 20

"The simplest and most effective way to sanctity is to disappear into the background of ordinary everyday routine" (Thomas Merton). Elsewhere in these pages you will read of happiness as the result of work well done, a useful life, rather than an end sought in itself. The same sort of approach needs to be made in regard to holiness. If one thinks of all the books and teaching on this subject in fairly recent Catholic tradition, one may recognize the need to do this. So often we have been treated to ladders of perfection, ways to holiness, stages in prayer, progressive detachment from the things of the body or of the material world. Or it has been in terms of successive degrees of self-knowledge and self-discipline. All these well-intentioned works aimed somehow at bringing the practitioner to perfection in a rather organized if not scientific way. They marked out the route and often suggested that it was a life by itself, a life little related to caring for children, loving one's spouse, doing one's worldly work. The "spiritual" life is the truly deficient term that has been used for all this.

We are coming more and more to recognize that there is only one life for any one of us, a human life, and it is either directed fundamentally to God and the service of God's creatures or to self-satisfaction. And all of that takes place in the arena of daily work, vocations, the relationships of human life, as well as in the rites of the Church, prayer, and special moments taken out of daily life. As Thomas Merton wrote, to recognize and love the demands and necessities of ordinary routine, of a life in which we are responsive to God and to others, to do that with love and reverence, that is holiness. Let us love and welcome what today brings to us and asks of us, not as a distraction from our pursuit of God but as the place and situation where we find and serve God.

February 21

"The Lord is my shepherd." Probably the most well-known and certainly one of the most beautiful expressions of trust and confidence in the whole Bible is Psalm 23, which has that famous beginning. Even if we have no familiarity with any other psalm, we have heard this one or know of it. And even if, like many people today, we have never seen a shepherd or a flock, still, the image, with the help of illustrations, is not all that strange. The concrete images of the psalm speak to all of us: "verdant pastures," "restful waters," and "dark valley," "my cup overflows," "you anoint my head with oil." Oil is not used today as it once was as a cure-all, but the image of something soft, penetrating, comforting, may still be alive for us. And the other statements are of the sort to encourage our complete confidence: "I shall not want." "He gives me repose." "I fear no evil; for you are at my side." "Only goodness and kindness shall follow me all the days of my life."

A psalm to quiet and calm our fears, worries, anxieties; a psalm to help us put all in the hands of the Lord; a psalm that takes all the scattered moments of our life, the worries and terrors, and puts them all trustfully in the strength of the Lord. A beautiful prayer to know well and use often.

"The Lord is my shepherd; I shall not want. . . . Even though I walk in the dark valley I fear no evil; for you are at my side. . . . Only goodness and kindness follow me all the days of my life."

February 22

If this were a self-help book from the local drugstore rack, it would tell you that the lesson of Peter's walking on the water to Christ is that if Peter had had more confidence in himself, he would not have sunk. If he had really believed he could do it, he would have taken all the gold medals. While that is the message of the self-help books and does have some place in our lives (learning to swim, to speak French, and so on), it is not the point of the Gospel.

The Gospel story does not say that we have nothing to do with being saved in this or any other situation. Rather, it commends Peter (and in him, us) for his willingness to get his feet out of the boat and to begin to move toward him who is already walking toward us with outstretched hand. The point is not how much we can or should do to help ourselves, but that there has to be some room in our life for the helping hand of this Other. If our life is so planned, so carefully bound up with our own little strategies and shortsighted wisdom that we have no place for the help of the Lord, there is something seriously wrong.

If Peter had not dared to go toward the ghostlike figure with faith, we most likely would never have heard his name. If Mary had found the angel's message simply too outlandish, the coming of Jesus would have met a roadblock. If Pope John XXIII and the Second Vatican Council had not been willing to launch the Church into the modern world and into some great changes of attitude, the Church today could easily be little more than a quaint and irrelevant museum.

Faith and trust, the daring that leaves something in the hands of God, opens us to the possibility of miracles, events that pierce the dullness and predictability of our lives. If we expect more of God, we often find solutions that our reason and imagination would never have conceived. Real trust asks us to look beyond all the lesser things we put our trust in, from our favorite columnist or religious leader to our bank account, to the one on whom our eyes should be fixed. Look to him. Hebrews says, "We must throw off every encumbrance . . . and run with resolution the race for which we are entered, our eyes fixed on Jesus, on whom faith depends from start to finish" (Heb 12:1-2).

February 23

"**I** will follow you wherever you go" (Luke 9:57). We should all at some time—or maybe many times—be seized with a similar fervor regarding Christ our Lord. Jesus' response to this in the Gospel is to strike while the iron is hot. He says: Come, then. No excuses, no delays. The form of these statements is absolute and very dramatic, and the point is clear: act now, cut out the quibbling, the hemming and hawing, the fudging. If I'm going to become more familiar with the Lord and with his teaching, his words, the Gospels, for instance, now is the time. Start today. If I'm going to give a few more hours a week to volunteering to teach CCD; if I need more familiarity with the beliefs of Christianity, now is the time to act.

Extending this a bit, we can say: If I'm going to develop and use my talent at something, now's the time to start. If I'm going to meet new people, now is the time. If I'm going to develop some new interests, try new and challenging activities, today, this week, is the time to start.

The excuses we think of today for holding off, postponing all this, whether spoken or unadmitted—studies, family responsibilities, work, football, beer, or television—will still be there in fifteen or twenty years under the same or different names: career, lack of time, my rest, age, and so on. As Jesus says, harshly and in hyperbole, let the dead bury the dead, but as for you, go and proclaim the kingdom of God; go, do what must be done. Now.

February 24

The history of Christianity offers many examples of ways in which believers have felt obliged to punish themselves. There are many examples of people denying themselves food; others staying on the top of pillars for long periods; others praying the psalms while standing in the North Sea in January; others burning jewels and fine clothes on bonfires; others dusting their food with cinders rather than cinnamon; wearing chains or spikes around their bodies; and on and on to such relatively minor things as not eating chocolate or drinking alcoholic beverages. Much of this has been accompanied by a grimness and dogged determination to kill something within the human being. It has been called, in fact, mortification, from Latin words meaning to make dead.

One has to wonder sometimes if the spirit of competition was not more in evidence in some of these endeavors than anything related to love, faith, trust. Too, there is the suggestion in all of this that the body and all that goes along with it is somehow bad or that whatever is beautiful, satisfying, pleasant, is, thereby, contrary to God's will.

But as a glorious saint like Francis of Assisi illustrates, the real purpose behind any rejection of the goods and comforts of this world has to be freedom. We desire to be free of the bonds that our attachment and dependence on all these things may entail, free to move and sing and serve like Francis, free of the encumbrances of wealth, objects, and greed.

The open road, the vagabond life, are not simply temporary ideals of the young who trek through Nepal or the Black Forest; they sum up the human desire to be free to be human, to be a person, rather than primarily a consumer or a custodian of this world's goods. No matter how remote this all may seem from our life at this moment, we must keep freedom, happiness, and traveling light as part of our ideal.

February 25

Who's in charge around here anyway? The weather or me? To varying degrees, extreme cold or very hot temperatures, sunshine, gray skies, oppressive humidity all affect us. It isn't always, of course, for the worse: We can be inspired by the weather, by the sunshine, by a nip in the autumn air, by the sudden softness and dizzying charm of a spring day. But one of the distinctive qualities of human beings is our ability to do something about nature around us. We see it all the time: We bend lumber, turn the most unprepossessing material into gleaming skyscrapers and handsome furniture; we overcome a vast expanse of water by a bridge or a boat or a plane. Our relationship with nature is no simple matter of either being subject to it or completely dominating it. And lots of questions arise about how we are to relate to it.

But today we could ask ourselves the question raised to begin with, Who's in charge around here anyway? Am I going to let an overcast day make me grumpy, gray weather make me snarl, a heavy rain or snow that limits my movement simply turn me into an ogre? Shouldn't we look beyond that to more important factors that determine how we feel and act? Doesn't our hope in Jesus Christ, our trust in his love for us, the goodness others show, give us reason to be more pleasant, more tolerable to live with? If faith and hope mean anything, shouldn't they have some impact on such basic matters as how we greet others, or the day, or our work?

Illness (serious or slight) is something else, another way in which nature does take over whether we want it to or not. That's the subject for another day's reflection. But for now, maybe even here, if the illness is slight—a cold, a minor headache, a sore arm—we can lessen its impact by thinking more selflessly of those who *really* are suffering. Can't we help them see beyond the clouds and downpour, the ice and wind, the bad weather in their lives?

February 26

Christians have sometimes—often?—acted as if freedom and liberty were non-Christian terms or opposed to Christianity, as if they weren't *our* ideals. But for the Jews and for the New Testament writers, the liberation of the Jews from slavery in Egypt was the great event, the one still celebrated every year in Passover and the background for Jesus in the Gospels. He is pictured as the one who frees us from sin, self, suffering, and death. I think many people today take it almost for granted that freedom is a pagan ideal and not Christian. We act as if constriction, limitations, a certain narrowness, were consequences of being a Christian. As if becoming a Christian were like joining an organization that gives you a bunch of new rules to follow. This especially seems to affect us in our middle years, our more respectable years.

Aren't the young and the elderly alike in having more freedom? The young often don't care what is "usually" done or how something has been done in the past (what has that to do with them?), and besides, their attractiveness and spirit often make even their brashness and flouting of convention engaging. The elderly often have clarified their vision of the world and its values and no longer see great importance in the issues or customs that are so crucial when we're younger. They'd rather practice hospitality and foolish kindness to children, visitors, relatives, than buy new furniture or keep up with the latest style. They don't care any longer what people think; they feel free to express what age and experience have taught them. In the most extreme case they say, What can they do to me now? I don't have that much to lose.

It's those middle years that can be so narrow and constricting. Isn't it possible for us to make an effort to be more free? To cast a more critical eye on all the practices of our society and feel more free to do what we know is good? Freedom, above all, from human and limitations should be a goal we think of much more often and expect to be helped to by our faith in Christ. Before and after Bolivar, Washington, Lincoln, or the GIs, Jesus was and remains our liberator.

February 27

Even if our life seems to be a minefield of difficulties and problems, of needs and worries, it often helps if we can for a moment put attention, our mind and heart, on something, on someone outside ourselves. Even our prayer needs a rest from asking and making clear to God how much we need. Psalm (99) 100 is a short and shining example of how we might turn from our self-concern, legitimate as we may think it is.

In four short sections, it expands our heart beyond its usual preoccupations. (1) It urges us first of all to praise the Lord with joy and music and asks the earth to join in the chorus: "Cry out with joy to the Lord, all the earth. Serve the Lord with gladness. Come before him, singing for joy." What a spirit! What a way to begin the day—or to end it.

(2) It turns briefly to ourselves only to remind us that we come from God, belong to God: "Know that he, the Lord, is God. He made us, we belong to him, we are his people, the sheep of his flock." When we're tempted to feel we are so alone and on our own, what a balancing thought.

(3) Thank, praise, and bless the Lord—something we tend to forget or to give short, formal attention only. Witness the way

people rattle off the *Gloria* at Mass when it should be sung or, at the very least, recited with some conviction. "Go within his gates, giving thanks . . . with songs of praise, give thanks to him and bless his name."

(4) The author's joy and praise lead him finally to state or, better, sing the obvious: "How good is the Lord, eternal his merciful love. He is faithful from age to age."

A great prayer to send our thoughts flying, to lift them from the dust, to reopen some thankfulness and joy in our so-often cramped selves. "Cry out with joy to the Lord, all the earth. . . . Come before him, singing for joy."

February 28

Too often we and "spiritual" writers have put conversion or the turning point of a person's life into a straitjacket. It has meant a turning away from the world even a rejection of flesh and matter. *The Imitation of Christ* reads: "As often as I was among men, I came back less a man." This view is not limited to Christianity; it is found in other religions, too, where the ideal person is one who after a shattering experience sees the uselessness of this life. While this ideal may have its place and serve in some situations, it is certainly not very helpful for most of us. And the Lord Jesus gives us a model of just the opposite. After years of quiet solitude he comes out of that and turns to the suffering and poor around him. He turns to our world, even to the point of surrendering himself eventually to death at human hands. Jesus does not take a look at the world and human activity, turn his back on them, and lead a group of chosen followers into seclusion.

His example and, more, his presence and power in us are there to help us transform our world and our ways of doing things. We are not given an example of how to turn our backs on it as just too awful for change. One of the great emphases of the Second Vatican Council was just this: that laypeople, ordinary Christians, have a most important mission to live the Christian life in the world, not in some retirement from it. Each of us is empowered to bring the Word, the grace of Christ, to the problems, the environment that is inescapably ours. Our responsibility is to the life and world before us. The movement to recognize our place in the world and to generously embrace it has a long history in Christianity. But, unfortunately, it is not the only history. The other tradition says: flee the world, live apart from it. Besides being impossible for most of us, such an attitude literally lets the world go to hell. Jesus says, rather, let it go to heaven, to the Father; and help bring it there. With all its inconveniences the world and life and work we face today are where God wants us to leave an imprint.

February 29

"Life's too short for worrying." "Yes, that's what worries me." A good illustration of how complex our human dilemmas are. That first, oft-repeated line we've all heard and probably recognized as true. Why waste time and effort in worrying when there are so many things to do, so much we wish to have done? There are better ways to pass the time: anything from prayer to reading to watching television to going shopping or to a ball game is probably preferable. And more useful.

The other half of the conversation is also positively on target. The shortness of life does worry you and me, is possibly often before us. In fact, do I need to say more?

Both sentiments are reasons for once more expressing our confidence in the Lord. Facing death, he himself, according to Luke's Gospel, prayed: "Lord, into your hands I commend my spirit" (23:46). None of us need wait for that moment to express the same trust. If the thought of death worries us a lot or appears frequently in our thoughts and feelings, maybe we should get into a habit of turning the thought into a prayer of confidence and trust each time: Into your hands, O Lord, I commend my spirit, I trust myself. You have the whole world in your hands. What should I fear? You have gone through death before us and for us. Be with us now and at the hour of our death.

March 1

Talk about self-giving always strikes a responsive chord. What's more natural and constant than self-giving, giving to myself what I like and want and expecting others to get into the act by doing all they can for me! Occasionally there's some resistance and then I find I easily end up compensating for it by doing all I can for me. I'm sure some of this is familiar to all of you.

But, of course, in Christian life self-giving refers to what Jesus modeled supremely for us in his life—an effort to use our energies, life, strength, in the service of God and of others. From our first moment in our mother's or father's arms, on through the years of childhood and our dependence on our parents, we are in many ways the object of much giving, the center of attention. Every morning, every day, is another Christmas for us. We're on the receiving end in most circumstances. Despite the efforts of our elders to lead us to think of others, to service of others, it still comes as a shock to most of us to realize at some point that we are no longer the center of the universe, that we are expected to give something to others.

Part of the purpose of the Eucharist is to place before us over and over again (after all, it's a lesson we don't take with much enthusiasm) the self-giving, even self-sacrifice of Jesus, who is now risen but still with us in word, sacrament, and Spirit. It's not just that our memory of him is jogged at Mass, but our ability to participate in his self-giving is reinforced there, too, as we enter into the action of the Mass, as we come prepared to offer ourselves with him. We pray to come away from Mass reinforced and strengthened in our ability to give of ourselves to our world, to life, to God.

March 2

"Don't worry; be happy," and "Please, don't be scared." Such song lyrics clearly have great appeal for many people. Undoubtedly, marketing people know that as well as theologians, writers, psychologists. We all like to be reassured. We probably all like to hear the words that tell us not to fear. Better yet, we like to be able to believe them. The fact that such a theme is marketable has led to some outrageous claims by preachers. They seem to say at times that trust in the Lord is so efficacious, the true believer will have *no* worries, *no* fears.

Our confidence in the Lord should help lessen our worrying, but to expect it to erase the ordinary conditions of human life is wrong. It would mean that somehow we think God owes us a kind of freedom from worry, sorrow, confusion, discouragement that was not even given to Jesus. Remember? The Son prayed that if it could be arranged he would prefer not to have the suffering he saw coming on Good Friday. No, the reality of Christian faith and trust in Christ is not so simple and unworldly. We remain in a difficult, not to say terrifying world, no matter how profound our faith and trust are.

Christian faith, the stories of the life of Jesus and of God's faithfulness to the people, all tell us we have every reason to trust the Lord. Every reason to have a more untroubled brow, a gentler, more peaceful countenance. Our confidence is not based on wishful thinking but on a recognition of what God has done for the new head of our race. The God who tells us not to fear, but rather to trust, also tells us we may have to in various ways share in the suffering and endurance of Jesus.

St. Paul says: "For we have been saved, though only in hope. Now to see is no longer hope; why should a man endure and wait for what he already sees? But if we hope for something we do not yet see, then, in waiting for it, we show our endurance" (Rom 8:24-25). Hope, trust, confidence, are inevitably mixed with endurance, struggle, difficulty. True, our salvation from suffering and death has begun. Basically, in fact, it is accomplished, but we will not feel all the results today. We do have every reason to hope, to trust, to even try to smile amid the darkness and chill of today.

March 3

"How long, O Lord? Will you utterly forget me? How long will you hide your face from me? How long shall I harbor grief in my soul?" (Ps 13:1-2). To all of us there come hours, days, weeks, months, longer periods, when these words seem by rights to be ours, mine. Whatever the causes—sorrow, depression, discouragement, loss of friends and family members, disappointment—the result is a feeling that we've been forgotten by God, that there is no end in sight to our misery. The Bible shows us people who have kept alive the greatest faith and confidence through just such trials, even abandonment. Think of Jesus on the cross praying: "My God, my God, why have you abandoned me?"

The enemy mentioned in the same psalm—"How long shall my enemy triumph over me?"—was probably for the writer some physical foe just over the hill or lurking outside the walls. For us more often the enemy is some circumstance of human life, a crushing and often unexpected setback to our plans by way of some disaster or health problem or hurt from another.

This short psalm, which expresses so well the grief and discouragement we can all feel, concludes abruptly with a couple of verses of trust and joy in the Lord: ". . . I trusted in your kindness. Let my heart rejoice in your salvation; let me sing to the Lord, 'He has been good to me.'"

Choosing this short and quite intelligible psalm to use in our troubles can probably, because of its confident and joyous ending, help us to see beyond the darkness that seems to surround us. There will be another day, another hour, another place where we sing again, rejoice again, know again the Lord's goodness.

March 4

Lent is often summarized for Catholics in terms of "prayer, fasting and almsgiving," a formulation taken over from earlier Jewish thinking. With that last rather quaint word, almsgiving, it may all sound pretty out of touch. But, basically, if we accept the three as a sort of shorthand summary for what our relation to God, self, and others should be, it can be helpful.

The problem with short formulas is that over a period of time the human tendency is to take them as complete summaries of the situation. Prayer, fasting, and almsgiving are what is asked—and often, that is all we think is asked. But, looked at from the perspective of the original intention behind them and as representing more than they literally say, the three can be very helpful.

Prayer is an abbreviation for our relation to God, for the necessity we are all under to keep contact with God, to worship, to speak to God. Something more in the nature of a dialogue, an ongoing conversation. After all, we do have God's part of it in Scripture, in the revelation given to us in the Church, in creation, in the events of our life and world. Prayer is simply a continued response.

Fasting refers to withdrawing food from the body, strictly speaking. Behind it is the idea that the self needs to be checked, limited in its tendency to turn the universe into a meo-centric one. In various ways we need to assure that self-consideration and self-satisfaction are not the only goals in our lives.

Almsgiving suggests giving a dollar to persons in need. But in a sense it's really the other side of fasting: It means turning in generosity and love to the service of the needs of others. It may not be primarily through the gift of money but through everything from involvement in politics and public service to charitable giving to volunteer work to just accepting joyfully the "obligations" we have to family, friends, neighborhood, community.

How we fulfill and understand prayer, fasting, and almsgiving is less a matter of prepackaged how-to lessons from the Church and more a matter of how we respond in love to the circumstances and calls of our world, our life, and our place.

March 5

For my birthday I received a card that one would only receive after a certain age. On the outside it read, "You are still young enough to have fun." Inside the text was: "But, hurry, hurry, hurry!" Every new beginning, either of the year or of Lent or the Advent season should put more urgency into our life, more spring into our following of Christ. The temptation to stagnate is very strong in most of us. And we tend to look for someone else to blame.

Some interpreters see the famous story about Adam and Eve and the snake as portraying the human desire to be more than merely human, to claim some divine condition. In another view of the same story—this is the great advantage of such stories, that they provoke such varying responses—we see pictured here the typically human refusal to be all that God wants us to be, a willingness to listen to some snake in the grass tell us what to do rather than to think for ourselves. Today, let's stay with this second view, the idea that we fear to make decisions, we shirk responsibility, we tend, once in place, not to move.

Presuming, as I think we can, that all of us have some temptation to simple inertia, we should ask ourselves if there aren't encouraging reasons for putting more into our life and actions. Why let ourselves come to an older age, for instance, wondering how we ever got there and why we didn't accomplish this or that? Looking further ahead and at other more energetic and committed people around us, couldn't we think, asking more of oneself is not something at odds with happiness and joy after all. It may be, in fact, the way to them.

The year, the season, our life, is still young enough for us to do a lot with it, in quality even if not in quantity. But isn't there a sense in which we should start today by putting more of ourselves into what we do, giving ourselves more wholeheartedly to the work, the opportunities before us, the people around us?

March 6

Not only because I do not like suffering, but for what I think are more theological reasons, I do not believe that we need to be encouraged to look for suffering, pain, the cross. When our Lord speaks of taking up one's cross as a necessary part of following him, I think it can perfectly well be understood to mean that the following of Jesus means accepting the pain, difficulty, disappointment—call it all suffering if you like—involved in living a life faithful to him. His own cross came as the consequence of his good life and obedience to his Father, not from some search. Love necessarily, in any form, brings suffering.

A genuine love means, as Christ's teaching tells us, a preference for the good of others, of the other. In loving him or her or those around us, we commit ourselves to certain demands on our energies and our time. Left to our good old selfish self, we'd be free of these. Without the intrusion of this person into our life, our welcoming of this person into our life, we would be free to do exactly what we like. But let a man or a woman or a child or a neighbor or anyone into our life and much of our existence is then defined, limited, qualified, refashioned, by their needs, what is best for them. Everyone encounters this in just the simple matter of what you and the other person will do this evening or this weekend. It would be most unusual if two people were to find that their ideas, hopes, or interests simply meshed at all times and in regard to everything. No, we often give in to be sure the other party is also happy, to try to please him or her and, most likely, the other person does the same.

Suffering, difficulty is simply the consequence of accepting the conditions of relationship and the conditions of our life, our work, our obligations, our commitments. No one of them is ordinarily going to be free of demands, sometimes difficult and painful, on our energies, our time, our disposition.

What better kind of suffering or pain than what is attendant on the good execution of work, the good development of a relationship, on the exercise of love?

March 7

Some words in Christian thought have been so overburdened with excess baggage or so caricatured that they "get no respect" in our world, even among Christians. Understood as they often are, they probably don't deserve it either. Take "humility." "Ugh," you groan, "You keep it." A downer, making a virtue of depression or of wimpiness, considering oneself the scum of the earth, dragging one's chin on the pavement. Who needs it? Many get put down enough as it is by life, unpleasant people, even parents, teachers, and bosses.

But a better, more respectable word for it today would be truthfulness, or simply truth. Humility (in its origins a word meaning to be down to earth) means really recognizing the reality that all that we are and have comes from God. That we are dependent on God for everything. To recognize that is humility. Recognizing the truth of our existence—that we did not make ourselves or our world but depend on God—is humility. And Genesis tells us that all God made including ourselves is good, worthy of respect. Why should humility or any other virtue mean denying that or lessening it? Humility has little to do with beating the breast and walking around with poor posture and a long face. It means rejoicing in the fact that we have our origin in God's love, and that, despite elements in our existence that terrify us, we are in the hands of a Creator who loves us.

March 8

Freedom, deliverance, liberation—all are closely related, and all are used often in the Bible to describe what God has done for those who trust in God. The prayer often is, You have set me free; you are my deliverer. The attitude suggests wide open spaces, heights, a broadness and spaciousness—freedom. Yet too often we Christians have spoken of our life in Christ as a matter of following commandments, feeling bound by rules, laws, regulations. Quite the opposite atmosphere from talk about freedom and deliverance. Yet freedom and liberation have a long history in the Jewish and Christian religions. We pray regularly: Deliver us from evil, free us from what is bad. The dominating event and motif of Jewish history is God's deliverance of the people from slavery in Egypt. The event was so important and vital that still today the main celebration of the Jewish faith is a recalling of that deliverance by a meal of remembrance, the passover meal.

In writing about Christ, Christ's followers who were Jews themselves spoke of him and pictured him as the new Moses, leading his people not from slavery in Egypt but from slavery to sin, suffering, and death. We in turn celebrate that each time we're at Mass: The Mass is a meal but a meal remembering what God does for us in Jesus, how he frees us from self, sin, death.

We should see our relation to God in Christ as a matter of freedom, our being Christians as a matter of freedom rather than being bound by more laws. Writer Flannery O'Connor in a letter to a friend who was thinking of becoming a Catholic Christian says that one should never do that unless one sees it as an enlargement of one's freedom. How far we often are from this biblical and expansive view of our faith! Too often our practice and speech about it only serve to justify those around us who see following Christ as a form of enslavement or, at the very least, a diminishment of freedom. Why not start our days more often with thankfulness for being freed by Jesus from what binds, cripples, suffocates?

March 9

Born again. Right. And again and again and again. For most human beings to expect that all is changed by one moment or one experience for all time is simply unrealistic, inconsistent with how God works through our human nature. Even Jesus, according to Luke's Gospel, grew in grace and wisdom. To insist that there must be some flashy or momentous new birth after which all is changed is dangerous and mistaken. If you didn't wake up today feeling that the power of some big past moment still dominates your every action, don't be surprised. Significant decisions about the direction of our desires and lives are not achieved in one fell swoop, but only little by little.

It certainly may happen that individuals will feel justified in dating their conversion to an exciting, even tear-filled moment, 5:03 PM, to be exact, on July 25 in the Miller Mall while looking at some new cords in the County Seat. It may indeed be a point of fervor that one can look back at for inspiration, but that it causes an indelible change in behavior I have serious doubts. Worse yet, someone wrote a book entitled *How to Be Born Again* as if there were some one pattern for spiritual growth. As if it were comparable to learning how to grow orchids in your window box or seeing Morocco on a camel and seven dollars a day. The whole idea diminishes the richness of human nature and the inventiveness of God. To expect that this will be the ordinary way of our development in Christ is simply dangerous.

It is mistaken, too, because maturing in our likeness to Jesus is a matter of growth, trial and error, progress and stalemate, even failure and backsliding. We must unquestionably in some manner say amen to our baptism, to the new life in Christ. But the amen may have to be demonstrated over and over again by the decisions we make, the little deaths to self and the rising to unselfishness that make up ordinary life. Thinking that it is all a matter of one emotion-filled moment or one decision easily leads to unrealistic expectations and possibly great discouragement when we face the fact of our enduring selfishness.

The Protestant Reformers rightly emphasized that the Church needs constant reform. The same is true for each of us. To review our day's actions and find selfishness and insensitivity, greed and misrepresentation of others is humbling, but it demonstrates the need we have to be born again, in a sense, each morning, each day. We get nowhere by letting the previous day's burdens and failures weigh us down. We allow Christ to work in us the more we begin each day with the recognition that we can begin again, with new hope in the grace of God. The Eucharist puts before us daily the death and rising of Jesus, the lifelong pattern for everyone who would be his follower.

March 10

Talking serpents, a tree of knowledge, a tree of life, a woman being formed around the rib of a man—all these are among the unforgettable and rich images that characterize the first book of the Bible, Genesis. Once we've read it or heard of the images, they linger in our minds, our consciousness (or maybe subconsciousness), our imagination. With a bit of reflection, they can continue to nourish our life in Christ over the years. The major difficulty is that we approach them too often with the wrong sort of attitude. Our problem is the one we have or seem to have so often with poetry, music, drama, and dance. So often our response to them is; What does it mean? But does everything have to mean something? Or must everything mean one thing only and no more? Can't some elements of our experience or our world just be, or just be beautiful, inspiring, exciting, refreshing, calming, wonder provoking?

The famous dancer and teacher of dancers Martha Graham once said after being asked what a particular dance meant, "If I could tell you, I would not have danced it." Music, dance, legends, poetry—like Genesis—are all of that nature. They don't exist simply to teach or even necessarily to teach at all. They don't tell us that in winter the days get longer, bones get brittle with age, the French don't use dollars, one's diet should include fibre. If living were solely a matter of accumulating such knowledge, there would be no need for these arts. But they do exist because there is simply more to life than meaning, than what can be expressed in such sentences as those above.

The great stories of a book like Genesis are stories rather than philosophical or theological treatises because there is so much more to say about life than can be put in ordinary words or language. Let's read them with minds open to the hard-to-form suggestions they may make to us.

Too, let's be open to the people and experiences of our daily life in the same way. They don't all have lessons for us either. Some of them will simply strike a responsive chord or awake a feeling of awe or excitement or evoke a "Wow!" Isn't it wonderful enough that a little six-month-old, for instance, can be so fascinating?

March 11

The prophet Jonah and his message have been pretty well overshadowed—understandably—by that famous whale. But there's much more to that strange little story. Jonah was sent to preach repentance to the Ninevites, a foreign people whom he and his folk would never have considered worth the trouble. God was more broad-minded. After dragging his feet but nevertheless doing the preaching, Jonah was then angry and disappointed that the Ninevites had actually listened and avoided the promised destruction by repenting. He seemed quite disappointed, too, that God was determined to be kind to people who didn't belong to Jonah's crowd, his club.

The temptation to resent or at least to look with some suspicion on those who are different from ourselves is with us all the time. Sometimes it takes the form of a national hysteria about some group, or it may be just a local problem. Politicians, jingoists, media, various individuals, all conspire to define as enemies or wrong those who simply have different customs or beliefs, look different, or have just moved here like our grandparents did. Despite some of that same tendency at times, the overall message of the Bible points to a God who is trying to widen and broaden the sympathies and hearts of those who hear God.

A book or story like that of Jonah tells us to resist the spirit around us, which regrets rather than welcomes signs of good will in others, in our so-called enemies, which is sad at their progress. This little book may have been meant to broaden the horizons of the Israelites about who can be saved, but the message is timeless. Everyone is invited to the banquet of the Lord. We are always on surer ground when we are tolerant, forgiving, and open rather than intolerant, stubborn, and closed.

March 12

Many places in Scripture seem concerned to lessen our self-love, our self-preoccupation, our plain selfishness. This is so strong, in fact, that some have seen Christianity as teaching a severe repression of self, as pushing negativity, self-hatred even. And some of the strong language used, if we do not allow for exaggeration, would justify that belief. But more honestly, Scripture is simply asking us to combat our aggressiveness, self-seeking, to limit our continual temptation to advance ourselves before everyone else, to push all the me-projects, no matter what the price to others. Our world offers many illustrations of self-exaltation destroying the lives of others, from egomaniacs like a war-mad dictator to individuals who walk all over others for their own advancement. The thirst for power, satisfaction, position, money stems from our overwhelming desire to see what we can do to make "me" happy. If it isn't a geocentric universe, we often seem to be saying, why not at least make it a me-ocentric one?

Admittedly, it is very difficult for us to leave out of consideration what is in it for me in whatever I do. Our Lord recommends in one of his parables that we show hospitality to those who can't invite us back for dinner, urges us to act at least sometimes without a reward or satisfaction in mind. It's tough! There's nothing wrong in inviting friends to dinner, he says, but what about doing good to those who can't or won't repay us? That's a higher level of imitation of Christ, who died for us when we had done nothing to deserve it, and certainly couldn't really repay him.

One observer has pointed out that even the person who denies himself or herself is in some sense congratulating the same self (in the back of the mind) for doing it. It's hard to get away from. To escape from the self and its influence is probably the most difficult and basic thing Christ says we should attempt. As someone else has said, "You can never really get away—you can only take yourself somewhere else."

While we recognize how our self-love, legitimate as it is, can easily become excessive, aggressive, become our great passion and turn us from God and others, we must trust in our union with the Lord for some of his expertise in self-giving to rub off on us. Christ both teaches and illustrates self-giving and makes it possible in us.

March 13

"Can't think of much going on. Trips to Japan, Sweden, and California coming up, plus a few other places. Work keeps me occupied most of the time. . . . You asked about my promotion. It means: title, recognition, more vacation, salary increase. . . . Betty called but I'm not holding my breath in anticipation of seeing her soon. . . . Very quiet, very dull, no excitement. Waiting for spring."

Part of a letter from a very bright young man, getting ahead fast in the corporation he is with; at the same time he is disappointed in relationships with women and the difficulties with meeting them in a large city.

The letter suggests, I'm sure, to many another that Luke (let's call him that) has it pretty good: very good job in a field he was trained for, lots of travel (with a good expense account, too), promotions, a secure future. Yet, life is dull, no excitement: "I'm waiting for spring."

We need to hope, plan, do better. *And*, we need to accept with love and gratitude what we have or have accomplished or been given. We need also to do a bit of comparison at times of our lot and that of others—to at least put our suffering in perspective. *And* we need to balance all these apparently conflicting attitudes and feelings somehow in our own formula, while, of course, making use of all the human means available to improve matters: singles' groups, changes in our own way of acting, and so on. "Waiting for spring." Who isn't? At anytime of the year. There is always more than we can envision, expect, hope for. The Christian's hope and desire should always ultimately be centered in Jesus, God's gift to us, the one in whom and through whom the fullness we all desire can and will come. "Hope springs eternal in the human breast; man never is, but always to be blest."

March 14

F. Scott Fitzgerald writes of a man who in his days of careless carousing has lost his wife to death and his little girl to relatives. Some years later, sobered and reformed by the Great Depression and other realities, Charlie goes to recover his daughter. While he and the relatives are discussing arrangements, they are interrupted by two drunken friends from the past whom Charlie is trying to shake. Despite his own reform, chances of getting his daughter back are dashed by the impression given by these ghosts (or more than that) from his past.

The call of Christ to us is one of repentance, conversion, new beginnings; we hear it in Lent, Advent, at the beginning of the year. A call to the life given us in baptism, to deeper faith and hope, to right relationships. But like Charlie, our past sometimes surfaces unwanted—somewhat like a bad memory of an accident or like those radishes we ate last night. We are tempted to quit, to resent having to begin again and again so often.

But it is just this despair that can block all change. It goes under other names, too: dejection, apathy, inertia. But whatever we call it, it closes us to any improvement. It excludes grace because it expects nothing! It is really spiritual death! This spiritless despondency, someone has written, shows us at whatever age with "the face of one who is already old beyond his or her years, who seems never to have known springtime."

We overcome the past best not by direct attention to it but by positive, state-of-the-art beginnings. Any genuine life is a series of fresh initiatives. The grace of God is always poised, ready to be activated at the slightest signal from us. We've failed and had to begin many times in many things: We fell down the first time we tried to walk; we almost drowned, perhaps, the first time we tried to swim. We probably missed the ball the first time we swung a bat.

Any Lent, any Easter, any Sunday, any day is the time to answer that call to new life, to turn our backs on the past. Unwillingness to start anew often amounts to a sort of pouting over the fact that *I* have failed.

We recover that lost daughter, our self, our dignity and wholeness when we regard each morning as a fresh start, unhampered by discouragement about yesterday's anger, laziness, pride, smallness, sensuality, or ingratitude. We begin anew when we look to the possibilities of today and tomorrow and not back at the wreckage of the past. If we keep our eyes on the one raised on the cross, power comes from him that lifts us up to a crisp and vigorous new life, to the ever-fresh life found only in the crucified and risen Lord.

March 15

The man called Buddha, for whom Buddhism is named, is often presented as being quite impatient with theoretical discussion. He is depicted as one who showed people how to do something about the problems of human life. In one story the Buddha uses the case of the man struck by a poisoned arrow. The Buddha says that the man is not going to spend his possibly dying moments or pain-filled breath in asking who did it and why but rather in asking that it be removed. A man suffering or in mortal peril is not going to ask theoretical, informational questions about his situation but rather that something be done to alleviate it. Christianity, too, despite what our ventures into theology may have suggested to us, is primarily concerned with doing something about our human condition, our suffering and pain, rather than with trying to present intellectually satisfying answers to all the possible questions reason can raise.

No matter how important the Scriptures are in Christianity, and they are most basic, words about religion, God, even about Jesus, are less important than his life, his example, his living power and presence among us for the solution of our problems, for an approach to the pains and perils of human life. What counts more than knowing that sin and suffering have been with the human race from the very beginning or close to it is knowing what we do about it. And we see that pictured and exemplified in the crucified and risen Jesus, the Lord.

In him we are told that persecution and suffering can be the result of complete goodness, can be the accompaniment of a life lived in accordance with the Father's will, can be expected in the course of living as a son or daughter of God. Jesus never tries to tell us why we suffer or where suffering comes from, but he does try to show us that obedience to the circumstances of our life (to God's will for us) may lead to suffering and a cross but also to glorification and resurrection. God sees the servant through all this to victory, to new life. The grain of wheat must die in order to be fruitful, reborn to a new life with God.

March 16

How to Win at Office Politics, How to Get the Upper Hand, The Right to Be Greedy, Winning with Deception and Bluff, and No More Mr. Nice Guy: Business Karate—all these titles express starkly how much of a contrast there is between the ideals of much ordinary life in our time and those of Christ's teaching. The antagonism must offer a real challenge or be a real pain to many a Christian facing the competition and realities of daily commercial life or simply of the parking lot. What do I do?

Think of the sayings of Jesus called the Beatitudes (Matt 5:1-12). Or much of the Sermon on the Mount (Matt 5; 6; 7). What do they do for the person whose business depends on being able to beat the other person to some part of the market? How does a manager compete for the best people while turning the other cheek? How could a real estate company turn a profit now if it were only concerned about inheriting the earth in some much more remote sense and time? Or how even think of profit when the poor are the blessed?

One revolutionary stance, of course, is to drop out of the system, to not participate, and many Christians have done that over the centuries. But it certainly seems that not all of us can do that; in some ways, doing that, tough as it is, is a luxury for a limited number. Immediately, what does one do who is part of the system and undoubtedly will be for years to come?

Doesn't it mean minimally that the Christian must temper, moderate all the impulses that go into the conduct of business and competition? That somehow in the midst of our involvement, we must realize that it is not the most important matter in our life? That taking into consideration the needs and weaknesses of others is what we must do? That our families and friends are more important? Obviously, all the answers aren't here in this short page. But for all of us there are some strong words of the Lord in the Sermon on the Mount, words about restraining our aggressiveness in the face of the needs and desires of others, of softening our hardness. Even apart from the books mentioned at the beginning, our society easily tends to sweep us into its round of competition, rivalry, insensitivity and self-absorption.

Somehow our Lord expects us to take him seriously. Shortly after the Beatitudes, he says: "You are light for all the world. . . . And you (like a lamp) must shed light among your fellows, so that, when they see the good you do, they may give praise to your Father in heaven" (Matt 5:14-16).

March 17

Maybe the reason Christian tradition speaks so often of eternal *rest* is that this life, no matter how we view it, seems so hurried, so full of hassles. Jesus' story about the return of unclean spirits even after the house has been swept clean of them (Luke 11:15-26), suggests that there will always be something new to combat, some new challenge to our peace and equilibrium. The "evil spirit finds the old place swept and put in good order," and it's as irresistible to him as suburban bodies at a barbecue to a swarm of mosquitoes. Sometimes it's the same vices that come back again and again to keep us humble and trusting in God. At other times it's new ones.

The ancient Chinese philosopher Confucius wrote to the effect that in youth we have to be on guard against lust; in our prime, against strife or aggressive ambition; in our old age, against avarice, grasping. I'm sure we can verify the truth of that formula. It reinforces the insight that life is a succession of trials, temptations, even battles. We are buffeted, if not in the same sequence, at some time or other by the demands of sex, the drives for prestige, power, or possessions.

Confucius backs up the Gospel message that if one vice seems overcome, there's always another one waiting to take its place. The battle to resist succumbing totally to some overwhelming drive is never quite ended. Possibly all these vices or variations on them are there to bother us in order to prevent an even more deadly vice: pride, a conviction of complete self-sufficiency. Such an attitude is even more radically opposed to God since it seals us off to help. Without these other temptations to resist, we could easily be persuaded by an unrealistic complacency and self-sufficiency.

That is the good thing about our temptations (fill in the blank with your own: _____). They can drive us to a sense of our dependence on God, our need to trust. And that should have the last word. That is the Gospel's consolation and good news, that God, the Lord, is with us and always available as we face the hassles of everyday life, of the different seasons of our life. God is with us to strengthen us or forgive us.

March 18

Writers and storytellers, including Jesus and the Gospel writers, at times seem to use distinct individuals to represent what are really only aspects of any one of us. We have the two sons in a story told by Jesus (Matt 21:28-32) who respond to an order of their father, one with yes, the other with no. And then both go and do the opposite of their word. What they ultimately do or don't do is what counts in this story. The real division, of course, most often is not between you and Tim or between Cindy and Jeff, but within each of us, between self-seeking and self-giving, selfishness and service. The two sons may be two aspects of you or me.

The opposite of this dividedness is what Jesus calls purity of heart. The term is something we could translate as singleness of heart, wholehearted aim in one direction, dedication to one ideal. What is most important in our lives for our consciences is this direction. What is my direction, my goal? At what do I aim? What do I most desire? Service or love, call it by any number of terms, should be the unifying ideal of the follower of Christ. It's what he came to model for us—to death.

We have been in the process for some time now in Christian Catholic thought, of trying to recover a notion of sin as referring primarily to the wrong overall direction of our life and intentions rather than to a number of specific, often very little, actions. To the unnecessary disturbance of many people, we have too often in the recent past found sin in too many specific actions, like finding electronic bugs behind every picture in the embassy.

We can contribute to our own maturity and the peace of mind of others if we learn to put the emphasis on the preference of our wills rather than on isolated actions taken apart from this intention. We might ask ourselves more often: For what, for whom, do I live and act? What is at the root of my life and its activity? Answering these questions can purify my life, make clearer and stronger the force I want it to have.

March 19

In the story of Jesus raising Lazarus to life in John's Gospel (ch. 11), Jesus is described as weeping when he comes to the tomb. The people around him say, "How dearly he must have loved him!" (vv. 35–36). In itself a beautiful testimony to the reality of Jesus' human nature: He sorrows over the death of a friend.

Some scholars in studying Scripture texts are at times tempted, possibly justifiably in some cases, to rearrange the verses, claiming that someone else along the line had done so to present a particular view of the situation. The scholars are simply trying to restore the text to its original state. All that is, obviously, very arguable. But it suggests to me a great spot in the Gospel story of Lazarus for this remark: "How dearly he must have loved him!" Another great spot, that is. Surely where it is it makes complete sense and expresses beautifully what Jesus experiences in the face of any death. He shares in our grief; in fact, he went through it with us. Early on in the story, Lazarus is called "the one Jesus loved"; he stands in a sense, like many a Gospel character, for all of us, loved by God, by Jesus.

Wouldn't it also be a fitting place for the expression, "How dearly he must have loved him!" when Jesus has called out to Lazarus and the latter has come out of his grave alive? "How dearly he must have loved him!" That, too, would express the fact that God's love calls us into being in the first place and restores us to life after we have been sick and even dead like Lazarus. God's love loves us back into life.

That love given to us is meant to do the same all around us and through us. Love brings to life, gives heart, gives hope. Our love, our kindness, gentleness, forgiveness, encouraging and complimentary words, all do the same for those around us. They serve to make concrete the love God has for all of us, to make it real here and now for them and us.

March 20

Loneliness is not just a sad state to be in or an indication of some failure on our part, it is also just part of being human. If we are as unique and mysterious and rich in personality as we are, then it's inevitable that no one can completely and satisfactorily understand us or feel with us. And that can mean plain loneliness: No one understands me. Absolutely.

But even granted this basic fact, we can and should avoid just sitting around feeling sorry for ourselves or lost in a cold, cold world. Practically speaking, as is most often the case, our life and world and the good of others do not allow us to sit around and feel how lonely we are. There are other approaches to take to the issue.

In terms of our character and the happiness of others around us and, indeed, of our own happiness, there are positive steps to take. Basically, we need to do something to take ourselves out of ourselves, to help ourselves forget the pitiable state we think we are in. In many ways the best thing is to think of the good of others, of something we can do for someone else who is probably as lonely as we are or in some other difficult circumstance. We can give her a call, write him a long-neglected letter, do something in the way of a pleasant surprise for her, offer to take him out, suggest something we can do together.

What better way to make concrete and real the love of God for others than to do something that makes them happy, lifts their spirits, encourages them, takes them away from their problems and difficulties? And in the process, we are able to forget our own misery for a short while or maybe for quite a while.

March 21

People in the public eye, like Julie Roberts, George Steinbrenner, and Magic Johnson, are often quite concerned about what people say about them. They pay large sums to assure the best image. They rebut unfavorable comments. They write letters to the papers and ask for equal time. Even Jesus asked his disciples at one point, "Who do the people say I am?" Their answer was anyone from Elijah to another prophet to John the Baptist. Finally, Peter said, "You are the Christ of God" (Luke 9:18-24). Interestingly enough, Jesus does not jump in and say: "That's it, Peter, you've got it!" Rather in the next verse he refers to himself by a very ambiguous term, the Son of Man. Son of Man, like you or I, is the son or daughter of human beings.

The way Jesus dodges titles in the Gospels suggests that he is saying, I don't really fit into any of your categories or descriptions. In the Old Testament God the Father had said something similar in answer to questions asking who he was: "I will be who I will be." In other words, it really is beyond you; there is no simple word for me. By his refusal to accept a particular description, Jesus justifies the comment his enemies will make all through his life: Who does he think he is anyway? They couldn't nail him down; when they tried, he rose to a new kind of life.

Jesus has been pigeonholed as everything from teacher to ruler to judge to superstar to revolutionary to social reformer. One good reason for studying the Gospels is to become better acquainted with what Scripture itself reveals about him. The big problem with defining him too well according to our desires is that such images prevent him from challenging us and assure that we stagnate. Why read of the words and actions of such a prophet if we already know all that he has to say? Leave Jesus be who he will, and he will be able to do in us more than we can expect or imagine.

March 22

Jesus did not die because his father's anger cried out for blood or to make satisfaction for us. That would be entirely out of character with the God Jesus proclaims. His death, as the controversies in the Gospel stories show, was the result of the opposition that built up against him. His life illustrates, once again, the truth that some of our popular evangelists apparently do not accept, that goodness and obedience to God are *not* always rewarded here and now with happiness or long life, success, wealth. The Son of God died on a cross at thirty-three years of age, only a couple of years after he began preaching, hardly what ordinary parents would regard as success for their son or daughter. Many a faithful believer in God does not get cured, does not make a bundle and live happily ever after on this earth. Many of them, of us, live in pain; others suffer want or abandonment. Goodness doesn't necessarily earn a reward in this life; on the contrary, it sometimes is accompanied by the cross of Christ. Many who follow him are led to say with him, "My God, my God, why have you forsaken me?" All the more reason why we whose sufferings and disappointments may be on such a small scale should avoid too easily saying the same thing.

But faced with the awful sufferings of friends and relatives, the world around us, we should more easily understand the temptation to feel abandoned, to despair. Jesus is being crucified again and again in his followers, his members, in the poor and oppressed, in the victims of greed.

The words of Jesus on the cross "Why have you forsaken me" are the opening words of Psalm 22, a hymn familiar to him and other Jews. Whether or not he went on to quote the rest or not, it is important to realize that the overall message of the same psalm is of hope and confidence, something to remember in our pains and in our anguish at the pains of others. "In you our fathers trusted; they trusted, and you delivered them" (Ps 22:5).

March 23

Nearly everything comes to us labeled "instant," "easy," "self-cleaning," "grease free," "no press," "worry free." And most of us are happy to settle for buying packaged ice cream rather than turning the crank of an ice cream maker ourselves. We don't regret permanent-press clothing; earth movers may prevent a lot of unnecessary back problems.

It may all seem at times to be in contradiction to the harsher statements in the Gospel about the necessity of discipline and entering by the narrow door. Is freedom from pain and sweat simply at odds with Christianity? I don't think so. A study of Christ's life does not support any idea that he purposely looked for suffering or taught us to; he was accused by enemies, in fact, of being a glutton and drinking freely. Our Lord's words about entering by the narrow door, taking the difficult route, sharing his cross, remain true but on a much more profound level.

They refer to a kind of discipline and patience involved in much more important matters than how we make coffee, shave, or build our house. Our Lord's words refer to the more inward, human effort involved in, for instance, educating children, strengthening the wife-husband relation, developing our character, growing in love, patience, courage, generosity, sustaining illness or accidents. For these there is no shortcut, no instant approach. Discipline is the continued effort over a long time in the pursuit of some aim, direction. Only through daily persistence and effort do we learn forgiveness, how to forget small, selfish concerns. We may open a can with a flip of a wrist, but to open a fearful heart is a slow and more sensitive operation; a pill may help us sleep a bit in the midst of suffering, but it will not make a serious problem between two people evaporate.

Our Lord's path, celebrated in every Mass, the path through suffering and death to resurrection and new life, is not just a pattern he happened to fall into. It's the pattern for human life.

Growth, spiritual maturity, requires that we go through the suffering and pain of self-forgetfulness and work for others, the alteration of our feelings and attitudes, the surrender of some cherished prejudices and smallness, the boredom of routine and everyday faithfulness. The question is not really do we want this way or some instant way; there is no instant way. But the question is whether we will willingly and generously accept the pattern written into our life or kick against it. The real crosses, sacrifices, in our life are not ones we choose but those about which we have no choice, those that are given to us by circumstances, responsibilities, relationships.

March 24

Those of us of the Catholic tradition seem at times more likely to deny ourselves a drink before dinner than to do the more difficult thing of being pleasant to the family and interested in what they've been doing. We may more easily forgo chocolate in Lent than visit the elderly lady upstairs. Or we add attendance at Mass and more prayer, all the while continuing to neglect writing a letter to a lonely or desolate acquaintance—because we have no time. It's the old temptation to substitute something quantifiable (a check instead of a visit) for the more difficult interior conversion we constantly need, the move from self to selflessness. We easily practice a kind of dishonesty when we involve ourselves in fasting and abstaining while leaving untouched our too-quick judgments of others, our lack of understanding, our impatience, our self-pity and our self-absorption, our tardiness or absenteeism.

Most of us have many reasons to maintain or develop a more positive and hopeful attitude, to be less whining and self-pitying, less willing to assume that we are among this world's victims, its persecuted, neglected, and misunderstood, than to cut out some little pleasure or add some devotion. Even worse, we can make ourselves feel like victims by withdrawing a few creature comforts from ourselves. We create an artificial purgatory that calls at least for self-pity if not someone else's pity too. Why not accept the health and ease we have, not as deserved but as a gift, a spur to more joy and gratitude in return, more generosity with the good or goods we have? Giving something up, as we say, in Lent, for example, often seems a luxury compared to the more obvious but left undone words and deeds of generosity and care that could light up other lives and lighten other burdens.

March 25

The outspoken people who challenge the despoilers of the forests of Alaska or the Amazon, the courageous men and women who point out the injustices in the treatment of the poor or the Native Americans or farm workers, those who give up jobs and carry signs to warn us against nuclear dangers, all these easily come under the umbrella of "prophet" in our day. Prophets in Scripture are those who speak for God by challenging the injustice of our mutual dealings, by pointing out the threats to human life and dignity.

As long as creation lacks the fulfillment that the Lord has promised, there will be need for prophets. But for those of us who have other callings and other responsibilities, it is important to understand and accept the fact that there *are* different gifts. Chapters 12 and 13 of the First Letter to the Corinthians have much to say on this. They tell us that there are many and varied gifts of the Spirit, all meant for service of the same Lord. "In each the Spirit is manifested in one particular way, for some useful purpose" (12:7). And some of the possibilities are listed: the gifts of helpful, intelligent speech, of clear expression, exceptional faith, the power to heal, to speak prophetically, to utter ecstatic praise. Elsewhere, Paul amplifies the list (Rom 12:6-7) to include administration, teaching, leadership. In our world today we could include everything from computer programmers to those who care for children, to nurses and doctors, lawyers and secretaries, people in public transportation, bankers, salespeople, and on and on.

Some of the tasks or positions strike us as having varying degrees of glamour or value, yet all serve some purpose. We need to learn to find our spot, to use our talents and gifts without constant over-the-shoulder looks of regret at what someone else is doing. The body of Christ, Paul says, the organism of all those linked to him by faith, is composed of many parts, organs, all necessary for the functioning. It is useless and unrealistic to yearn to be something we are not (possibly cannot be) while shortchanging the life and opportunities right before us. Lord, help me to love and do well what you put before me this day and every day.

March 26

In a complaint about the unresponsiveness of his contemporaries Jesus compares them to a bunch of hard-to-please children (Matt 11:16-19). Someone plops a popular disk on the CD player and they won't dance; someone says, "Let's play sad" and they won't mourn. It's a bit like the situation where the wife complains that her husband never wants to do anything but sit and watch TV in the evening or on weekend. He's no more attracted to a concert or a dance than he is to a wake or a PTA meeting. The tendency to inertia, to a kind of unresponsiveness like that facing the football widow, is common to many of us. Others often wonder what it would take to move us. We are so inclined to get comfortable with what we are and where we are that we seem actually immovable. Any time, but especially Lent and Easter, is a good time to question ourselves about this heaviness, this inertia.

When do we pass from being justly comfortable to being simply inert? When do we pass from being settled and sure of ourselves to being just rigid? When does routine become rut? When do we pass from being serene and tranquil to membership in the living dead? When do we cease being simply carefree and become just unconscious?

We need periodic reminders to shake us up a bit, to make us at least think about the possibility that there are worthwhile changes yet to be made, that grace could still do something new in us. That there is more to come.

March 27

An article on a British billionaire reads: "Maxwell does not collect art or attend concerts and rarely reads a book or sees a movie. . . . He sleeps only four hours a night. . . . Though his wealth could mean a life of ease, he values working. 'Most rich people just shop,' he says with disdain. He has no personal friends: 'I don't have the kind of time one needs to give to friendship' " (*TIME,* November 28, 1988).

This book has nothing to say to a man like this. He is on such a different wavelength that the values and ideals espoused here are incomprehensible to him. Still, maybe this book has everything to say to this kind of man: It speaks of and expresses the belief that art, music, human achievement in general, and above all, friendship and love are the matters that count most in human life, way ahead of work and wealth.

Two contrasting pictures emerge. One is of the person devoted to money and power at the cost of all that seems to make human life worthwhile. The other picture values human life and deeds for bringing before us vividly the reality and presence of God.

Loved ones and friends, from wife or husband to friends and loves—what more concrete, reassuring, and real signs do we ever have of God's love for us? Without them even the greatest and most important message of Scripture has no reality, no flesh and blood. God's love—from the care and concern of parents to that we receive from those who love us and whom we ourselves have chosen to love—is what keeps human life going, what moves any of us to do anything good. Oscar Wilde said somewhat outrageously, as was his wont, but correctly: "Christ did not die to save people, but to teach people how to save each other. This is, I have no doubt, a grave heresy, but it is also a fact." No, Oscar, it's no heresy; it's just the actual meaning of "Christ died to save us." It becomes real to us when it comes through a word, a smile, a touch—from a friend, someone who loves us.

March 28

Even though the evening television news is sandwiched in between perfume, jogging equipment, and deodorant commercials, and certainly presents a domesticated view of the horrors and tragedies of our world, there are people one hears of who don't want to see it or read the news. It's too depressing, they say. And, after a day of constant confrontation in the course of one's responsibilities, it may be understandable that we'd prefer a tranquilizing experience to something that will open up all the limitations and frights of our world. It is easy to escape from terrors outside ourselves and even those within by means of enough distraction, noise, activity.

But whatever form it may take, we all must in some way or other face the frightening experiences, the temptations to despair and discouragement, the questions about the meaning of everything. Otherwise our faith, our religion, our life lacks a certain amount of depth and realism. We may be living in an illusion. To experience lostness, emptiness, meaninglessness, fear, a genuine sense of how utterly fragile my life is, all that is a necessary backdrop to genuine, illusion-free hope and trust, to faith. Someone has said that holiness means knowing oneself to the point of being horrified; paraphrased a bit, we might say that there is no holiness, no opening to it without some profound awareness of what life is without faith or trust.

Hard as they are to endure, most of us who have had some experience of hopelessness, of wanting to give up, of seeing life as empty and pointless, have realized from that experience what faith and trust really mean, what we are being saved from. Perhaps we have to share Christ's "My God, my God, why have you abandoned me" cry to be ready for resurrection, for new life, for hope and trust.

We only really believe what God is and what God can be for us when we have tasted discouragement and loss.

March 29

George Burns: "I'm very fortunate. Let me give you a little bit of advice. Fall in love with what you're going to do for a living. It's very important. To be able to get out of bed and do what you love to do for the rest of the day is beyond words." One couldn't agree more: "to be able to get out of bed and do what you love to do for the rest of the day is beyond words." It must be everyone's ideal: to be able to bounce out of bed looking forward to what you will spend most of the day doing!

If we look carefully at Burns' words, certainly not meant to be an introduction to philosophy or theology, we do find some helpful qualifications for those of us who *don't* bounce out of our beds excited about what is before us today. He says, "I'm very fortunate." You bet. Not everyone has that kind of job; whatever else it is, we can certainly call it a kind of good fortune. And it seems as arbitrary at times as other blessings: Why do I live in a relatively safe and prosperous part of the world while other humans live in an earthquake-stricken area, already one of poverty? No matter how much we want to lay our blessed state at the door of hard work and thrift, we must admit that our circumstances are not all deserved. We're fortunate.

To get from being not so fortunate as to love one's work, Burns seems to suggest a solution: "Fall in love with what you're going to do for a living." It's somewhat related to the old axiom, if your work bores you, try doing it well. It also suggests, do for a living what you're going to love doing. Maybe more people beginning their life's work should look at it that way. I'll try to do something for a life work that interests me, rather than simply something I know will make money. Falling in love with what you're doing is also a great idea; however, I'd hate to try and push it too much with some of the jobs we human beings must have.

Possibly for those of us who are not in the ideal position of George Burns—happy in his work in his mid-nineties—there are some more-provisional measures we can take. We can look at the job as positively as possible and emphasize that side. We can concentrate on doing those parts of the job that are least painful in the most generous and satisfying manner possible. Maybe we must look beyond the job itself to some other reason for enduring it: At the basic level, of course, is the fact that we and family have to eat and be sheltered. Maybe love—for that same family or someone else who is being helped by the job and us—should lead us to do our best with it. Our work, what it means to us, how we go about it, how we can make it contribute to our happiness and that of others, is a huge issue, worth reflection and action. God grant that I find some good, some hope, some joy in what I do today.

March 30

Even if we can be forgiven some nostalgia for our youth or for the old home and the days past, it is still a bit sad when we think that all good things are in the past; that the present just marks a decline from all that has been and the future can only bring worse. Such an attitude is often linked to or meant as a support for religion: The idea is that "back then" people were more religious, morals were better, the pope, priests, elderly people all got more respect. While on the surface this seems a longing for better times, it can suggest a great lack of hope and confidence in God's plans and God's grace in us and our world.

Even at the Lord's Supper, the heart of Christian practice, we do not simply thank God for what *was* or recall with nostalgia what Jesus did, but we express our hope for what is yet to be, for what God can still do. Such hope and confidence drove the great Pope John XXIII in his late seventies to call the momentous Vatican Council of the sixties. Even old age, he demonstrated, "does not have to mean that your heart dies and dries up." And he showed, too, that not only could an old man initiate change but that an even older institution, the Church, could respond. So can we.

Each morning should be a new beginning, a looking ahead to the possibilities of today and tomorrow, not back at the wreckage of the past. Some lines of the great and eternally hopeful Cardinal Suenens about the Spirit express it well: "We must be ready to expect the unexpected from God—I am a man of hope, not for human reasons, but because I believe that the Holy Spirit is at work. To those who welcome Him He gives each day a fresh liberty and renewed joy and trust. . . . I believe in the surprises of the Holy Spirit; John XXIII was such a surprise. To hope is a duty not a luxury. To hope is not to dream, but to turn dreams into reality."

March 31

Oysters can be grown in on-land tanks under such well-controlled conditions that they never encounter a whale and mature with lightning speed. Instant oysters. Though there may be a lot of pearls among us, we are not homegrown oysters or products of accelerated technology. Our character, our growth in Christ cannot be that hasty. Our Lord warns against this when he tells the parable about building on rock and not on sand. Without solid foundations the wind and the rain blow away the building. We've all had the experience of quelling our temper for possibly even months only to find it still capable of a volcanic explosion. Liza Doolittle (in *My Fair Lady*) is passed off as a princess after being taught the necessities of manners and language, but breaks out into some indelicate language under the excitement of the Ascot races.

Jesus doesn't seem to think that character formation, following him, is simply a matter of learning techniques and externals, of acquiring the accessories of virtue, of attending a weekend seminar or a retreat. The joy of being something, someone, in his teaching presupposes the pain of becoming, of an interior and deep change, often taking much of our life.

It all means patience on our part with slow and plodding attempts to follow Christ, willingness to be formed by his words (daily reading, some reflection), by the sacraments. What can be accomplished within by the grace of God working on a willing heart and through an open ear is what counts. From within will come the lasting change. "The glad heart lights up the face," says the Book of Proverbs. Any other way of lighting up the face is merely cosmetic.

This doesn't mean we shouldn't smile till we've reached sanctity, shouldn't be kind till we're really transformed! But while we encourage ourselves and others by our spirit, our hopeful attitude, and some joy, we continue to work at foundations that are more stable, less dependent on the weather, our health, or our moods.

April 1

"Don't let worry kill you; let the church help." Someone reported seeing this on a billboard outside a small town. The second half of the slogan seems bitterly true at times to some.

It suggests for one thing the overemphasis on sin in the history of Christianity, on finding sin in too many places, especially in regard to the senses, seeing, hearing, tasting, touching. The strong injunctions of Christ against greed and the desire for wealth have often been neglected despite their frequency in the Gospels. At the same time, a complicated structure was developed detailing how many ways one could sin in regard to sexuality. By contrast, one must search long and carefully in the Gospels to find pronouncements by Jesus on that subject. Too often the Gospel, the good news, has been turned into the bad news, into a collection of sayings of doom and gloom. Too often, instead of bringing the saving help and word of Jesus, the Church has seemed to come only to make us worry about petty matters and uneasy about anything smacking of pleasure.

One good antidote to all of this is a more careful reading of Scripture. The message over and over again is of God's unfailing love and concern, God's desire to save all. When the message is demanding, as it is, it is in requiring that we in truth love our neighbor, that we see and carry out the implications of treating him or her as members of Christ.

Would it not be a good and justifiable understanding of our faith if we expected that it give us consolation, inspiration, hope, encouragement, strength? Rather than depress, deflate, discourage, and sadden us? Even the cross of Christ is not conceived in the Christian message as an end but always seen in conjunction with the resurrection as a sign of God's love and a cause for hope and joy.

April 2

Christian moral teaching has recognized that if we have done something wrong, injured or robbed another, we are bound if at all possible to make amends, restitution. Someone who has cheated an employer or employee or has promised a certain kind of work or performance and failed to deliver must repay as time and circumstances allow. People guilty of injuring others through some fault of their own have an obligation to assist in the treatment and its expenses. Both parties are responsible for the care and welfare of a child, whether they are married or not.

Presuming our efforts at restitution, our need is to recognize our sin, ask forgiveness, and be willing to begin again. Probably the greatest danger is that we feel overwhelmed by our failures and hopeless about any other kind of life. Great stories of Jesus like that of the Prodigal Son (Luke 15:11-32) show us repeatedly a loving father who "jumps" at the chance to set us back on the right path, to accept us back into his heart. "I tell you, there will be greater joy in heaven over one sinner who repents than over ninety-nine righteous people who do not need to repent" (Luke 15:7).

April 3

The way marriage and the essentials of the Christian faith mesh is truly astounding, especially in a world where marriage doesn't often get a lot of respect or is regarded as a very chancy affair. But if another's love for us is a sign of God's love, a way in which the care of God is made manifest, then marriage, above all, illustrates it. In marriage, by virtue of the mutual commitment, each assures the other that we, I, or you live in a world where we are welcome, loved, and destined for good, for happiness. In a lasting marriage each party has a daily visible reminder, a concrete realization, of the love of God for us. Through Tim or Mary I know what it is to be loved by God.

The commitment of marriage says, I will always be here for you, with you, Tim, Mary, as someone committed to your good, to console, strengthen, help you, to share joy and sorrow. Faithfulness is just this intention of always being there for the other. This character of marriage becomes richer the more we are aware of the depth and imperishability of God's love, of how it persists throughout the whole history of the chosen people, despite *their* unfaithfulness and capriciousness. Their unfaithfulness, in fact, is spoken of as adultery, a sin against the one who has promised lasting love to them.

Closely linked to this faithfulness of God to those loved (and who isn't included?) is God's willingness to forgive. They are hard to distinguish. Faithfulness and forgiveness are qualities that married couples and friends of any kind must bring to any lasting love. No matter how glorious and inebriating our relation to another is (and spring has brought that experience to everyone, one should think, at least a few times), the reality of an enduring love is that it requires from both parties a willingness to forgive. Our justly prized individuality means that we inevitably rub each other the wrong way, are misunderstood, cause injury or pain. The sin of self-centeredness that afflicts me also afflicts all my friends and associates. They must often forgive me and I must often forgive them. None of this means that we need give up our best convictions; it means rather a recognition that any lasting love depends on a willingness to forgive, forget. The two, faithfulness and forgiveness, serve well as the essential demands we need make of ourselves as we look at our friendships and loves.

April 4

Those of us who have lived long enough can remember religious books and likely sermons and retreats that emphasized our unworthiness, our sinfulness, so much that we could almost see a sort of cloud hanging over ourselves. In an effort to exalt what God does in us, Christianity at various times has seemed to put down the human very much, to attempt to depress any natural excitement, pride, joy, or satisfaction we might have. "All who exalt themselves shall be humbled, but those who humble themselves will be exalted." Get over your self-centeredness; learn to be less pushy and defer to others' needs and comfort; forget yourself, deny yourself. Self-love is the enemy, and it's a hard habit to break.

More recently, at least in the secular world around us, we've been bombarded with encouragement to love and esteem ourselves more, and have been told to avoid negative thoughts. We are told to be ourselves, our wonderful selves, to affirm ourselves. We are to accept and love what we are. Book titles tell it all: *You Are Your Own Best Friend* and (my favorite title) *Ain't I a Wonder and Ain't You a Wonder Too?"*

Undoubtedly there's a balance to be struck here somewhere. There does seem to be evidence that we do spend a lot of time being our own press agents; people are willing to walk all over others if it suits their purposes. There are individuals who see their neighbors as doormats at the entrance to financial, social, or sexual satisfaction. We have lived in apartments or dorms where someone always leaves the dirty dishes for others to do. There is evidence that many of us are involved in a romance with ourselves that goes back to the crib. If we had our own intercoms, we'd probably ring ourselves up several times a day and say, "I just called to say I love you." But granted all that—and haven't I perhaps spent too much time making it clear?—the more recent emphasis on self-affirmation and how okay you and I both are does make a necessary point. Possibly we would respond better to being told how important and fruitful our self-concern can be. Without it we'd probably do little good for anyone else or for ourselves. It's an inevitable part of us, something in us that pushes us to act, to work, to do, and to do better. The best and most selfless-appearing accomplishments of human beings seem inseparable from some legitimate love for self. We can only to a limited degree ever get away from it.

Even efforts to turn ourselves to God's service, the service of others, to learn to give ourselves away, presuppose that we value the self given us by God, that we think our nature, our talents, our lives, are God-given and worth being offered back to God. We give ourselves to God in humility because God has exalted us with gifts worth returning and using for others.

April 5

How much we look for signs from God or about God is evident from the rush to any unusual event with possible religious significance: a weeping statue of Mary, a sign that someone perceives in the stars, or an image on a refrigerator door. In First Corinthians, St. Paul says that the "Jews demand signs and the Greeks seek wisdom but we preach Christ crucified, a stumbling block to Jews and folly to Gentiles" (1:23). The sign we look for can be some spectacular event in the world around us or something more private. We may say, "I'll know that if such and such happens I'm meant to do this or be this." Or we take some spiritual excitement, an emotional lift at Mass, in prayer, from a religious movie or book, as a sign confirming our belief and trust in God. These may all have or not have a lot to commend them; that's matter for some other time. The point today is the one St. Paul is making: The main sign we are given is Christ crucified. What can that mean for our life in Christ, for our thirst for signs and confirmation of our belief? To say that instead of signs we have Christ crucified?

It may be telling us that we should regard a life without exceptional signs or emotional mountains as part of our sharing in the suffering of Christ. And even the suffering, for many of us, will not necessarily be so unusual, so world-shaking. Couldn't it mean simply that we are to realize the importance of the faith that so often does not see or feel but still hangs on? "Blessed are you who have not seen but have still believed," Jesus says in John's Gospel (20:29).

Our participation in the cross, the crucifixion of Jesus, is in pretty down-home ways: in daily faithfulness and care in the midst of often dull and even exasperating activity. Certainly, the day-care person doesn't always have a picnic with the little dears. Nor the person working painstakingly on lining up the dull and demanding facts for a report. Much of daily life comes under the heading of a sort of low-grade suffering that doesn't even have the romance and dignity we attach to great distress. Yes, most of us in our own undramatic and unnoticed way have the opportunity to share in the cross. Blessed are you who have not seen or felt but have continued in belief and trust and hope. Because of Christ, the suffering and desolation of the cross are forever inseparable from its bright sequel.

April 6

That famous story that we usually call the parable of the Good Samaritan (told by Jesus in Luke 10:25-37) really has an odd title if you think about it; it's a bit like saying the Good Canadian or the Good Angeleno, as if it were so exceptional to find a decent one. Well, for his countrymen to whom Jesus was speaking, the Samaritans were a pretty lousy people. They were descendants of some Jews who had gone against Jewish law by marrying people of a different race with different beliefs. So they were regarded as a bad race and unfaithful in their religion. Jews and Samaritans apparently regarded each other with about as much affection as some groups in the Middle East today or in Northern Ireland. Yet, as a slap in the face at this kind of hatred and prejudice, Jesus makes the hero of this story a Samaritan.

In the story, you may remember, a poor man is mugged, robbed, and left half dead by the highway. A priest and a Levite (another religious functionary) both passed by and ignored the fellow. Only the Samaritan—you wouldn't expect anything decent or humane from this type—stops and helps the victim. In our world, depending on who you are, it would be like making the compassionate one a Commie, a nerd, a Libyan, a bum, even a capitalist.

Jesus told the story in answer to a question about who this neighbor is I am supposed to love. Like all of us, the questioner was hoping there would be some limits in the answer, making it a little easier to "love your neighbor." But Jesus' answer leaves no room for limitations. Anyone in need is my neighbor and the real neighbor doesn't ask for credentials from the hurt or suffering person before offering help. It's not a matter, apparently, of finding the "deserving" poor or the deserving victim.

For today, let the story remind us that loving our neighbor or our enemy—Jesus doesn't make any distinction between neighbors who are friends or enemies—may be the only injunction Jesus ever gave that is absolute, without qualification.

April 7

I hope you find the story of the disciples of Emmaus (Luke 24:13-35) as rich and thought provoking as I do. More than that, I'd like you to sense the joy and strength I find in it. Tennessee

Williams sums up well one of the points of this story. One of his famous characters is known for a line: "I've always relied on the kindness of strangers." Memorable movies, plays, literature, the Gospels themselves, have such continual power over our imagination because the authors have expressed something many of us feel but probably never put so succinctly. "I've always relied on the kindness of strangers."

In the famous Emmaus story, the "stranger" turns out to be Jesus. The walk of the two disciples from Jerusalem to Emmaus (like Jesus' own lifelong trek to Jerusalem) is like the way of any human life. For knowledge and know-how, for consolation, for help, for strength, for many more ordinary earthly things, we all depend a great deal on people who are at some stage strangers to us. In them we often find what we need or are looking for. A teacher we meet in the fifth grade for the first time on some September morning turns out to be a vital influence on the rest of our life. Above all, the man or woman we first sighted "across a crowded floor" turns out to be the joy of our life, the ever-present proof in our lives that God lives and, more, that God loves us.

Often this truth of how grace filled strangers can be for us stands out more clearly the more isolated or lost we are. Living in a foreign country and speaking the language poorly, I experienced this truth. The failure of a word processor forced me to look for repairs quite a ways from where I lived. Getting there was a matter of a couple forms of public transportation, with the hope of finding a taxi to take me the last miles to an industrial zone. But there were no taxis, no clear indication of what direction I should go to find the shop, and the real threat of rain while I carried this portable machine. For directions I asked an electrical repairman who was working at a box marked danger. He not only found the place on his map but took me there in his truck.

In my situation, this young man turned out to be the bright light of the day, of the trip. There are so many like this in our lives. Instead of counting up, as we easily might, the grumps and grinches we meet, we have good reason for thinking of how often we encounter or meet graces, people who are gifts to us in a particular moment, who turn out to be signs of the presence of God, of Jesus on our way.

April 8

I think it was Dag Hammarskjöld who is supposed to have said that the greatest achievement is not to have run away, not to have given up, but to hang in there, as we say. It sounds sort of minimal when we're in our take-on-the-world moods but, at other times, we can see a frightening truth here. Possibly we can only appreciate that remark if we've been close to or have actually hit the bottom, felt despair. I suspect we're all tempted to run away at least for a time—from our obligations, our commitments, our efforts, our jobs, our boredom. And we do it in accepted ways. The weekend or the vacation is some kind of break like this. There are darker and more dangerous escapes in drugs or alcohol. Some legitimate breaks like vacations are necessary safety valves, ways of relaxing in order to be able once again to accept the wearing obligations of daily life. T. S. Eliot said that we can't really take an awful lot of reality. We lose patience so often with the gadflies among us who cannot for a moment forget the sufferings of the world, who have no small talk, who cannot laugh as long as anyone in the world is weeping. We turn away from the starving faces on the news or turn to the consolation of some loved one when everything and everyone else seems false and disappointing, harsh and burdensome.

But in the long run, apart from these moments when we hide, put on the earphones and go away in some sense, most of us recognize that a certain persistence, stability, and commitment are intrinsic to a happy life and a good conscience. There is, many have pointed out, no real virtue, no good quality in us, unless it is there with some regularity. An isolated act of kindness is not enough. Love isn't love that fades with the first dark cloud. Perseverance is an ingredient of the qualities that we value.

And prayer, our Lord tells us, must include perseverance. "He spoke to them in a parable [about the persistent widow and the unjust judge] to show that they should keep on praying and never lose heart" (Luke 18:1). And very likely persistence in prayer is at the root of any other persistence we have.

What sometimes prevents us from continuing in prayer is our merely "human" foresight. We think to ourselves that nothing better or good can happen, that obviously nothing is happening. We give up on prayer. But what we can see as possibly happening, in accordance with our reason, is not the measure of what *can* happen. That would presume that our intelligence was the sharpest in the world or that we have the mind of God.

Because we cannot know all that might be, that is reason for hope and joy. Because we cannot foretell what might happen, we have all the more reason to persevere, to continue in hope in one who has the deeper, longer vision. Our experience can verify this for us, and we will have the experience if we persist in prayer.

Lord, I pray poorly, mechanically sometimes and with little hope. Help my poor prayer: strengthen it, enliven it, fill it with persistence and hope.

April 9

"Wherjumeetim?" I overheard a bunch of young women, probably college students, in the restaurant talking. "Where did you meet him?" "Where did you meet her?" In a sense, the more basic question is, as one hears so often from young people on their own, working and living away from home, "Where *do* you meet him or her, that person?" The letter or the refrain goes like this: "I often feel like I'm drowning. It is getting so hard being alone. It wears on me, and makes me crabby and short with people. Having my two best friends in the area move away in the space of three months hasn't helped. No weekend visits to look forward to."

Someone, somewhere, said something to the effect that life is all about meeting, about finding, *that* person. To be a person really means to be in search of another person. The other side of the search is the demand it makes on each of us; there is a need for us to be ourselves the persons who can meet and be that person for another, for others. The need, the search requires that we allow God's love for us to blossom in the form of love, consideration, respect, sensitivity to others—the qualities which make relationships possible. Putting questions like where did or do you meet him or her at the center of our life is not a bad idea. What else is of such value, such worth? To love and be loved, as many a poet and songwriter have put it, pretty well sums up the core of human existence.

Christian belief tells us that God does love us. Like every other great love in our life, it is something unearned, a gift. After "Where did you meet him?," probably the next most frequent utterance is, "I can't believe I should be so blessed, to love Kate and know that she loves me, something I could never deserve." Or words to that effect. Meeting is everything; let's put more of ourselves, our concern, our hearts, into those relationships, which almost add up to life itself. Nothing else is quite worth it.

April 10

The spirit of our religion, of our following of Christ, is not simply a matter of personal choice. It is also of concern to the world around us. If the society we live in has so often such a poor idea of religion, of the Church, possibly of God, it is partly due to how we, consciously or not, picture these. From the very beginning God comes to our world through other human beings; God is mediated through what we say, do, and how we act—though we also must realize that what we believe and what we do are not identical. Nevertheless, given this as God's ordinary way of acting, how God is presented and how religion is presented is not a matter of indifference.

Like anyone else, Christians can expect some allowance for bad days, the aggravation of a toothache or a worry, a bad background or an unbalanced religious education. So we are not on display every minute. But to look at poor images that others have of religion, the Church, God, could help us to purify our own image, our own beliefs.

Religion certainly comes across to some as a burden, a kind of constriction of human life when Christians identify the following of Christ with a kind of behavioral prissiness that has more to do with social practices than with religion. If human interests and joys seem foreign to Christians or something to be apologized for, it certainly is insulting the Creator of all. Religion can come across as small, petty, concerned with unreal and irrelevant problems—what one wears, whether women can distribute Communion, or whether they can appear in the sanctuary. Some of the issues that disturb Christians or occupy their time and breath seem to be cases of fiddling while Rome burns.

Or God comes across as bloodthirsty, arbitrary, punishing. The Son had to die for our sins; he had to be crucified to soften up an angry God! Whew! What a conception of God! Along the same lines, God may come across as unfair when we see disease or evil as punishment for sin.

Religion, the Church, can be seen as a snoop, concerned about the details of personal life in a way that does not respect human freedom and conscience. Or the Church comes across as some sort of dictatorship, a legal labyrinth, a kind of enslavement, a form of thought control, like primitive communism or some brainwashing technique.

The God who comes through the Church and its spokespersons and through all of us should be seen for what Jesus is in the Gospels, loving, liberating, cheering, hope inducing, expansive, and generous.

April 11

In the crucified and risen Christ we have the final picture of the future that is to come, of that for which we hope. The more we look at the teaching of Christ, the less excuse we have for thinking of it in abstract, unreal terms. God's answer to every question and desire that we have is given us in pictures, stories from a concrete, vivid human life. Even the hopes we have for that life, which will fulfill this one, are given shape in the man who after his death appeared to his disciples by a lake, breakfasted on fish and bread with them, and had Thomas touch his side. There is nothing ghostly, dreamy, or even simply philosophical about what we are promised.

Philosophers and theologians, thinkers in general, tend to be suspicious of the concrete, the visible, the individual. Or else because of years of a particular kind of study, they've forgotten it. They would rather deal in what we so often call the "eternal truths." But who cares about eternal truths? What we care about, hope for, desire, is the assurance that what and whom we have loved, what we have desired in our moments of unspeakable longing, will be found or refound forever, or, more likely, surpassed. We have in the resurrection of Jesus an assurance that a transformed and brightened life will be ours, even when this one falls apart. Jesus risen and appearing in all those very concrete episodes to his followers tells us that our hope is justified, that a future awaits us that will be not only recognizably what we have longed for but incredibly more. Christ has risen, alleluia. So will all who believe in Christ, alleluia.

April 12

In the film *Chariots of Fire*, Eric, a runner and future missionary, exclaims, as has many another surely, how exhilarating it is to break that tape, to be the winner. But he then goes on to say that faith has to persist in those less-glamorous moments when dinner is burned or the doctor has just come up with a bad diagnosis or you're out of a job—when you really aren't in any sense a winner. For every time we have a spectacular win there are probably many other moments when we're just surviving or doing simply okay but not brilliantly.

We'd all like to have more frequent and clear indications that we're doing great and we can, of course, help each other in this regard by not being too sparing with the compliments and encouragement, by being willing to recognize the accomplishments of others around us. But we're often going to have to persist without that.

Isn't it one of the lessons of the cross to realize that the greatest progress may be occurring in the most unlikely and painful moments? If God brings new life out of the cross, God may also generate more growth in us during those plodding days and gray months than in those more appetizing times when emotions flame, lights flash, and crowds applaud. Shouldn't we trust that God is working when we persist in trying to pray, when we persist in worship, though neither brings us much consolation? The kingdom, Jesus tells us, grows quietly like a seed.

"Happy are they," he says, "who have not seen and yet have believed" (John 20:29). Faith grows in depth by being exercised in boredom, drudgery, daily obligations, in the unavoidable routine of any life. Faith grows through our endurance of depression, despair, doubt, our sharing in the pains of Christ. None of these is anything welcome in itself, but even when we have done all we can, some of these miseries will be inescapable. They will try our hope, our faith, and certainly will dash our joy to the ground.

I keep telling myself to persist in these small and unappealing bits of drudgery, in the gray and unrewarding days, with the hope that in more serious and really devastating times I may find myself possessed of a deep trust in the presence of the Lord. His words about being with us to the end of time seem to make most sense when we realize that the Lord is with us in suffering, disappointment, and death.

April 13

"You have come to disturb us, O Christ" (words of the Russian novelist Feodor Dostoyevski). This truth is evident throughout the Gospels, especially in the uncomprehending reactions of Jesus' disciples to his actions and words. After he tells them how difficult it is for those with money to be saved, they are properly dumbfounded and say; "Who then can be saved?" Jesus' reply is, "Things that are impossible for you are possible for God" (Luke 18:26-27).

Despite the fact that we can ultimately take some consolation from the reply of Jesus, it is still most important that we take his shockers for cash. And let them disturb us. To rush too quickly to the consolation or the promise in God's word can easily mean trying to avoid the necessary confrontation between our values and God's.

Not to be disturbed by what Jesus preaches and teaches often means we do not really hear what he says; we aren't really listening. He has come to disturb all of us, not just nineteenth-century Russian novelists or first-century disciples. Think of the people in our ordinary life who "can't" disturb us. So often it's the elderly or the very young, and it just means we are not letting ourselves take them seriously. We have written them off as not having enough experience or as having become soft-headed or incompetent, not really worth hearing, not people who could really teach us anything.

How sad if in actuality we treat the word of God in the same way. It should disturb us; it must shake us up, scare us, worry us, at the very least puzzle us. Eventually it can and must mean consolation, peace, joy, but that must be in a sense won, not taken for granted, assumed too quickly, too easily. A little disturbance keeps the blood moving.

April 14

"Born to lose." Losing is a word we use in many different ways in our language. We lose everything from our hearts to our tempers to our glasses or keys; we lose time and we speak of people losing their minds. Some of us can even lose a car in the Disneyland parking lot. "Born to lose" ordinarily means we're the sort who would have no luck at all if it weren't for bad luck. When we look at that list, we realize we don't want to recover everything we lose.

In a superlative sense, Jesus tells us to "get lost," to lose ourselves. It means in practice, he says, that we do not resist if someone slaps us or takes our shirt or forces us to go further than we wish. We must lose ourselves, he says, in order to find ourselves, to become the persons modeled after him.

The paradox about how we find our real life, a more rewarding, true life when we forget the self and its preoccupations in the service of God and others—this paradox cannot simply be understood. Like much of Jesus' teaching, it only yields some sense in the effort to live it out, to practice it.

Getting lost, losing ourselves, in his teaching is never the end. The end is more and richer, deeper life, existence. Once we get over feeling sorry for our poor selves, for being lost, for being unselfish, for being concerned for the good of others before our own, we learn how all this leads to new life, a new self. We are not really born to lose in the teaching of Jesus but born to gain, to live on a more profound and happy level than anything high-tech, money, human ingenuity, or selfishness could achieve.

April 15

Many influential forces and people try to reinforce the idea that Christianity, the following of Christ, is a matter of morals; or they wish to limit it to that. Governments, politicians, law and order forces all like the idea that religion makes people more law-abiding, less inclined to disturbing the peace. Even nonbelievers appreciate religion if it serves this function for society. In fact, some would go further and be even happier if, besides making people law-abiding (not stealing, killing, harming others), religion would just make them more meek, accepting of what any authority has to say.

While this may be understandable, even forgivable in those who are not acquainted with Christianity, still it is a serious reduction, emptying out of the following of Christ, to see it as simply a system of morals. Other religions and movements often duplicate the same set of morals. What is more important for the believer to have is not a set of commandments that forbid this and allow that but a vision and an ideal of what can be through the power of the risen Christ among us. That vision tells us that human effort and activity are not useless, that a new and better world is in the making and can be hastened by our surrender to the grace of God. It tells us that all peoples are meant to live in mutual respect, even love; are meant to share and enjoy the goods of this world and the greater good that comes with the risen Christ. The vision tells us that no matter how many times we hear today of friends suffering from cancer, accidents, grief, great disappointments, how much we read in the papers or hear on TV of catastrophes such as the riots in Los Angeles, war in Kuwait, and ancient hatreds, all that can be changed and become something different, not just in another world, but beginning here and now through the healing activity of Christ in those who trust in him.

Good behavior is the consequence of a vision of what might be. What we need and what inspires us most is trust about the future and God's plans for us, that tells us everything we do can be of eternal worth, can help build a new earth.

"He [God] will dwell among them and they shall be his people, and God himself will be with them. He will wipe every tear from their eyes; there shall be an end to death, and to mourning and crying and pain" (Rev 21:3-4).

April 16

Everyone has noticed how often part of the preacher's task seems to be to remind us of the words of Scripture that we just failed to really hear. It is so difficult to listen to God or even to other people. We often listen only with the idea of finding a place to break in with our own precious contribution. It is even more difficult to listen to God or God's word. We stand at attention for the gospel only to find ourselves musing about that deadline, an upcoming concert, or what's for dinner. Yet, to truly listen seems synonymous with being open to God. Think of how much Jesus promises in John's Gospel, chapter 5:17-30. "Those who hear my word possess eternal life." And "the dead shall hear the voice of the Son of God, and those who have heeded it shall live." And, finally, more dramatically: "An hour is coming in which all those in their tombs shall hear his voice and come forth." The voice and words of the Lord give us life, revive our dull and lackluster spirits. Even more basic in our lives as Christians than what we say or do is our willingness to listen to the word of God, to be truly receptive to God. Some silent time is an absolute necessity for every one of us if we are going to truly hear the word of God.

April 17

To be "christened" really suggests that we are Christ-ed. That term for baptism means more than that we belong to Christ or are made like him. They are both a bit weak for the meaning of baptism. "Christened" means to say more, that we are made Christ, become members, parts of the risen body of Christ. He is the head of this body of which we become members, not members like members of the lodge or club but members as in the word "dismember." "Member" in that word refers to a part of the body, a limb or an organ. From him, the figure means to say, comes the life and vitality that moves through us all. We have "put on Christ" is another way of saying it (Gal 3:27). Being a Christian is not simply a private, personal matter or a matter of a declaration on our part but being joined to the body of believers, the body of Christ. We are Christ-ened.

And the body of which we are members is that of the risen and ascended Lord, a body free of the limitations of time and space. He is no longer present simply in Palestine in the first century A.D. but in Stockholm, Singapore, and San Antonio, here and now, in all who are joined to him. Because our union with him is this close, because his life flows through us (we call it grace), our following of Jesus is not simply a matter of straining every muscle to figure out how we can do it, but of *allowing* him to act in and on us. Imitation of Christ is too weak a term; it suggests that we are looking at a model, a picture, or sculpture some feet away and checking ourselves against it every once in a while. We are closer to him than that; he is in us, or put another way, we are in him.

During the glorious time of Easter and ascension, when the texts used in Mass are so full of the risen Christ, we should make a point of repeatedly coming back to a recognition that this is *the* truth about our salvation. It is primarily a matter of allowing the Lord to work in us by faith, receptivity, trust. His grace in us can more and more identify us with him, make us altogether more "one Christ."

April 18

We in the Northern Hemispheres generally rejoice in the way that Easter, the rising of Christ, and spring, the rebirth of nature, seem to coincide. To see crocuses, tulips, blossoming trees and bushes, lilies, flowering dogwood all reappear and winter and snow recede at the same time that we celebrate the Lord's overcoming of death emotionally reinforces our joy.

However, it doesn't always work that way. I remember an early April newsletter crowing about Easter and warm, inebriating spring weather. The letter had been put together on a Friday. It came out on a Wednesday, by which time the Minnesota weather had asserted its independence: The temperature was ten degrees above zero and snowflakes were in the air. Still, it was the Easter season.

Or we could find ourselves in Australia or Argentina, and there Easter will coincide with fall, with the dying of vegetation.

Both the unseasonable and discouraging interruption of spring and the experience of life in the Southern Hemisphere suggest that Easter is not the same as the reappearance of the grass, the budding of trees, the return of the perennials.

In fact, we need the reminder. Christ's return to life, his new life, is not what was expected (as with the tulips) nor will ours be; it is a *gift*, a sign of God's power and love in our world of suffering and selfishness. In a sense, whether the tulips come up or don't has little to do with his rising. The reality of his new existence is independent of nature, goes way beyond it, and assures us that nature (which, for us, inevitably means death) does not have the last word. In the midst of cold and snow, gray days and discouraging ones, too, the resurrection and its hope must shine for us, and we must let it shine for those around us. After all, we should be celebrating it not only in April and May but in November, December, and February.

April 19

Many of us find a certain kind of Christianity somewhat imperialist, disrespectful of others' privacy and conscience, of their dignity and person. I say imperialist because like the superpowers telling the little nations what to do, this approach tells us what must be our response to God, in what terms and language it must be made, or in what specific practices. A phrase like "born-again," for instance, or "I accept the Lord Jesus as my personal Savior" or wearing the Green scapular or observing the First Saturdays becomes the magic formula or password. Along with what *we* see as the appropriate answer to God's love in our lives, we need to realize that each of us answers God in a different manner. It is true that faith, hope, and love may be essentials of that response, but *how* we express them is not dictated.

Too easily one falls into this form of magic by making *this* word or even *this* experience the norm for determining the value of another's following of the Lord. Or looked at another way, a concern to tell others exactly how God wants them to respond becomes a kind of fussy, self-conscious piety so intent on doing good for others that it forgets to respect their freedom and individuality. In its push to "save" others, it is in danger of losing its own humanity and exhibiting little trust in God. Do-goodism means the self-righteous tendency to think that we know what is best for others and are going to tell them or give it to them whether or not they understand how badly they lack it.

This kind of Christianity fails because in its zeal to "save" others it overlooks the fact that the following of Christ is bound to be somewhat suspect if it does not also lead to a better humanity, more love and trust, in the one intent on doing so much good. In the process of sharing our faith and hope we are only following the steps of the Lord if we ourselves are being reformed and made more faithful, loving, and hopeful at the same time.

April 20

We understand better and profit much more from the Gospels once we realize they were not written to give us a lot of interesting history but were written to model Christian life for us. Mary Magdalene weeps at the tomb of Jesus, and the angel says to her: "Why are you weeping?" (John 20:11-18). Friends or the person in the mirror may ask us similar questions, maybe many times in our lives: Why are you, why am I, sad, down, grim, hopeless? And Mary's response easily fits us in this situation: "They have taken my Lord away." I do not see Christ or his providence in the awful things that happen in my life or in the world or among my friends. I just don't see or sense his consoling presence in the daily miseries of life either, in the disappointments and failures of life, in the unresponsive, unpleasant people I must deal with or meet. At the very least, God, Christ, seems hidden. But all the while, "she saw Jesus standing there but did not recognize him."

As in a number of the resurrection accounts in the Gospels, the disciples do not recognize Jesus. Like them we, too, have limited too severely how he must appear. We may be ready to see him in a flowing mantle and amid celestial fireworks but unable to recognize him in a cemetery or walking the street. Like Mary looking for the dead Christ, we are unable to recognize the living and risen one.

It's a reminder that we can hardly be given frequently enough: to be much more open to the presence of the risen Lord and his grace in unlikely persons, places, and happenings, in unexpected turns in our lives. I'm not saying that every moment of our lives, therefore, is potentially full of electric joy in the awareness of the risen Lord. But, possibly there should always be some joy at any recognition of his presence, even if, as will often be the case, that risen presence is still marked by the wounds of the crucifixion. In both joy and sorrow, there is reason to say with Mary, "I have seen the Lord."

April 21

Read chapter 16, the last, of St. Mark's Gospel. It's only eight verses long. Many scholars who have studied the ancient texts believe that the Gospel ended there. (What follows in most Bibles was probably added by an equally early writer or writers of the community.) However, taking the Gospel to end with 16:8, we have a thought-provoking conclusion. The story in that chapter tells of the women coming to the tomb of Jesus and hearing the angel say: "Fear nothing: you are looking for Jesus of

Nazareth, who was crucified. He has been raised again. . . . But go and give this message to his disciples and Peter, 'He is going on before you into Galilee; there you will see him, as he told you.' " The last verse, even more abrupt in the original Greek, reads: "Then they went out and ran away from the tomb, beside themselves with terror. They said *nothing* to *anybody*, for they were afraid."

Whatever may be the complete story, one can only say, what a way to end the Gospel! The women are given a message for Peter and the disciples and are too scared to say anything to anyone! (In a contemporary horror movie where the dead are always reappearing in some frightening way, the witnesses invariably give an earsplitting scream and tell the whole world.) But the women at the tomb are scared into silence. Beyond our wonder about them is the more immediate question: What is our reason for not saying more about the resurrection, for not being more obvious witnesses that the one we believe in has risen?

Commentators on this odd ending to St. Mark's Gospel have suggested that the message for the reader is that the women were too frightened to say anything. Saying something, shouting the good news, filling the world with joy over this victory over death, is left to us. The joyous confidence we exhibit, with which we face life, the ability to rise again from sin and despair, the willingness to work for the good of all, a trust that with Christ risen and living among us our world can be changed for the better—through all this we show that he is risen indeed and still lives. Without a lot of preaching—in the streets, at home, or in the pulpit—our lives should be such that they only make sense to observers because we trust in the risen Lord.

April 22

Elvis Presley dropped in at Burger King in Wichita last week; Jim Morrison is not really buried in that cemetery in Paris but is still living. These seem actually rather popular beliefs among many Americans. Probably a good number of the same people never think of Jesus Christ as risen and still with us or think it is an outrageous proposition. For believers, that Jesus is risen is not simply a statement of some kind of ghoulish conviction that he came out of the grave; it is rather the certainty that in him death, sin, and suffering have been overcome, that he truly lives.

Jesus may not have been "seen" recently in the Burger King or at the bank, but Christian belief is that he is there—and everywhere: at the supermarket, the cocktail party, the soccer game. Like the two disciples walking away from Jerusalem on that first Easter Day (Luke 24:13-32), we, too, can expect to run into him on the way, on any street, in any place, disguised as Joe or Cindy, or, as for those disciples, as many others we do not know by name. Finding him in all these places, situations, and persons is a matter of faith and love. Faith, because we need the conviction that risen now from the grave, Jesus is present not just to the Jews of first-century Palestine but to the residents of Walla Walla and the remotest part of the Sahara.

We demonstrate and carry out that faith when by love we show toward all those we meet in any of these places, in any part of our daily life, the honor and respect that we would give to Jesus himself. The Lord is risen indeed and is still with us—in the patient we visit in the hospital, the lonely friend we write or call, the miserable we try to help, the victims of war and famine for whom we work. Christ is risen not just to console and comfort us but to challenge us to console, comfort, and change the world around us.

April 23

Theology and philosophy have often misled us. Most of us would probably find little difficulty in believing that about something we find so obscure and irrelevant. I'm not going to settle here who's fault that is! One constant temptation of philosophy the world over and of many religious movements has been to make the religious life, a life according to the will of God, into a matter of choosing between the body, or flesh (bad, base, inferior, source of all sin and evil), and the soul, or spirit (good, superior, source of all good, battled by the body). This always sounds so "spiritual." And it's been around so long and popped up so often even in Christianity that it's hard for us to speak except in terms of body and soul. It's easy to accept this simple distinction. And it certainly has struck many a philosopher or theologian as a more lofty approach than one that gives more due to the body.

But according to the Gospels, Jesus rose from the dead in his whole person, body included. "I believe in the resurrection of the body. . . ." The Gospel stories make quite a bit of his sharing a bit of fish with his disciples after rising. The point is that the Jews, from whom our Bible, even the New Testament, comes, believed that the human being was a unity, that John Smith is just what you see, one individual, clearly visible and having qualities and powers that aren't simply visible but which are a real part of him. When that John died, in Jewish thought, the whole John died. If he was to have another life, it would have to be the whole John again that would share in it. The body is an intrinsic part of the human being, not just some inferior bit of baggage given him or her to make things tough. The body, like everything else God made (Genesis), is good. Christians need to resist "spiritualizing" tendencies that would deny this. Maybe if we valued the body more we would use it more for good, treat it with greater respect, have more concern for the living conditions and life of those around us.

April 24

"From the beginning American blacks were introduced to the rewards of Christianity, heaven and resurrection, for the good of the plantation owner in this world and for the good of the slaves in the world beyond." A historian's comment on slavery in America. You assure the slaves of rewards and joy in the world to come and you are assured of good work, good harvests, good income, here and now. The slave puts his or her sights on the world to come and is willing to put up with work and misery in this life. This kind of thinking has led many a contemporary religious writer and theologian to soft-pedal the resurrection and eternal life. They don't want to seem to justify present injustice and apathy about this world's problems by turning our gaze elsewhere. Because we have here no lasting home does not mean that we don't need a good roof and adequate plumbing. Living with an eye continually set on reward in another life only diminishes our commitment to a better earth.

Some lives, of course, seem to blend efficacious action and commitment to this world with firm faith and trust in the risen Redeemer; take, for example, Archbishop Romero, Dietrich Bonhoeffer, and probably many others known to us personally. These people used their lives well for God and, despite martyrs' deaths, seem to have achieved fulfillment. Many of the wealthy and fortunate of our world certainly feel fulfilled to some degree and appear that way to many of us. Others among them, of course, as suicides and addictions testify, find something lacking even in the midst of plenty.

A student once commented to me on the ending of the film *Bonnie and Clyde,* when the two main characters are killed in a gun battle: "Is that all?" He could have meant, "Is that all there is to the story?" or "Is that all there is to human life, to anyone's story?" For most of us, human life is always short on the fulfillment we imagine there could be in it. All the more when that human life is one of misery, suffering, poverty, and loss. But the message of the resurrection of Jesus is that there is more to human life. That young man, cut off in his thirty-third year, is brought by God's power to fulfillment beyond what even thirty or forty more years of life could have brought him. In Jesus we see the future of our race and have now the hope that makes today's search for fulfillment worthwhile. We, too, will rise again.

April 25

Hope has had a history. The people we meet in the Bible have not always hoped for the same things. In much of the history of God's chosen people before the time of Christ, hope was that God would intervene in some national crisis (attack by enemies, threat of war, exile, and captivity) and save the people from disaster, humiliation, imprisonment. For much of that whole period, hope was for something exclusively of this world. Those who obeyed their parents, according to the commandment, were promised a long and prosperous life. Hope went further eventually to the expectation of a Messiah who would come and bring perfect peace and prosperity.

Over the course of the centuries, as these Jews discovered that the good and faithful did not always receive these good things and that the wicked and self-seeking often lived in happiness and prosperity, the belief in another life where these injustices would be corrected grew. Christ confirmed this new belief. Here the good and faithful, totally obedient son of God did not receive wealth or long life for his pains but, instead, poverty, suffering, and death at an early age.

But in his resurrection God pictures vividly the reality for which we hope, a life with God, victorious over sin, suffering, and death, something that goes beyond anything the earlier kind of hope could have envisioned. Keeping our eyes on Jesus and his death and resurrection should protect us from the temptation to expect that God here and now always rewards virtue and faith with good things. God didn't do it for Jesus, why should God behave that way toward anyone else?

April 26

Someone has said that the religious situation of Americans is not so much denying God as simply ignoring God in daily life. The other side of this is or can be our absorption in money, things, possessions, getting and acquiring, having. If this doesn't go the full length of being idolatry, putting lesser matters, concerns, objects in place of God, at least it easily means losing the other dimension of life, losing our interest in more human matters, matters that relate us to God and others rather than to objects and possessions.

One of the ways in which St. Paul makes the resurrection of Christ and our share in it of practical consequence is to remind us that in our baptism we were given a share of the life of the risen Lord Jesus. Our resurrection has already begun because of God's grace, God's life, in us and with us. Our more profound life is with God, with Christ, not just with possessions, necessary as they are. Paul says we should put to death that lust (desire, grasping, greed) which is idolatry. He calls it idolatry because we easily, in terms of time, attention, energy, put all these before God and the good of others.

With some daily reflection in faith, some genuine prayer, we can solidify our conviction that despite our involvement with the world, our bank, our job, our IRAs, our worries about paying for a good education for ourselves or the children, our more profound life must be beyond that.

"Since you have been raised up in company with Christ, set your heart on the higher things where Christ is, at God's right hand; be intent on things above rather than on things of this earth only. Your life is hidden with Christ in God" (Col 3:1-3).

April 27

"And if the while I think on thee, dear friend, All losses are restored, and sorrows end" (Shakespeare sonnet).

Why not think of our friends more often, above all when we're feeling low and discouraged, unloved and forgotten, tired and without incentive? Where else did these people come from who love us and who have made our lives so happy with memorable moments if not from God? What do they represent except the grace of God, a gift, something undeserved? What are they but signs, evidence of God's love? What makes friendship and love so much to sing about is that out of nowhere (even if we think it was Iowa, France, or Ontario) have come these people who have given us love, friendship, good company, and joy, who have made us sit miles away from them and smile at the thought of their charm and kindness, their laughter, their love. They are grace, or graces.

Grace is one of the most fuzzy and impossible concepts for most of us to understand. What does it mean? The term itself comes from a word meaning freely given: Our English term "gratis" is related to it. The love of family and friends is just this, grace, an undeserved gift. Here are people who love us no matter what, who forgive, who feel responsible for us often despite the way we disappoint them. Our friends are people who have come into our lives, have come to love us, to share themselves with us. What better sign of God's love, of grace, which likewise is there not because we were so irresistible but just because God chose to love us.

In every relationship there is this element of unexplainable choice, Why do I love so and so? Why did I make the effort to get to know him or her better? Why did he or she make the effort to know and meet me? The answer is that there is no simple reason why this has happened. Like God's love, the love we give or receive is the overflow of goodness, the overflow of the goodness of someone. As long as that exists, there is something to sing about. As long as that exists, losses are restored and sorrows end.

April 28

In one of the Easter accounts in the Gospel of St. Luke, two disciples of Jesus are walking away from Jerusalem on Easter Day pretty hopeless about the crucified Lord (Luke 24:13-35). As they walk, this stranger joins them and explains how the Scriptures teach that the Lord had to be crucified and rise again. After they come to recognize that this stranger is the Lord by the way he breaks bread with them, they say: "Were not our hearts burning inside us as he talked to us on the road and explained the Scriptures to us?" From what we see and hear in many a church on Sunday morning, we must wonder at times if anything is burning besides the candles. If our hearts *are* burning, we are certainly masters at hiding our feelings. We often seem like robots at a cold ritual.

Most likely there are a lot of reasons for this, and the blame can be well divided between priest, people, musicians, architects, and others. But rather than trying to find our scapegoats, it's always better to look first to ourselves.

A great deal of what happens or doesn't happen at Mass or worship depends on us individuals who come together to form one body of worshipers. What do we—what should we—bring to worship? Or to our daily prayer? The word of Jesus still comes to us at Mass and in reading Scripture. Why doesn't that hearing of the word, why doesn't the celebration in general, light more fires in our hearts?

Understanding and expectation are two important elements. If the risen Lord does not ever inspire or move us, it may be a matter of poor understanding, an undernourished faith. That we can help by reading and reflection.

But even more, we need to come to Mass, to prayer, with high expectations. What we take away will partly depend on what we bring to it. Maybe it's too much to expect that we will always come with the anticipation we'd bring to the opening ceremonies of the Olympics or to the chance to see our favorite performer in person. But shouldn't we at least awaken our faith along with our bodies before beginning, so that we can put some energy and alertness into it? Too, once we are at prayer or worship, we need to give it wholehearted attention rather than sandwiching it in between the really "important" things in our life like tennis and brunch. Any coming before God requires that we come with some effort, some alertness, some hope and expectation. Maybe then there will be more burning than just the candles.

April 29

The man whom Christians believe was also the Son of God seemed bent on overturning in his life and words ordinary expectations of what a God should decently be expected to do. On a divine level, it's a bit like the glimpse the world got in Pope John XXIII of a man in such an exalted position being able to laugh at himself and push aside some of the formality and protocol considered proper by the guardians of the papacy.

Similarly in Jesus, God becomes a helpless human infant dependent on your everyday man and woman for nurture, protection, shelter, for burping and help with his first steps. At the end of his life it's the same: He becomes the object of sympathy and scorn on the cross; dependent on others for a decent burial.

The philosophers and theologians of our history have often come up with characteristics that *must* mark or qualify a being as God: freedom from suffering and emotion, unchangeableness, the ability to do anything and to know everything. Over against all that, in Jesus we have God taking on human weakness, from that of a child to that of the ordinary mature human being (John tells us he was angry and tired, that he wept for a dead friend, that he was disappointed in his followers), finally letting himself be put to death on a cross.

Even more than announcing the need to revise our notions of God, all this tells us something of more import for our lives. It tells us that God is not indifferent to human struggle, pain, death. Jesus has gone through it, and beyond that, he is with us every inch of the way; we are never alone, never completely abandoned. Even though we may feel very genuinely Jesus' own cry "Why have you forsaken me," his resurrection tells us that it is not the last word. Born a child, he is called Emmanuel (God with us), and his last words in that Gospel are his promise: "And be assured, I am with you always, to the end of time" (Matt 28:20).

April 30

A Zen Buddhist story tells of a man named Bankei who was preaching to his followers when he was interrupted by a priest who was heavy into miracles. In order to quiet him, Bankei asked him what he wanted to say. The priest said: "The founder of my religion stood on one shore of a river with a writing brush in his hand. A disciple stood on the other bank with a sheet of paper. The founder wrote the name of God onto the paper across the river through the air. Can you do anything so miraculous?" Bankei answered: "No. I can do only little miracles. Like: when I am hungry, I eat; when I am thirsty, I drink; when I am insulted, I forgive."

If, as some of the after-the-resurrection accounts in the Gospels indicate (e.g., Mark 16), the risen Christ shows his presence among his followers by signs, we need to realize that signs come in various sizes and shapes with varying degrees of importance or value.

The most reliable signs of the power and presence of the risen Jesus in us are that, like the Zen man, when insulted we forgive, when irritated we are patient, when passed over we do not whine, when successful or praised we do not become boastful or overbearing. That we are not quick to feel offended or to keep a record of others' wrongdoing, that we do not rejoice in the sins of others, that we are persevering, joyful, encouraging, hopeful, courageous, in the face of the monotonous demands and unsung duties of everyday life. By *these* signs those around us will know that Jesus is risen and ascended but, even more, that he is still living by his Spirit in his followers, in this world.

May 1

Writes a former student in his late twenties: "I like my job . . . but I still feel that I'm made for a life of leisure." The thought has crossed the minds of all of us, I'm sure. Work is an important part of our life—think of all the hours of our life that are spent at it—also often a very prickly part. We can't really live without it but we'd like to try. Some years ago Studs Terkel conducted interviews with many people about their work and found that something like eighty-five percent were not really contented with their work. From the fifteen percent or so who were happy with what they were doing, the temptation was to generalize and, consequently, to be unrealistic.

We could all agree with the theory that claims that the kind of work God calls you or me to is (*a*) what you or I need most to do, and (*b*) what the world needs most to have done. Ideally the two should meet. If your work is that of a doctor in a leper colony, that may well satisfy (*b*) the world's needs to have this done—but if you are bored and depressed by it, then (*a*) can't be satisfied and what you're doing is probably no help to others.

It all sounds great to me, but I suspect it is mostly a paper dream.

The reality seems to be that in our kind of world, in our kind of economy, one may conceivably have either (*a*) or (*b*) verified in one's own case but seldom both. And, again, given the economic realities (how could I move thousands of miles with my family, drop this job, etc.), I think many people rightly feel trapped or at least very restricted. Mobility is very much related to an easy economic situation. Our daily work for most is either (1) what the theory described, something that answers my needs and also serves those of the world and is, therefore, for me a real blessing, something to be thankful for; (2) or my work is not that satisfying to me or that significant for the world either, a type of suffering from which there is little escape; or, finally, (3) my work is a mixture of satisfaction and pain, reward and disappointment, the two mixed together in varying proportions probably even from day to day or from week to week.

Maybe with work, as with a number of other givens in human life, our best response is to accept it as this mixture and to see it as part of the cross that marks the follower of Christ. We Christians do pray for the dead that they may have eternal rest. This seems to be a recognition that much of human life, work included, is something from which we need relief, something that has undesirable and unsatisfying characteristics. Having said all this, having accepted in fact a rather grim view of much human labor (why do we all look forward so much to the weekend, to vacation?), it remains to say that part of the solution is up to us. We can work for changes in working conditions, in our economy. Here and now we can bring to our work whatever there is in us that might humanize it, make it more pleasant, more agreeable for our fellow workers, for all those affected by it. Like every other facet of human life, there is something in it that we can adjust and to which we can bring some light, strength, joy, healing.

May 2

In John 5:25, Jesus says, "The time is coming when the dead shall hear the voice of the son of God and those who have heeded it shall live." The words certainly seem to have a general application in which all of us can trust. But they also find a specific application later on in John's Gospel, when Jesus calls Lazarus forth from his tomb. We have in this just one concrete picture of what Jesus intends for all who listen to him.

Before Lazarus can hear the word of the Son of God and be called forth to freedom and new life, the stone had to be rolled away from his tomb. "Take away the stone," Jesus directs. It must have occurred to the witnesses that rolling the stone away should hardly have been a problem for one who was about to raise a man from the grave. Possibly again, as so often in John, this is laden with meaning for the reader. Doesn't it suggest that what is in our power to do, *we* must do? We cannot raise ourselves from death, but we can roll away the stone. We can open ourselves more to the word of God. We can reject false self-satisfaction, unrealistic self-sufficiency, the bondage of stale habits and ways, the *always* premature hardening of our hearts. We can remove the barriers that seal us off from the voice of God: distraction, too-avid pursuit of other matters.

When the boulders are rolled away, the call of Jesus to us can be heard. We can respond with loving faith and trust and hear Jesus say, "Let them go free."

We are always in the state of hearing the Lord but not hearing perfectly. We hear enough to know that he can make us free, but often we are hesitant to accept that. We owe it to the rest of the world, to those around us, to believe more firmly that trust and faith in Jesus mean freedom, liberation from fear and timidity, an opening to generosity, large heartedness. That being a Christian is cause for joy and exuberance, for hope and confidence, freedom from the bonds of death and selfishness.

May 3

The Shroud of Turin has been shown by carbon dating (approximately 95 percent sure) to be no earlier than the thirteenth century. Not, therefore, the material in which the body of Jesus was wrapped after his death on the cross. While the genuineness of the shroud is not confirmed, we are confirmed in a conviction that our faith cannot rest on any such tangible evidence. That Christ lived, suffered, died, and rose again for us is not something we can know in the same way that we can know who was our great grandfather or how many people set sail on the Mayflower. The relatively unimportant matters of human life can often be known with what seems to be absolute certainty. But the big matters, the important things, no.

We believe that Christ died and, above all, rose from the dead (dying, after all, is not that unusual) because somewhere along the line we decided to believe in the word, the preaching, of the early disciples who believed that he had risen. None of them saw him rise from the dead. They saw the risen Lord; he ate with them, talked to them, but none of them saw him rising from the dead. Their belief in him, shaped and made durable after so much hesitation, doubt, questioning, even denial, is what we have to fall back on. We believe because they believed. Or, more immediately, we believe because someone who taught us and whom we trusted believed. He or she in turn believed because of someone before them, and so on. Our belief is part of a long chain of belief stretching through centuries of Christian belief and practice. Something we cannot pin on any one safe, sure thing, like finding out for sure that there was no body in the tomb on Easter morning, or finding the sheet in which his body was wrapped.

We believe in you, Lord, that you are our Savior, our Lord, the one who saves us from sin and death, because those who have gone before us and whom we have trusted believed in you. We are blessed, you have told us, not because we have seen and believed but because we have not seen and yet have believed.

May 4

An ancient Chinese writer says, "To know when to stop, to know when you can get no further by your own action, this is the right beginning." This is a truth also taught by Christ and St. Paul in different words. It is the liberating attitude we need.

Our tendency, if we're serious enough to read even this sort of book, is to think that everything more and more depends on how much we do, how well we plan, how carefully we look ahead, how tense, in fact, we are, and how keyed up. But even in such matters as learning any skill, how to play a game or a musical instrument, there comes a point where progress depends not on gritting our teeth still further, on straining, but on letting go, relaxing, letting some power within us act. We've all been told in the course of trying to learn some skill to "relax" and we know how difficult it is to take that advice. But when we can and do, there is a difference. Things easily wing their way ahead, sail smoothly.

As we look at our lives, examine where we have been or where we're going, it's necessary that we put *in perspective* our own activity and effort. That activity certainly is of value, but there is always a sense in which we need to realize that letting go a bit can allow the power and spirit already present within us to carry on.

"To know when to stop" requires listening, paying attention to our whole personality, our body, our self, not simply pushing on as if we were directing some spiritless machine. It's a form of self-knowledge to know when to stop pushing, when to relax, when to let the reins go slack, when to rest. And for the Christian it's a recognition that we are not the sole agents in our activity, our lives. We're in the hands and under the influence of one with more foresight and power than we have. Why not put more trust there?

May 5

"What if it was all a big joke?" The question came from a longtime, traditional, practicing Catholic in her mid-sixties. Further conversation made it clear that she presumed that I, the priest she was having dinner with, must have answered that question for myself at some time. And it demonstrates very well that doubts and questions of the sort are not limited to young radicals or disillusioned middle-age people.

I agree it is a question or one way of phrasing a doubt that has occurred to me or has lurked behind my study of religion and theology. There are at least three parts to my answer. (1) We must question, think, reflect, try to understand more about our beliefs and their bases. There is no end to what we can do, since the object, God, and all that relates to God, is endless. Most of us probably need to do more of this than we ever take the time to do. Possibly we've had the questions raised and discussed in a class in our younger days, but so often we are more interested in how to get a job, how to find a spouse or where we'll go for our vacation than we are in such—at the moment—far-off topics. To study, read, take a class, join a study group, and the like, all take effort and time. Shouldn't we probably take that time and effort rather than putting it off again and again because of more immediate concerns about taxes, job, children, politics, and retirement?

(2) At some time, not to foreclose all further questioning or thinking, but to enable us to live productively and generously, we must make a decision. We must decide in some firm sense somewhere along the line that this is right or wrong for me and that I will try to live and act accordingly.

(3) And that leads into the third part of it. Our manner of living is part of our solution, part of the answer. Just as we learn the correctness of our decision (our promises) to love someone by what results from that, so we learn the rightness of our commitment to the Lord by the fruits of the life that follows.

"The believer, like the lover, has no conclusive proofs to give him complete security. But the believer, too, like the lover, can be completely certain of the Other by committing himself entirely to the Other. And this certainty is stronger than all the security established by proofs" (Hans Küng).

May 6

To be ready to accept the death of people close to us as something we do not understand but that is in the hands of God is certainly commendable. To grieve deeply, to be crushed, and to feel abandoned and hopeless is also most understandable. I think of three deaths during the past couple of months: a robust twenty-three-year-old dying suddenly of a heart attack; a forty-two-year-old father of two teenagers dead of cancer, and the senseless murder of a fifty-six-year-old father of six by someone who apparently wanted his car. One can understand how the mother of the six children could be reduced to uncontrollable sobbing. There is really nothing we can say to "explain" such deaths—or really, when it comes down to it, death itself.

Probably the most common approach is to deny death in any number of ways. Usually we do it by finding words that mask its presence and soften the reality. Centuries ago a famous Roman philosopher did a good job of doing away with death in a few lines: "So death, the most terrifying of ills, is nothing to us, since so long as we exist, death is not with us but when death comes, then we do not exist. It does not then concern either the living or the dead, since for the former it is not, and the latter are no more." Avoiding death by playing around with words.

Probably the only denial of death that makes real sense is to deny death as just an idea and accept it as something that will happen to each of us. "There is . . . no death . . . There is only . . . me . . . me . . . who is going to die" (Andre Malraux). If it's only a vague idea or someone else's problem, it may not be much of a reality for us but it becomes real when seen as an eventuality in my life.

The ultimate answer for those who believe in Jesus Christ is that because we have been joined to him by baptism and faith, to him who overcame death, we, too, will share that overcoming. "By baptism we were buried with him, and lay dead, in order that, as Christ was raised from the dead in the splendor of the Father, so also we might set our feet upon the new path of life. . . . But if we thus died with Christ, we believe that we shall also come to life with him" (Rom 6:4, 8).

May 7

"For seven days and seven nights they sat beside him on the ground, and none of them said a word to him; for they saw that his suffering was very great" (Job 2:13). "They" refers to three friends of a man named Job of the Bible. Their names, which have never really caught on among us, were Eliphas, Bildad, and Zophar. They had come to comfort their friend Job, who had just lost everything—family, livestock—in a series of disasters, and was sitting dumbfounded and miserable. They came to console him and sat for seven days saying nothing.

What kind of comfort or consolation is that? Often the only and the best kind we can give. We too often feel we must rush into words when just our quiet presence nearby—"They sat beside him"—is enough. Especially in the grief of others, we are known for rushing in with words that—if those mourning were able even to think at all—are completely devoid of sense or are even basically insulting to God. People say, "God wanted him." Do we really mean that the Lord of the universe needed the only child of this couple more than they did? Or, "It was God's will," when we are trying to console parents whose child was molested and killed. God's will? What a picture of God we paint in this attempt to console others. Evidently, in saying these things we are not thinking, just grasping for something to say. As Job said after his friends finally broke their silence to give him some advice: "Ah, if you would only be silent and let silence be your wisdom" (Job 13:5).

Another expression, closer to the original approach of Eliphas, Bildad, and Zophar, is probably more helpful and honest: "I don't know what to say." And, if we must say more: "Let me know if there is anything I can do." Or, better yet, do what we know needs doing: the dishes, answering the phone, picking up friends and relatives, making sure there are meals. And, once again, just to be near, handy, available may be better than any words can ever be in the face of the awesome mystery of death and suffering. "For seven days and seven nights they *sat beside him* . . . and none of them said a word to him."

May 8

There is much insistence in this book on the hope-inspiring, confidence-building power of our belief that Jesus is risen. There is also, I hope, no encouragement to think that our belief makes it possible to bypass the real miseries, pains and disappointments of human life. Nothing of the sort happened for Jesus himself; why should we expect it for ourselves?

Jesus faced death, and in the midst of speaking about it expressed his trust that those with whom he was eating a last meal would be reunited with him at another banquet. After giving them the pattern of the supper to be repeated, he said, "I tell you this, never again shall I drink from the fruit of the vine until that day when I drink it new in the kingdom of God" (Mark 14:25).

Only a few verses later in the same Gospel, Jesus tells his disciples, "My heart is ready to break with grief" (v. 34). And in prayer to the Father he asks if there isn't some other way for all this to be done: "Abba, Father, all things are possible to you: take this cup away from me. Yet not what I will, but what you will." This lesson made in the Gospels is one that hyper-salesmen of faith in Jesus have tended at times to ignore in assuring those who believe that faith will smooth the road, short-circuit the pains, avoid, in fact, the cross.

Besides giving us the hope of rising with him, the whole story, by its realism, by not suggesting that somehow Jesus went to the cross smiling, tells us that God in Jesus is with us in the midst of any horror that can befall us. With us, not removing or hiding the difficulties!

As we read this, presumably most of us comfortably enough situated to do it without much pain, we should pray that we grow in confidence that Jesus is with us and that we will be with him.

May 9

Like most of us, I'm aware (helped along by comments from others, friendly or hostile) that I have some disabilities. They go from deficiencies in my character and personality to ineptitude with machines. Yet I'm sufficiently within the "normal" range to be forcefully struck by severe physical or mental disabilities. Recently, on a very mild, bright spring day, I came across two severely disabled people being pushed around in wheelchairs by family members. Another day, I saw in church an older woman with a somewhat younger man with apparently serious mental problems. While I did actually drift off for a moment during the sermon, the sight of this man mesmerized me and, like those in the wheelchairs, kept raising questions in my mind.

What does the fulfillment and good life the rest of us seek—at the health club, the country club, in education, travel, music, art—what can that possibly mean to one who is either unable to comprehend it or who comprehends it but is prevented from pursuing it?

While we legitimately pursue our fulfillment through the use of our talents, time, abilities, it is good to look at that fulfillment in a broader way than just as *my* fulfillment. Think of the vast number of people for whom just finding something to eat is the only pursuit for which they have time. Think of all the handicapped, suffering, bedridden, paralyzed, or emotionally disturbed people who are fortunate if their suffering can be eased a bit. Is fulfillment only meant for you and me living in the comfort of middle-class America, the suburbs of Chicago or Dallas?

I think the only answer to this disparity is to realize that fulfillment in its most complete sense is a gift from God, helped, surely, by our efforts. The incompleteness of our own fulfillment tells us this, and the apparent impossibility of it for others points in the same direction. We need to do all we can to better the lot of the suffering and underprivileged while knowing that for all of us, our complete betterment, morally and otherwise, is ultimately God's gift. "I have come that they may have life, and may have it in all its fullness" (John 10:10).

May 10

In thinking about the Eucharist or in trying to teach about it, you find such a variety of images and concepts that you feel lost. What can you say? And part of the answer is, of course, that you can say only so much. We find the rest of the answer in the doing, in participation, preferably in an appropriate way over a fairly long time. Because the Lord's Supper is an action, an experience, it can only unfold its meaning when we enter into it; it is never simply a matter of the right words. It's much like the way a favorite picture or piece of music reveals more and more to us over the years. There is simply no substitute for taking part in the Mass at St. Peter's or St. James's or Our Savior's.

Every single description we use of the Mass is inadequate and, therefore, by itself one-sided: meal or banquet, sacrifice, thanksgiving, remembrance, presence of Christ, promise of the world to come, celebration of liberation, reinforcement of the community, the actual formation of the body of Christ, the unifying of human beings.

Nevertheless, we can try to see how they are interconnected and what they have to say. For example, the Eucharist is a banquet welding together those who partake into a community, reinforcing their love. As it does this, it is a sign and picture of the world to come, where we will form one risen community in and around the head, the Lord. Or, in the bread and wine of this sacrament, we also recall the Lord's sacrifice and remind ourselves that true community, living and working together in peace and good will, presupposes a sharing in the self-sacrifice of Christ, a willingness to curtail our own demands for the sake of others, a willingness to prefer their good to our immediate good. A loving union of people, a banquet of friends and resurrection are, in a sense, the obvious result of a life lived in generous and sacrificial love. That community of friends is formed, too, by our coming together to do this in remembrance of the Lord. The beginning and the end of the process is good will, friendship, love. The preface for a wedding says it well: Love is our beginning, love is our end. Every Mass or Holy Communion should remind us of that beginning, that end.

May 11

"Be kind; everyone you meet is fighting a hard battle" (John Watson). And a French writer is credited with a famous remark: "To understand everything is to forgive everything." Such absolute and sweeping statements often leave us with a bit of doubt, but we don't have to settle that now. Rather, let's see what value they have for us.

The combined statements invite us to look at everyone we meet as having more to understand than first meets our eye. And that what is often not observable is some conflict, some private worry that may account for the fact that they seem to us (1) distant, cool; (2) abstracted, uninterested, snooty; (3) crabby, quick tempered; (4) morose, unhappy; (5) not interested enough in me and my worries, problems, or needs. Often we have some inkling of what is wrong, at least partly: The person is in a job that is very demanding and aggravating; is poorly paid; works bad hours; holds down a couple of jobs and takes care of a family; is obviously afflicted with some illness.

We're implementing a truly loving attitude toward them if, whether or not we can imagine a host of excuses for them, we at least accept that there must be something that excuses what to us is offensive or insensitive in them. A further suggestion: If we look into ourselves we will see we have worries and difficulties that we think would be cause for special consideration if we were to make them public. If we, why not them also? "Everyone you meet is fighting a hard battle."

May 12

Since reading somewhere a historian's belief that villagers in the average little medieval town probably never saw more than a hundred different people in their whole lives due to limited transportation and the lack of all the ways we have of transmitting images, that has struck me very forcefully. Undoubtedly such a limited experience, such lack of external stimuli, which we take for granted, would have its advantages and affect one's thinking, possibly even in some good ways. Though one can easily see people in such a situation being frightened or suspicious of outsiders, provincial.

My reaction is one of relief that I don't live in one of those villages. One of the most amazing and refreshing evidences for God's unpredictable goodness is the beauty and variety we see in human faces and persons. The types of character that shine through the faces we encounter in a large population strike me as signs of an inexhaustible and even more beautiful source of all this, which I call God. When some extraordinary beauty in human beings or in nature or in some creation of human beings—art or music or dance—hits us, it comes as a gift, something out of the usual that could not have been anticipated in any sense. It is like nothing else in our lives.

Well, maybe there is something else very much like it: love. When someone loves us, other than those we so often unfortunately take for granted, it is also a gift, something we could not possibly have expected or thought we deserved. All this is what we mean by grace. These are graces, gifts from God, of which there are an infinite variety. Praise God from whom all blessings, all gifts, all surprises, flow.

May 13

Encouragement. Who doesn't need it? Further, is there anyone among us who does not give it? We may not—thank goodness—consciously think of what we do and say as being encouragement, but much of it is. Our friendliness, good cheer, interest in others, a pat on the arm, sharing a funny story, willingness to help with burdens—all this constitutes a kind of encouragement to others. Much of our ability to survive depends on encouragement from someone, from somewhere. It tells us that what we are doing is worthwhile, helpful, good.

As apostles like Paul and Barnabas traveled to young Christian communities in the first century, the Acts of the Apostles tells us that they gave reassurance and encouragement in the midst of trials and difficulties (Acts 14:22). They told these new Christians their own story and encouraged them by the account of all they had been through. If we, Paul and Barnabas say, can still hope and preach the good news, why not you? Giving encouragement could well be a matter of recalling the gospel, the message of Christ, for our friends and those we want to help. On the other hand, it may not always be so obvious. We can encourage by simply affirming the good others are doing, backing their efforts and good will, letting our own faith and trust shine through in a good spirit and hopefulness. Often our spirit and manner is more helpful and contagious than anything we have to say.

May 14

Jesus is "our strength, our song, our Savior" because he has truly risen from the dead. Today, as in many a day past, there are efforts to make "he is truly risen" stand for something much less. Among some who apparently wish well to Christian belief but are really close to dealing it a death blow are those who say we should understand it to mean that in his influence and the honor people gave him for his life, he "rose" from the dead. One could possibly say the same thing about Abraham Lincoln or Karl Marx. Others say it means that his followers, after a moment or two of extreme disappointment, were emboldened by his example to start new lives for themselves; he "rose" in their new lives.

No, the resurrection of Jesus meant—unless we ignore the ordinary way people use language—for the New Testament writers (on whom we base our faith) that after his death on the cross this same Jesus entered into a new kind of life. Because of this and because with the creeds we believe the same is our human destiny, we have the most profound and absolute grounds for hope, for seeing beyond present misery. Without it we have every reason not only for sharing the misery—that we must do in any case—but also for sharing the view that there is no light at the end of the tunnel. As St. Paul says, "If it is for this life only that Christ has given us hope, we of all are most to be pitied" (1 Cor 15:19).

Not only the whole Easter season but our faith itself should keep before us all year round this great and final source of our hope. Most Christians have forgotten or never knew that Easter is the center of the Church's annual celebrations. Santa, the reindeer, the gift giving and the kids have all put the emphasis elsewhere.

But "We wish you not to remain in ignorance, brothers, about those who sleep in death: you should not grieve like the rest who have no hope. We believe that Jesus died and rose again: and so it will be for those who died as Christians; God will bring them to life with Jesus" (1 Thess 4:13-14).

May 15

The blasts of Jesus against some of his opponents are unmistakable: "Woe to you scribes and Pharisees, you frauds! You are like whitewashed tombs, beautiful to look at on the outside but inside full of filth and dead men's bones" (Matt 23:27). They give an exemplary appearance of observing regulations of their religion but are inwardly something much less. He accuses them of hypocrisy.

Without—we pray—being consciously hypocritical, we are all in the bind of claiming ideals that are superior to our behavior or that we fail to consistently carry out. I say it's a bind because our ideals to be truly ideals seem always to be above and ahead of us, pointing to something not yet realized. We know that Jesus has the words of eternal life (John 6:68); we recognize his teaching as the guide to genuine living but still, of course, show plenty of evidence of selfishness, aggressiveness, arrogance, vengeance. Ronald Goetz has said that we have neither the firmness needed to follow him nor the consistency to reject him.

Our following of the Lord means an unending dissatisfaction with ourselves. The good we know we should do, we so often do not do. The solution, again very human, is to imagine that clenching our teeth and putting more iron into our will is what is needed. But this, too, like our surprise that we do not better live up to our ideals, reflects more of that self-reliance and self-sufficiency that is part of the problem. These may be most desirable qualities in running a business or learning a new technique but are out of place in relation to God.

Living up to our ideals has to be another powerful reason for trust in him. Salvation is more a gift than an accomplishment. "My strength and my courage is the Lord, and God has been my savior" (Ps 117:14).

May 16

Christians easily lapse into talk about the will of God (even at funerals!), and we do pray that it be done in us. It is certainly important in the following of Christ, yet discerning it leaves us little reason for glibness. It is rarely ever known with scientific clarity. Older forms of the Christian life have often suggested that knowing the will of God was extremely simple. For the members of a religious order, all that was necessary was to drop in on the superior, say fairly early in the morning, and come out with an almost hour-by-hour description of what God wanted of you. For the laity with less-immediate access to an abbot or mother superior, it was sufficient to do what the bishop or pastor said and, in the case of women, what the husband said. Others, usually in a more Protestant milieu, would open the Bible at random and find the answer to each moment's difficulties. Some of this, of course, continues today. Televangelists claim to have an especially sure knowledge of the will of God for themselves and for the rest of us. And lesser lights too: The newspapers, a summer or two ago, reported a baseball coach who decided not to play a certain player because, as he said, God had told him not to. The will of God was very clear at least to this coach; God's word was: "I don't want Al Schwarz pitching."

The reality is that ordinarily God's will is made known to us with blood, sweat, and tears. To the extent that we are able to use our reason and think and plan, God seems to want to use it, too. After all, God made it. Knowing God's will is often a matter of reconciling diverse elements in our life and surroundings, knowing where our responsibilities are, and putting them in proper order. We need to be open to the will of God first of all by and through our prayer, some listening to God's words, and some silence. We need similarly to be open to the needs of our community, our families. We need to give attention to the voice and opinions of authorities and weigh them in terms of who is speaking and of how little or how much we are competent in the same area. It is by no means a matter of simple, uncritical submission to others. Another element in knowing God's will is some awareness of the givens of our condition, of our daily lives and vocations, of place and time. Again, it is not simply a matter of submission; the will of God can be that we change an unjust and wearying situation.

Thy will be done, on earth as it is in heaven—definitely. In one sense, that's the easy part; knowing what it is in our situation is the first and very demanding part, a part that requires honesty with ourselves and our situation, a being alert to the world and the many voices in it that have a right to be heard by us. Accompanying all this with prayer can help us sift out the voices according to their value.

May 17

The theme song of a TV show set in a neighborhood bar goes, "You want to go where everybody knows your name." Apparently, that's where the singer, at least, feels comfortable. More loftily, we'd say that's where he or she finds a genuine community. For some Christians, especially those who are members of small religious groups, that may also be true of their Church. There everybody knows their names. Those of us accustomed to large and fairly anonymous parishes may dismiss all this as hopelessly ideal. Yet the desire to be known and to know, to be in the company of friendly, welcoming people, has been a reason for the success of what are often called cults and sects.

The situation is quite different, often, in many large urban Catholic churches. And with fewer Catholic priests available, there doesn't seem much likelihood that Catholics are going to find their local parishes becoming smaller and more intimate. But in a belief so person-centered as the following of Christ, this hope of being known cannot too quickly be left behind. I'd guess if people can't and don't find it in their church, which is rightly billed as a "community," they'll find it at the bar, the club, where they work. And no one can object to that.

But doesn't something have to be done about the coldness, indifference, institutional appearance, of our parishes? People can enter the church building for the Lord's Supper, a rite celebrating the unity and love of believers not only for God but for each other, can do this without being recognized, greeted, acknowledged in any way. The peace greeting can be performed so perfunctorily as to lack value; one limply shakes hands while looking in another direction or greets warmly just the people one came with. There are probably thousands of neighborly ways in which we can overcome this, but today I'd like to urge one approach. So often one is still able to enter Catholic churches totally anonymously and leave the same way. Many of us could do a lot to help overcome this by being concerned about, taking some individual responsibility for changing this. Why should there be any church service or church where there are not people greeting and welcoming those who come? Eventually, we might even find ourselves coming into Mass and discovering that someone knows our name.

May 18

Someone has said of the gospel word about letting your light shine before others and for them that "God's revelation begins as a private discovery and ends as a public responsibility." The insight or strength we have received is given to us in order to be passed on. It's like the old saw about how you lose something by hanging on to it but get more by trying to give it away. It's one of those paradoxes that only experience can confirm for us. Common sense certainly can't justify it.

We don't have to wait to fully understand what we are discovering or feel finished with it to be able to pass something on to others. Often elderly people feel they have so much to say but don't know when to stop. It's also the young with fresh insights who should be encouraged to pass them on. The Lord's word and our own perception of it require that we use any light from it to brighten the world around us, to strengthen and comfort those with whom we live and work. No matter what doubts still nag us, we should be able to offer others some cheer, hope, encouragement. We resolve our doubts and problems not only by prayer and reflection but also by acting, especially by unselfish doing.

If we're young and heavily engaged in study, work, the life around us, there are still many of our contemporaries who are going through either the tormented teens or the turbulent twenties, even the threatening thirties. If we're older, of course, we know how our contemporaries are more and more afflicted with ills, aches, loneliness, temptations to doubt, and discouragement. The power present in the Lord's word and the Lord's Supper is there to be tapped by us, and through us to give some encouragement, strength, light, and hope to those around us.

May 19

While Mark's Gospel sometimes strikes us as odd with its great number of miracles, at the same time it presents Jesus and his followers as most fully human. The disciples are pictured as slow to understand and believe: "They were completely dumbfounded, for they had not understood the incident of the loaves; their minds were closed" (6:52). Peter's lack of comprehension so exasperates Jesus that he calls Peter Satan: "Away with you, Satan, you think as men think, not as God thinks" (8:33). And when he is arrested: "Then the disciples all deserted him and ran away" (14:50). Jesus' message about following him in loving service, sharing his sacrifice, giving ourselves for the building up of his community, is one the disciples took to as quickly and generously as most of us take to disappointment, failure, pain, or a broken leg. They are slow, reluctant, really puzzled; probably attracted and repelled at the same time by this unusual man.

While the essential message of the New Testament invites us to change our lives, give them in sacrifice and love, share the burdens of others, still, there is also a most realistic recognition that we are going to have a hard time picking up steam in pursuing that ideal. We may trudge and stumble and only come painfully and slowly to embrace his message. Even after his resurrection appearances are reported by the women and others: "They did not believe it" (16:11). "But again no one believed them" (16:13). He had to reproach the eleven when he appeared to them for "their incredulity and dullness." What familiar qualities if not words: lack of belief and simple dullness. So often the Christian life of any one of us is marked by the same uninviting marks.

Yet eventually these same people were able to give witness by their lives and even deaths to belief that he was the Savior and that he lives. Lord, strengthen our belief, our trust, our resolution; take away our slowness, hesitation, dullness, indifference.

May 20

After repeated commercials for Reeboks, Sluice, and Poliflex in the course of a two-hour TV movie, we easily turn off our hearing completely. Or, after a season of speeches by politicians, we learn to do the same thing. Why listen, we think, when "misspoke," "disinformation" and "memory lapse" all mean just plain old lying? We quickly become like the hard, rocky ground mentioned in the Gospel, incapable of absorbing anything (Matt 13:1-9). It becomes very difficult for anyone who is not a Johnny Carson, Colonel Kadaffy, or Julia Roberts to keep our attention. We are so saturated, bombarded with words. But St. Paul tells us that faith comes by hearing, that believing is a response to a message we have heard. What is said here about hearing also holds for our reading, too, with necessary qualifications. Printed ads and information fill our eyes and minds. How can we remain open, hear or understand what is of worth around us? Two points should be enough today. One, we need occasionally some silence, some retreat from the bombardment of our senses by the oral and written word. We need to do this to "remember" what silence is like, what real hearing is like.

Secondly, we need to remind ourselves that genuine hearing or listening, paying attention to anything, is not a passive matter. It requires effort, exertion. The experience of trying to attune one's ear to hear and understand people speaking in another language is a good lesson in how demanding hearing really is. It's genuinely fatiguing.

Especially we owe better hearing to the Word of God, whether in our private reading of it or at worship. We often take a lot of trouble to get to Mass or worship: finding the kids' shoes, making sure we have our envelopes or checkbook, getting the ice off the car windows in some climes, setting the sprinklers, and so forth: Why not make it "quality time"? During this one hour let's forget the cost of our apartment, the plans we have for the afternoon, or that mess in the garage, and give the Word of God and even the words of the poor preacher our complete attention. We honor God's words not just by saying an unthinking amen but by listening and asking how we can make this pertain to ourselves, no matter how badly the preacher may have done his part. In that way, God's word will have a chance to break in and be effective.

May 21

"Do this in remembrance of me" are the words of Jesus telling his disciples to celebrate the Lord's Supper. As the New Testament makes very clear, he is not telling them this because he will have disappeared and they need to try to remember who he was. Rather, he says: do it because it will remind you that *I am present*, that I am still with you. Remembrance that makes present what is remembered is what we're talking about in the sacrament that Christians call Eucharist, Mass, the Lord's Supper. We do not celebrate an absent Lord, Savior and God, but one present to enliven and inspire us today, the twenty-first day of May.

In the sacraments and in Jesus' word we have something much more powerful than we would have in even a color video taken by one of the apostles or than we would have if someone found the garment he was wrapped in at death (the shroud) or if we had his sandals or staff. In concentrating too much on something such as the shroud, a Christian would be in danger of ignoring the more important fact that Jesus is present here and now by his Spirit, his Word, in the sacraments and in the community of believers. "Where two or three are gathered together in my name, there am I in their midst" (Matt 18:19).

Even the ascension of Jesus recorded in the Gospels is not meant to mark the disappearance of the Lord but the end of his special appearances. As someone has said very well: anxious concern about the details of what Jesus was like in hair and clothes or whether we have bits of any of them or an imprint is really a distraction from the more important task of hearing God's Word and experiencing God in our hearts. As the angels said to the disciples at the ascension, "Why do you look at the heavens?" (Acts 11:11). Look around you; realize he is always with you. "And be assured, I am with you always, to the end of time" (Matt 28:20).

May 22

It is certainly commendable to be able to say things clearly and even confidently. From seeing the success of TV evangelists, other gurus of various kinds, and politicians who use this approach, it is apparent that it works. But it seems also evident that one of the greatest dangers in religion is to extend this certainty and clarity to matters that are just not that easy for us to nail down. Part of the charm of young people is often a kind of confidence and brashness in these matters; it is also something very dangerous. In something I read recently, a bright young man is described as "a clever young man to whom had fallen a rather larger share of self-assurance and intolerance than even clever young men usually possess." Along the same line someone else has written, "Too many people, too early in their lives, are certain of too many things." This confident certainty is capable of being used to dupe, seduce, brainwash others' minds and hearts.

Most of all such certainty about religious matters is just inconsistent with the fact that religious matters are, by definition, so much beyond our understanding. To resist the temptation to give all the answers to every complex human and religious question seems to me to be the higher and more truthful approach. And the longer we live, the more we may come to realize the relative character of all statements about God and religion. It makes it all the more inappropriate for the old, whether institutions or people, to make clear but brash declarations about complex matters. It is bad enough and maybe more forgivable in the young, but can it be tolerated in those with more experience who have lived long enough to know better?

Why not emphasize that absolute trust in God that we can have but be a bit more modest about specific questions that have many facets, many qualifications. "Education," someone has written, "is the process of moving from cocksure ignorance to thoughtful uncertainty." A more positive way of putting all this is that we must recognize that the more we think we know, how much more mystery there is to everything and everyone.

May 23

Do we use the word love too vaguely, too broadly? It seems to mean in ordinary conversation everything from the love of God for us to the affection of parents for their children to sexual relations.

Do we know too little of it? Do we throw the word around too easily, sign too many letters with it, claim that we "love" too many people? Would something short of love be a better term?

Do we romanticize it too much, blow it up into more than it can possibly be, and hence always find ourselves disappointed, disillusioned? Do we expect more of it than it can possibly give? Maybe these questions are destined to remain provocative matter for discussion, for poetry, for songs, for philosophy, for theology, for everyone, while the reality remains or is too complex a matter to be captured by anyone of us in words. What we can do, however, without worrying about meaning and definitions, is to practice what is in reality a most welcome form of love: consideration, patience, concern for others, deference to their needs, thoughtfulness for neglected persons, interest in the good of others (when they allow it). No matter how beautiful, provocative, thoughtful, and insightful words can be, most of us would welcome—and accordingly should give—these signs of what we can all recognize as love: selflessness, generosity, consideration, helpfulness.

May 24

Life is a celebration but not an entertainment. If we think of dear friends gone from us, often prematurely, it must urge us to celebrate, to *live* the life we for some strange reason still possess. Do a little review of these people in your life as I do here: a very good friend, a talented writer and budding poet, killed in war at nineteen years of age; a relative who suffered poverty and marriage failure and in her forties died of cancer; a loving mother who after a life of hard work and constant illness died in her seventies; a brilliant professor-priest who died suddenly of a heart attack at forty-five; or another in his fifties after a long lingering illness; a young college student killed on a bicycle in his freshman year—and on and on. All of them possessed qualities holding more promise than their lives were able to fulfill. All were loved. It would be very easy to sit in tears and discouragement over the injustice and incomprehensibility of these deaths.

But that might indicate self-pity and selfishness or a lack of trust in God, in whose care we must believe they now are. Kept far better than we or this world could ever have kept them. The more fruitful attitude for us is to celebrate, utilize, benefit from the life, health, and talent we have. We can do nothing now about *their* deaths. We can do a lot about *our* lives. We can celebrate life, live it generously, joyously, making all we can of it here and now. What better way to honor those whose lives cheered, helped, and blessed us? Insofar as we can, why not begin each day intent on using well our time and talent, not wasting effort and energy on pettiness, recrimination, brooding over imagined or real injuries, but rejoicing in life and time, opportunity and friends. Entertainment is certainly a part of any life—in fact, we probably all provide it to each other often unknowingly, but it recedes in importance whenever we take it on ourselves to celebrate, to rejoice in the gift of life itself.

Entertainment, as we often understand it, is a substitute for a willingness to celebrate, an easy, even more passive way to spend the time, which celebration sees as an opportunity, a treasure. Celebration carries with it the notion that we must contribute something, act, move, initiate. Life is not just entertainment, not just a cabaret, but truly a celebration of the gift of life and all the other gifts that have come with it.

May 25

Our witnessing to Christ is so pale, so low-keyed—to put it mildly! In making this complaint, the idea is not that we should go looking for ways to make ourselves really obnoxious, to bring on persecution. But it does seem that our faith in the Lord could permeate us more fully, be more influential in our lives, at least to the extent that others see it as intrinsic to our identity. They should sense that the good in us is somehow related to our belief in the Lord.

We may not be called to ringing doorbells, passing out religious literature, or preaching at the mall on Saturday afternoon, but in some way a genuine belief in the Lord requires that we let it flow over into some visible, audible consequences. We might suggest to a despairing, inconsolable neighbor that we will pray for her or that she might try prayer. We might tell another miserable friend why we hope, why we have some joy amid difficulties. We might put more effort into finding something to read for a confused or uninformed friend. We could invite a lonely or neglected acquaintance to a welcoming parish liturgy. We might meet the cynicism of fellow employees with some trust in the possibility of change, improvement. The ways of witnessing are as varied as our lives and opportunities.

May 26

"Some fellows look and find the sunshine; but I look and find the rain. Some fellows make a winning sometime; but I never even make a gain." Dramatizing our ills and problems, our difficulties and pains is almost a standard way of making conversation, small talk for many of us. It's the pay dirt of country western music and many a popular ballad. "I don't know how I'd ever go through another night like that." "You can't imagine what a hellhole the place is." "I've never in my whole life felt so humiliated." I think we can allow for some of that as a cultural thing, a way of speaking, the injection of a bit more drama into our daily life, which we so often think is pretty gray and dull.

But when we start taking our drama seriously we may be in trouble. Many of our daily difficulties might be better off with less attention. Generally, we need only look around us a bit to see reasons for thankfulness and less self-pity if we have a tendency to really take our little ills seriously.

I stayed one summer recently at the rectory of a large city parish in the heart of the downtown area on the border of the financial district and the tenderloin. Coming into the house evenings, I would almost invariably have to step over a sleeping man, one of many to be found in entries and storefronts of the area. Imagine how humbled I felt one evening in the course of stepping over an elderly man lying in the entrance. As he noticed me, he moved aside, called me "Sir" and excused himself for being there, promising to be out of the way by 6 A.M., all this in response to nothing said by me.

As I went to bed that night: What if I did have a few arthritic pains, what if my typewriter was acting up, if so-and-so had missed an appointment, if I had a bit of a cold, if my steak was burned, if I got caught in the rain, what if . . . So what.

May 27

The Marlboro man with his firm mouth, steely eyes, and granite jaw typifies one of the ideals of our society. This ideal fears or suppresses feeling and its expression. For men, at least in our society, giving vent to feeling (except maybe at a ball game) is seen as unmanly; it may even be a setback for one's career. But it's broader than just men. Christian tradition has, rather oddly, developed an anti-emotion, an anti-feeling attitude. Despite the Bible's open and clear appreciation of the body and passion, Christian teaching was, somewhere along the line, led to fear and suspicion of all this. One person blamed for this is St. Augustine, a theological writer of the fifth century.

But even he had his more positive moments in regard to feeling and opposed the idea that a good follower of Christ had to suppress all feeling; that this was the way to peace. St. Augustine says that stilling all our feelings is not the way to peace but the way to loss of genuine human qualities. The Christian ideal is not to be unmoved, above human feeling and excitement, but to let these carry us along to more generosity, joy, and enthusiasm in our following of Christ.

Our feelings are suppressed at times, too, by a kind of false pride that will not allow us to express them. Or by too much regard for stuffy customs. Both keep us from spontaneous expression of feeling, from a more expansive and less stiff attitude, from an occasional tear.

St. Augustine goes on to say; "Do not try to keep your soul free from emotional influences." If we believe that God made the human person good and that even our tendency to sin does not destroy that, then our sexuality, our feelings, our passions, are good, too.

We should be more worried about being hard of heart, insensitive and indifferent, than about letting go, acting a bit foolishly. After all, Christ did not think that his status as the Son of God was something to be held on to but willingly took on the lowly form of a human being (Phil 2:5-11). God wasn't worried about what the neighbors would think.

May 28

As he returned to his Father, Jesus told his disciples to show and tell the good news. They were to tell it and accompany that with extraordinary miracles, according to Mark 16. That text indicates that some people in the early Church apparently had the same fascination with the marvelous and exotic that still flourishes among us. Witness a few years ago cars lined up for miles to see the supposed face of Jesus on an oil tank. In that chapter of Mark (vv. 15–20) the disciples are told they can expect to cast out devils, speak in strange tongues, handle deadly snakes, or drink poison and be unharmed and, finally, cure the sick. Some of those should raise eyebrows: We will speak Afghan or Seminole? Be able to handle rattlers and copperheads? Be able to drink arsenic and strychnine? In terms of the rest of the New Testament, expelling demons and healing the sick are more comprehensible, but these others sound like material for a *National Geographic* special on a recently discovered tribe.

Elsewhere in the New Testament we have quite a different attitude toward flashy and freakish wonders. When the devil urges a hungry Jesus to make some Big Macs out of the stones in the desert or to throw himself off the top of the Temple to test the angelic safety net, Jesus refuses. He will not do showy or acrobatic miracles (Matt 4:1-11). When the Pharisees ask for special signs, Jesus says no. When Paul's contemporaries want miracles, he says he will only give them Christ crucified. Finally, after writing about such gifts as speaking in strange tongues, Paul insists that the higher, even the greatest, gift is doing the works of love.

That business in the Gospel about handling snakes and drinking poison reflects, it seems, a faulty attitude of some in the age in which Jesus lived, which looked for God in the abnormal, expecting more magic than mercy. The same temptation persists among us. But the more consistent and central message of the Gospels is that God's presence is manifested in healing, mercy, love, and daily patience. If we work at these day by day and build up hope and joy in those around us, we needn't regret our lack of expertise in handling rattlers or downing arsenic. We're doing something better, more demanding and, in the long run, more helpful.

May 29

In my book, St. Paul gets two citations. First, a complaint for the difficulty and obscurity of his writing. And, secondly, a scriptural Oscar or Emmy for the exuberant hope and encouragement of his writings. I'm not going to even claim to resolve the first matter, but I think we're allowed, even if we can't follow all of Paul's twisting thought to benefit from his spirit, his faith. In Romans 15:13 he writes: "And may the God of hope fill you with all joy and peace by your faith in him, until, by the power of the Holy Spirit, you overflow with hope." Behind the difficulty of some of Paul's writing (even St. Peter wrote—2 Peter 3:16—that "they contain some obscure passages.") is his strong faith in the risen Christ and how we share in that risen life by faith and baptism. "You must regard yourselves as dead to sin and alive to God, in union with Christ Jesus" (Rom 6:11). By our baptism and faith in Jesus Christ we have begun our own resurrection; we live a new life; we are dead to sin and raised to new life in Christ, he says. Because of this, no matter what gloom and grayness seem to swamp our vision and our lives at times, we have reason to hope, to expect to see sunnier days, to offer others hope. We counter pessimism and despair in ourselves with trust that the night of suffering and discouragement will be followed by the morn of resurrection, the dawn of light and hope.

Our reflections should more often be on such verses as the one quoted above, reminding ourselves (after all our minds, memories, and hearts are part of the process, too) that our faith should lead to and support hope. And the two should provoke joy and peace. If the words of Romans 15:13 do not enliven us or cheer our dismal days and faint faith, let's turn them into prayer.

God of hope, may our faith in you fill us with joy and peace; help us to overflow with hope. Jesus has risen, and by your power and love we, too, will rise from this present trough of discouragement or indifference. Strengthen our faith and hope. Alleluia.

May 30

Snapshots, tapes, and home movies of family and friends gone before us or absent from us provide us with the kind of memento that people in other ages could never have. Such things are real reminders in a sense, real but still powerless. What can pictures or recordings of a voice gone from us do but produce some smiles or regrets, at times even tears? They cannot make the person walk with us or sit for a cup of coffee or discuss family affairs. What would a videotape or movie of the actual life of Christ himself do for us? Move us deeply, possibly, but it would be no substitute for his presence and power.

But Jesus has left us something more powerful than home movies or even videos made by Peter, John, or Mark. He has given us his Spirit to be with us. He has left us much more than souvenirs of himself. Before ascending he had told his disciples, "I am with you always, until the end of the world." His human life was around thirty years, spent in a very small country about one hundred by fifty miles at its largest among a very small portion of the world's population. He was never in Chicago or Calcutta or Millerville. He probably never met a live Irishman, Pole, or Chinese.

To make up for this, he has left his Spirit, the Spirit of himself, of Jesus, to be with us. Through the Spirit, a being by definition not limited to one place or time or body, he is at work in every part of the world through all time. Correctly but often too easily, we think of the Holy Spirit as given us for our consolation now that Jesus is no longer on our earth. True, the Spirit should and does console us; comforter is another of the names given to the Spirit. But we should not stop there; the Spirit is given to guarantee the continuance of the work of Jesus in healing and saving our world.

The Spirit does this through the free cooperation and ingenuity of human beings who believe in the Spirit. Generally God heals and cares for our world through doctors, parents, and good neighbors; God will cheer the depressed and despairing through our friendship, the music we make, the pleasure we give, the time we spend.

May 31

A friend's attentions, the sensitivity and faithfulness of husband or wife, the thoughtfulness of a son or daughter, the brilliance of someone's achievement (athletic, artistic, academic, etc.), the encouraging words of another, the unfailing presence of someone in the midst of grief and disappointment—these are the ways that we ordinarily sense the love of God for us. They give it flesh, make it real here and now in this difficult moment or humdrum day, and we can do the same for others. "The heavens proclaim your glory, O God, . . . day unto day takes up the story . . . ." (Ps 19:1-2). And friends, parents, and good people all around us display your love, put it in a handshake, an embrace, a kiss, a smile, a word, an action.

Even our belief in the resurrection of Jesus, on which rests all our hope, comes to us through others. No one has promised, no one assures us that God will reveal it to each of us in some personal, vivid way. We know and believe that he has risen because of the witnesses he chose. The women to whom he appeared, the disciples to whom he spoke and with whom he ate. Like God's love for us, our belief in the rising to new life of Jesus, too, depends on others and has come to us from them.

Those who had known him before his crucifixion recognized that the risen Christ was the same person, that he had indeed risen from the dead, that the cross had not been the end. None of them saw him rise, but they saw him risen, and their irreplaceable obligation was to proclaim it to the world. This they have done, and we have the record of this in our Gospels. Beyond that, we who have received their witness and been blessed with hope because of it have the happy obligation of showing by our lives and words that we, too, believe. That we want to help the whole world believe that he has risen. That overcoming death, sin, suffering, and injustice does not merely depend on our good will and efforts but ultimately on the power and love of God. Our faith and hope have come to us through others; the faith and hope of still others will come to them through us.

June 1

In big city buildings, subways, and similar places, one is met by continual commands to push this, that, or the other thing.

And it becomes evident to anyone moving to the city from the quieter, slower life of the country or small towns that pushing is the name of the game. If we don't just push doors and buttons, we frequently end up pushing each other all over the place.

But pushing in deeper and more profound ways is a tendency in all of us, whether urban or rural, except, perhaps in the case of the most indolent and unmotivated. Often understandably, we push ourselves, push employees or students, push this or that person to get things done well and on time. We have ideals for ourselves and for our families, for those for whom we have some responsibility. And in seeking to realize the ideals, we must push, demand, insist, encourage very strongly, goad, or motivate others. And ourselves.

The more difficult thing is to know when to stop pushing—myself, my son or daughter, my friend or employee. This is probably one of the most mysterious things in our life or our living: knowing when to stop pushing. When there has been enough pressure, when we should put some trust in the power of nature itself or of the person or of God and allow something to happen that is not the immediate result of *my* so-important pushing.

Both in our own lives and in those of others on whom we have influence or for whom we feel strong responsibility, there come moments—if we are sensitive enough to them—when the right thing, the more productive thing is to stop the pressure, and let go. That is tough! Probably even more difficult than constantly exerting pressure and demands. It requires more of a sacrifice of our sense that all depends so entirely on me. As an ancient Chinese writer, Chuang Tzu, writes, "To know when to stop / To know when you can get no further / By your own action, / This is the right beginning."

June 2

Sometimes a particularly outrageous statement serves the good function of highlighting the truth for us by suggesting its opposite. For instance, "In Hollywood, if you don't have happiness, you send out for it" (Rex Reed). Put that way I think we see more clearly the outrageousness and wrongness of that idea, that happiness is some kind of object or service that one can find in a store or obtain through an office, something on the same level as a cheeseburger, a fur coat, a rented car, a new suit, an airline ticket. Most of us probably have no difficulty in seeing that happiness cannot possibly be any one of these, any combination of them or even in the same category, something we can choose from a counter or display.

Not only is happiness not an object, it is also not something we can directly seek in any sense of the word. An English artist of this century, Eric Gill, said that if the artist took care of goodness and truth, beauty would follow. Rather than being so concerned about the pursuit of happiness, we are told by Scripture to seek not happiness but goodness, honesty, respect for others and for our world, concern for others, healing and caring, service, work that needs doing. Doing our work well, serving the needs of those around us, being grateful for the gifts given us and using them well, all this easily brings with it a sense of worth, of legitimate satisfaction, a sense that my days and hours are not just dragging by or being thrown to the wind. We experience a certain glow that we call happiness.

Possibly the main ingredient in this whole process, the main reason why this work is so successful, is that the emphasis is not on me and my needs, but on others, on matters beyond and outside myself. Happiness comes from giving ourselves to these matters, these persons, not in trying somehow to gild and polish this little self.

June 3

I imagine that if most of us had been given the task of writing the scenario for Christ's rising and subsequent appearances, we would have arranged things a bit differently. Think especially of the people to whom Jesus appeared. In one sense it seems a bit like "saving the saved." He showed himself to people who had been, to varying degrees, favorable to him, devoted to him, even if at the crucifixion and death they may have been sorely tempted to wonder if it hadn't all been a mistake.

He *didn't*, however, appear to the Pharisees or others of his enemies, or to Pilate or Herod. You would think it would have been a good occasion to allow himself at least a few "I told you so's." But he didn't rush over to wake up Pilate or to interrupt brunch that morning at the high priest's.

Of course, just on a very basic human level, that doesn't seem to be the sort of thing he ever did. He never forced people's devotion or faith. He didn't seem interested in scoring points. The whole matter as recounted in the Gospels, in fact, is a procedure that leaves very much intact the human being's ability to respond, the right to make choices. You might say that Jesus downplayed the whole matter of impressing those who did not want to be impressed. In fact, he appeared to women first of all. And women were not regarded in that society as reliable witnesses!

The whole procedure emphasizes that in order to see Christ risen, to believe that he has saved us from sin and death, requires that we show some minimal good will. Possibly that is the first action of God's grace in us: to pry us open further when we begin to be ever so slightly open. It suggests that in all of human life, in all our efforts to allow growth to occur, we need to accept the possibility that grace, God, inspiration, light, may come from sources and in ways we don't expect. Grace is truly all around us.

June 4

"He reached out from on high and grasped me; / he drew me out of the deep waters. / He rescued me from my mighty enemy / and from my foes, who were too powerful for me" (Ps 18:17-18). The words of the psalm may strike us at first glance as a bit dramatic for our use. But looking back on our life, don't we see examples of where things could have gone much worse or gone in a dangerous or sordid direction from which it would have been hard to pull back?

Wasn't there possibly a relationship or a network of them that could have been very destructive? Weren't there possibly decisions we could have made that would have prevented us ever knowing some of the great people we do know now? Wasn't there possibly a shortsighted decision that with the help of a good advisor or friend, we were able to avoid? And even when things have gone badly, have there not been bright lights amid them all that have balanced the darkness and gloom? And there are all the people who have given us hope or restored it to us so often by a word, a smile, a look, their very presence, the gift of their time.

The experience of most Christians who have remained so through many a change and trial is that life has been full of such moments, such people, such events—what theologians call grace or graces. Freely given, undeserved signs of God's goodness and love. A great part of Christian life, like that of the Jews from whom came the psalm quoted above, must consist in thanksgiving for the signs we see in our lives of the goodness of God, most often in the immediate goodness and kindness of those around us. Sure, others may see all this as chance, as the result of "lucky" circumstances. Christian belief is that God has the whole world in his hands; that goodness and love come to us from one who, despite the more bitter moments we endure, wants our good, loves us beyond what even we egotists could rightfully expect. He "drew me out of the deep waters."

June 5

Many people looking for a book of daily reflections seek, I'm sure, a collection of pep talks, goads to activity, inspirational words. We all do, after all, face sluggish days, days when nothing seems particularly worth the effort, when we wonder why, why, why. Days of boredom, of being simply tired of the whole thing and needing, we think, someone's good words, encouragement. That seems to me undeniable. And we do provide that service to each other, not just by giving homilies or pep talks but by words of encouragement and praise, words that reassure us that our life and our work are worth it.

But there's another and very opposite side to this whole matter that deserves some attention even if it may seem at times beyond us. It's this: we *can* take ourselves, our striving, our efforts to be better, *too seriously*. Our striving itself, our hot pursuit of excellence, above all in our relation to God, can be another form of the self-centeredness and self-concern we all recognize as part of the problem.

To forget ourselves is obviously part of the solution according to Jesus. If all our effort is centered on making me better, more virtuous, more spiritual, more perfect, isn't this a matter of just more *self*ishness, even if it isn't concerned with getting me more power over others, more wealth, more material security? It may, as someone has said, feed the very vice it intends to destroy, self-centeredness, self-concern.

We need an occasional reminder—really more than occasional—that our perfection is more a matter of allowing God to act in us than our own striving to figure it out with our small minds and weaker wills. An ancient Chinese writer, translated by Thomas Merton, wrote: "Do not try to hold on to Tao. / Just hope that Tao / will keep hold of you!" We might vary that for our purposes: Do not try to hold on to God, to perfection. Just hope, trust, that God will hold on to you. Everything else will follow.

June 6

A theologian known for his insistence that belief must show itself in concrete action, in changing the wrong conditions of our world, says, nevertheless, that our first response to God, to knowing and believing in God, must be "awe, silence and contemplation" (Harvey Cox). After that comes action for one's neighbor. And finally, maybe a distant third, comes theology: reflecting, speculating about the message of God. For most of us the temptation is to rush on to the second response, probably much less to the third. But we do need to linger more at the first. Awe, astonishment, wonder, appreciation, silence, a willingness to listen, to exclude worries about the microwave and the investments for a while. Contemplation: time to turn over in our minds and hearts the insight or perception we have of God and all that relates to God.

It all adds up to being willing to do something so unproductive by worldly standards as sitting quietly and opening ourselves to God. It may not be in the silence of a church or chapel; it may have to be as the baby dozes off in our arms and we have a moment to breathe, or on the way through the tangle of urban traffic to the job or the office. The radio does not have to be on every minute. It comes equipped with a knob to cut off the power.

Part of the necessary motivation and power we need to live as followers of Jesus in a joyful and confident manner must come from having been able to make more perfectly our own his words of assurance and encouragement. Because we have reached some personal conviction that God loves us and is with us in all we do, we can face it more hopefully. Because we know from having been able to think and pray about it for some moments that he is with us in everything and able to come to us through the most unlikely means, we see our world full of his presence and can smile and hope through its miseries. The silence, the awe, the contemplation anchor us in the one in whom we can hope, trust, and rejoice.

June 7

The letter from an energetic, successful young man of about thirty years of age is typical of what one hears from many a young, unmarried person. "I just got 'slam-dunked,' as we would say in the dating game. . . . I met this girl who really was delightful, lots of fun, caring. . . . We dated for about a month. . . . Suddenly one day I found a message on my answering machine saying she was getting married—obviously not to me. . . . Anyway, it's not the first time that's happened to me and probably won't be the last. And while it hurts, I always recover. Sooner or later though, I'm sure I'll meet Miss Right." The case may be a bit dramatic and, one hopes, exceptional, but the point is more universal. Relationships that look so promising and are so good do not always work out; something happens, and it's all over. One is back to cold dinners alone and hoping someone will call or vainly calling others, only to find that they are busy with so-and-so, their new flame, making one's own hurt all the worse.

The problem may be especially acute for young people, out of the family home, working in a strange new city, who are looking for new friends or for the one who may be their companion in marriage, some lasting love. But the problem is often of longer duration than that and can hit many persons even in later years.

Satisfying love or friendship is probably among the highest, deepest goals of most human beings who haven't settled for power or money in their place. But the way to it seems strewn with misfirings, failed relationships. The very idealism that makes us so disappointed in all this should keep us looking and hoping and believing that it is possible and can come about. As the fellow quoted says so well: "It's happened before and this will probably not be the last time. It hurts, definitely, but I always recover. Sooner or later, though, it's bound to click." Such hope and optimism is certainly half the battle.

Along with hope we need an honest assessment of our selves, of our strengths and weaknesses. It isn't simply a matter of finding the right person but of ourselves becoming the right person.

June 8

Elsewhere in these pages I've been frivolous enough to suggest that we need to come to our daily life with more of a sense of humor. I know: what a light-headed, unproductive approach; how do you ever expect to get ahead that way, etc.? But anyway, since I've betrayed such a frothy, insubstantial approach to life, I'm emboldened to do more of it, with Scriptural blessing, no less.

Look at the attitude expressed in the opening verse of Psalm 146:

> Alleluia! Praise the Lord, O my soul;
> I will praise the Lord all my life;
> I will sing praise to my God while I live.

And you thought the writer of these pages was an airhead? Look at that verse. Obviously, I don't really agree with my imaginary antagonist in that first paragraph. I think that verse offers an ideal, wonderful way to face life.

The verse invites us implicitly, once again, to look at our lives, our relationships, the world around us and see all the truly beautiful and inspiring people and realities there. "Praise the Lord, O my soul." There will be days of despair of indescribable sorrow and pain, of disappointment of the most fundamental kind—I doubt whether you or I ever escape meeting one or the other. But we meet them better if we aim to praise and thank the Lord for all the good that we do encounter and that is by no means a small matter. Our intention and hope must be to "praise the Lord all my life."

When you meet people walking down the street or corridor whistling, singing to themselves, you know there is a certain amount of basic happiness there, some sense of well being and, whether they think that way or not, a kind of thankfulness, gratitude. We may be even guilty of it ourselves! Why not? "I will sing praise to my God while I live," while I have so many gifts around and in me, while life moves relatively well. If we make enough music now, maybe the melody will linger even after the good is gone.

June 9

One of the first and most lasting problems in Christian history has been concerned with balancing and understanding how Jesus is both God's Son and a truly human being. Generally the tendency is to make him as Godlike as possible. We accept that he died on a cross, that he got tired, as John's Gospel tells us, that he ate and drank, that he even showed some anger, but as recent discussions show, we have a difficult time imagining that he had any hesitation, fears, or doubts about his vocation. In any case, most would agree that Christians need to take the humanness of Jesus more seriously in order themselves to be helped. The title Jesus preferred to use of himself was "Son of Man." While the term has other, more exalted references in Scripture, basically it is a Jewish way of saying that one is human. A member of the human race. Even after Peter calls him Messiah, Jesus in response calls himself Son of Man, once again emphasizing his solidarity with us, with human beings. Elsewhere, in allowing himself to be baptized, too, a rite for people who had something to repent, he showed again the depth of his involvement in our humanity.

Part of the idea seems to be, too, that Jesus, the Son of Man, is not just the Son of Man as you or I might be a son or daughter of man, a human being, but *the* Son of Man, the ideal, the model of what a human being should be. The measure for all of us of how our living stacks up in the eyes of God. He is "the true self of the human race." In him we see the ideal human response to suffering (in oneself and others), to hatred and persecution, to sin, and to God the Father and to our neighbor.

Because we believe he is also the Son of God and rose from the dead to send the Holy Spirit to make us "sons and daughters" of God, we believe that he is capable of transforming our humanness into his own likeness by his word and by our sharing in the Eucharist.

June 10

So often we live in the hope that real life, joy, happiness, good or better friends are all further on, somewhere else than in this plain, unromantic, even dead today. And one can't deny that the hope for something better, for the future, is a great part of what spurs us on and puts a point to life and activity. But somehow we have to balance that with some recognition that real life is always here and not elsewhere, with these people not with some we've never met, doing the work we must do or have committed ourselves to. If we think of real life, good friends, satisfying work, as all being "just around the corner," we find that we're on a circular track; there are no corners.

We get nowhere by constantly postponing all for the future. Most of us have had the experience of enjoying a good dinner, a concert, a performance of some kind, but have had it spoiled by being with someone who can't forget or put aside some worry or concern. They're not really with us and hence make our enjoyment also less. Or we ourselves are distracted by some worry and let what is before us pass unappreciated.

To think that real life is always somewhere else, with some other people, in some other environment, can be a ploy that only leads to never facing life, never really enjoying it. So often it isn't really our work, our routine, the circumstances of our life that get us down. It is our unrealistic expectation that other people and other places would be free of all the disappointing aspects of this time and place.

The truth about life is certainly rooted in the attitude Christ enjoins in the face of the end of things: be awake; pray. It is also strongly present in Zen Buddhism, and we Christians could benefit by some of that emphasis. Live now and here. In many ways what we call being a saint means simply living wholeheartedly and generously from our depths at this moment, seizing opportunities, being really present where we are. A willingness to do this is what makes life satisfying and productive; what frees it from useless hankering after what is gone or not yet here.

June 11

If you've gotten married recently you may have consulted one of several booklets suggesting readings for the wedding Mass. Or, if you've simply attended a wedding or two recently, you've had experience of the texts that are read. You've probably heard I Corinthians 13 enough to know that most-beautiful text by heart. When choosing a Gospel text, the couple often have put before them the few texts that explicitly mention marriage in Christ's teaching, texts about whether or not divorce is permitted (Matt 19:3-9; Mark 10:2-12), texts that are really not all that inspiring for a couple entering marriage.

One does better looking for texts that touch more on what kind of human being one must be to make a happy marriage. Christ's teaching is directed to all of us and concerns the more basic issues about how anyone of us becomes a good person. From really assimilating such texts, it should follow that marriage and work will be carried out with honesty and integrity, faith and love.

One text I suggest often and which has application to all of us is found in Matthew 6:25-34 and Luke 12:22-31. It has a generous, spring-like quality that should be appropriate not only to the usually buoyant atmosphere of a wedding but to any day of anyone's life. "Put away anxious thoughts about food and drink . . . clothes to cover your body. Surely life is more than food, the body more than clothes. Look at the birds of the air . . . ." Read it, over and over. What a beautiful invitation, reminder, of the care and love of God as two people enter a life together, a life that must be built on love and trust. Facing an unknowable future, what is more basic than this trust not only in each other and in their love but in God, who is its foundation?

No matter how much preparation has gone into the wedding, there is a sea of unknown possibilities that make the very fact of the marriage promises so moving. What more generous words do human beings speak? Even if we aren't getting married this month, we can benefit by reading and reflecting on these generous, expansive, hopeful verses. "Set your mind on God's kingdom and God's justice before everything else, and all the rest will come to you as well."

June 12

"Give us our daily bread," we pray. And it seems a most obvious request to make. Give us the sustenance we need to function as human beings, to be able to work, to love, to think, to serve, to create, to run or walk, to cook or repair. And a just distribution of the world's foodstuffs so that fellow human beings do not starve is an obvious corollary. But all that is still minimal in a sense. Our Lord says that we cannot live by bread alone but only by every word that comes from the mouth of God. Our spirit needs nourishment, too, needs to be encouraged, moved, strengthened, filled with hope, love, generosity.

Today, let us expand that even a bit further. If we see all the good that humans achieve as coming from God, who has given us such powers, then besides daily bread, there is more that we need. There is more we can provide for each other by the use of our talents. Can't we include in that "more" all the great expressions of God's rich life that appear in human achievement? Jesus was not simply the Word of God in the sense that he was God's expression verbally of truth; he was also in his flesh the vivid expression of God's mind and heart. Far beyond human words (oral or written), which, admittedly, have a power to thrill and enliven us, there are all the other ways in which human beings express what is in them through the gifts of God: art, music, dance, athletics, compassion and caring, forms of service.

Besides bread, we need and can provide for each other something of beauty, love, joy. The excitement we may feel, the sense of being raised from the ground a bit, of having "slipped the surly bonds of earth" for a few moments that we experience in the face of many a human achievement, this is something we *need*. Longings and desires we cannot put into words find some response and encouragement when we witness a moving play or movie, an athletic or dance performance, even a humorous picture of life. In them we can catch a glimpse, momentary as it is, of the perfection and beauty, the joy and love, the happiness and peace, for which we work and which exist fully in and with God.

Praise the Lord for dancers and singers, musicians and poets, gymnasts and swimmers, painters and potters, rugby players and farmers, winemakers and bakers, film directors and actors, playwrights and composers. Praise the Lord for them, for their performances, their art, their work, their play.

June 13

My father is older than I am—as happens in so many families. In fact, he's reached the age where he has minute recall of many scenes of his youth. Some of his most vivid memories are of the First World War spent on a navy transport going between New York and France. He recalls how a man fell off the ship while it was leaving an East Coast seaport. The other men were able to get some sort of cable ladder to him, and he was coming up the long distance from the water to the deck. Near the top he looked down, became terrified, lost his grip, fell back and was drowned.

In the time before my father's navy days, in the days of the big sailing vessels, when a new man was climbing the narrow rope ladder to the crow's nest, the veterans on the ship would keep calling to him: Look up, look up. If he looked down, he'd easily become dizzy and fall.

In the famous story of Christ calling Peter to come to him across the water (Matt 14:22-33), Peter's problems, too, began when he took his eyes off the Lord and, as one translation puts it, "saw the wind." "When he perceived how strong the wind was, he became frightened" and began to sink. Even when we seem to be drowning in problems and worries, if we can keep our eyes on our rescuer, our Savior, and not let our attention be diverted by the waves below, there is hope.

Recently I was pleasantly surprised when a young couple chose this Gospel reading about Peter for their wedding Mass. When I mentioned that to a woman married long enough to have a couple of teenagers, the appropriateness struck her immediately. She said: "Sure, keep your eyes on the ideal, the essentials, on Jesus, like Peter, and don't let the hassles and fears overwhelm you; otherwise you sink."

The force and drive of our faith depend on this kind of singleness of attention, a concentration of our spirit, not something we learn overnight. We start moving toward it by trying daily to make our faith, our trust, more wholehearted, letting it include more of our life's worries and concerns, putting them all in the Lord's care.

June 14

"Man was made at the end of the week when God was tired," wrote Mark Twain. Despite his famous stories that we identify with all that's good and American, Twain had some very bitter and biting remarks to make about belief in God and Christianity in some of his writings. The remark just quoted may not be outstanding for bitterness but it does express his disappointment in human beings. He says, in effect, that in making humans God did not give it the best shot. God was worn out by the strain of making rhododendrons and rhinos, palms and pumas. Twain is obviously speaking of God in very human terms.

But the book that has the story about God making human beings (Genesis) also tells us repeatedly that when God had finished making everything, man and woman included, God saw that the whole was good, very good. Obviously, the disappointing traits we and Twain see in each other and, if we're honest, within ourselves, come from elsewhere. Often we blame the devil ("the devil made me do it") or the woman (Eve) or women, or in some way, pass the buck. But Scripture in general puts the blame and praise at the feet of each of us. To simplify somewhat, God made us responsible and respects that ability. With it, we can even say no to the Creator.

Scripture over and over again appeals to our ability to change, to make a complete turnabout (repent), all based on the presumption that ordinarily we are responsible for our actions. Without saying that we can do everything, Scripture at least presupposes that the ordinary human being has something to say about what he or she does or does not do. (Clearly we're not primarily concerned here with factors that seriously limit our freedom.)

Part of our dignity as human beings consists in our ability to make decisions, to give our word and to have it taken for cash. Along with this goes the possibility of being sorry for our wrong decisions, our bad judgments. And we can be happy that with God's grace many matters are going well; we have made at least some of the right decisions. Why not recall now how much there is that we can do by way of response to God, how many ways there are for us to say yes?

June 15

Christians have at times pictured God's reaction to our sins so humanly that we see them as literally ruining God's day. We almost imagine God sulking in a corner. Inevitably, of course, we conceive God according to our human experience. There are many examples: A Hollywood convert to Christianity in a well-meant effort once termed God a "living doll." Scripture itself speaks of God as jealous, shooting arrows at the enemies, enjoying an evening walk in the cool breeze after a long hot day. Other religions have spoken of God as not merely having a wife, something fairly expectable, but also as stealing other men's or gods' wives. To express God's great power and inexhaustible creativity, Hindus picture God as having many arms. Obviously, personifying God, thinking of God in personal and human terms, has both attractions and dangers.

What's the alternative? Often it is to think of God as the Supreme Force, some stainless steel or plastic machine, the Intergalactic Dynamo, the All-Knowing Computer, the Absolute, the Great Idea, Truth, Goodness, Beauty. This view tries to avoid making God share petty human traits by making God impersonal—somehow more than or other than human.

Dangerous as it may be to model God on Tom, Dick, or Mary, nevertheless it seems to be closer to the truth than the second. When we speak of God as he or she or personal, as Father, Mother, Lover, Shepherd, King, we are thinking of a being who, like us, can know, love, feel, communicate, interact. At least such a being can get some response from us. What would bring us to worship or to love a God conceived of as some unresponsive power mechanically moving the parts of the universe? The martyrs we read about in Christian history did not sing among the flames or their pains for some great idea or master computer. No, we suffer, sing, love, worship, only in response to a person. While we may need to avoid making God too human with unbecoming human traits, still, to think of God as a person, able to respond and love, is necessary, something not to be given up even to avoid calling God him or her. God as Father or Mother is a quibble really when or if the alternative is to think of God as an It. No, God is a person who loves us and expects a return. God must have a face, a glance, a voice, a heart, a name. We're happy that it is that way.

June 16

Often we define miracle much too narrowly. When we hear the word we think of the sun dancing in the sky, a divine face or figure appearing suddenly, a severed limb being instantaneously rejoined to the body, a train being stopped moments before it would hit a child. In a way, these are almost like cartoon versions of a miracle. Or magic show or circus types, the type Jesus refused to do in the course of his temptations.

Our desire for such miracles may stem from our fear in this difficult world or from a need to be reassured that God acts, is present, cares. The trouble is, we only know God acts, cares, is present, if we have some faith, trust that this is so. As you'll read elsewhere in these pages, Jesus did not use his extraordinary powers to impress or overwhelm those who were not receptive to him. Why should we expect him to do so today? The kind of miracles mentioned in the first paragraph would, theoretically, be such that no one seeing them could have any doubts. Faith would have been made unnecessary.

But throughout Jesus' own ministry he demands faith, complains, in fact, that he can do no healing because people lack faith. Miracles always occur when God's love meets human faith and trust. Rather than complaining that in our day there are no miracles or that God seems to have done it all during the New Testament period, we should widen our understanding of "miracle" and see that where we see God's loving action occurring we have a miracle, a sign of God's power and presence. God does not substitute miracles for the events of ordinary life but allows those with faith to see miracles in all of ordinary life. The unexpected and wonderful love I have received from someone, the way many of my hopes have been realized, the way I have been rescued from despair—these are miracles! What does it matter if others accept them or not? They, too, will see and recognize miracles, God's action in our world, when our lives show ever-more clearly thanksgiving and joy in the presence and loving care of the miracle-worker.

June 17

If there is anything we want more than financial security it may be a similar security in our minds and beliefs, certainty about everything that will be or could be. This explains some of the human pursuit of fortune-tellers, astrologers, and, too, our following of spiritual leaders (gurus, evangelists) who offer all the answers in a clean, neat format. It explains even the attraction of the Baltimore Catechism still in our day for some: It is all there so plain and clear. God is this; sin is that, the result of sin is also clearly this here and now and in the world to come.

More and more we have come to realize that life and God are not so easily captured in our phrases and formulas. Salvation is not simply reducible to something like the directions for putting together a deck chair, a valid baptism or the repetition of some phrase like, "I accept the Lord Jesus as my personal Savior." Just as we cannot treat God as such a simple and manageable commodity, so we trust that God who made us so complex in our emotions, dreams, and possibilities does not treat us like robots either.

False clarity and precision, extreme simplicity come from minimizing the reality of God and the mystery of God and our relationship. Think of how justly insulted a man or woman would be to have someone else's love for them reduced to "All she sees in him is a great body and a lot of money." No, Christian belief and life, too, are full of paradox, of unresolvable mysteries, of tensions that only grace and living can resolve in any sense. An ancient Zen writer said, "Those who know don't say, and those who say don't know." Those who really have an insight, we could say faith, know it is not simply expressible in this or that formula or ritual or practice, and those who claim to have it all bottled up have missed the point. We should rejoice in the mystery, the depth of our relation to God and not envy those who claim to have reduced it all to the wearing of a medal, the saying of this prayer, the practice of so many Masses or some magic words.

June 18

"Even a turtle has to stick its neck out to get anywhere." This folksy way of putting it expresses an important truth of Christian existence. Growth in our following of Christ, in our development as human beings, depends on some initiative, some daring, some foolishness at times, some willingness to do the rash, generous thing.

And this "sticking our neck out" has been modeled for us by God. What foolishness by the standards of human thought: that the immovable, happy and complete, unchanging, all-supreme being would take on human form and risk trying to teach this unpredictable and often violent group of people. God's Son, Jesus, entered fully into our life, being born of a simple couple in Palestine and finally encountering severe, ultimate hurt at the hands of those he came to serve. "It is by this that we know what love is: that Christ laid down his life for us" (1 John 3:16).

None of us likes to look forward to the same kind of end. But with trust that God is with us if we attempt to follow the Son's example, we can at least imitate God's initiative toward us by our love toward those around us. The love of God is poured out on us in baptism through Christ in order that we continue that love and be carried along by its power. St. John puts it simply and clearly: "We love because God loved us first" (1 John 4:19). As God took the first step, we need not simply react to others' love but to let love drive us to be daring, to make a new effort, to try to do even the most extravagant things we're prompted to do. Less concern is in order about whether we're going to be seen as softhearted or softheaded and more that we carry on the gift we have received.

"Fools rush in where angels fear to tread" is said of romantic love. If God has been so foolish as to send Jesus, we can risk the joy of being foolish, too—in daring to love, serve, and interest ourselves in others.

June 19

One fall a freshman on some class assignment came to my dormitory residence to interview me, a Benedictine and a member of this particular community. His first question was about how long I had been a member of the community. Since he was sitting down I felt it was safe to tell him. I did; he was obviously flabbergasted, and then he stunned *me* by asking, "Are there some who have been members *longer* than you?" (There were.) Fiftieth wedding anniversaries must have a like effect on eighteen-year-olds.

Whether in marriage or religious life, by our promises we take on the responsibility of being something for someone or for God and, possibly, for being somewhere too. I'm sure some of us almost take this for granted; others find it hard to imagine or at least find such a commitment inconceivable. Or they can think of it only in terms of the next ten minutes or later today. The German writer and philosopher Friedrich Nietzsche wrote that only human beings are capable of making promises. They indicate that we are willing to go beyond the feeling of the moment and assure someone else or some enterprise that we will be there tomorrow or longer. Even though poetry, songs, theater, and movies all glorify passion and spontaneity, we need to reflect a bit on how important to all of us are the commitments we and others have made. How important it is to know that the trash hauler will come or that the doctor will be there for my appointment, no matter whether either of them is being carried along by a great passion. Passion and excitement are there to draw us into matters that otherwise might be too frightening. In relation to marriage, isn't love, for instance, the "tender trap" that leads us on to do more than we had originally ever imagined? Getting ready for a date, one doesn't often think of diapers, school bills, and a large enough home. But commitment ultimately may be the real proof of passion or, better, of lasting love.

June 20

My recommendation of Matthew 6:25-34 ("Do not be anxious about your life, what you shall eat or what you shall drink. . . . Look at the birds of the air . . . .") as a wedding Mass reading often raises questions and eyebrows in the persons to be married and, I'm sure, in those who attend. Isn't this kind of advice, granted it is from our Lord himself, a bit dangerous to be giving two people who are already dizzy enough because of young love? Doesn't it just encourage in them a thoughtless attitude about the future? Love will take care of all. Who needs an income, a house, a job? "Look at the birds of the air; they neither sow nor reap . . . ."

Or, it may strike us that the advice, after all, is more appropriate, if they needed it, for plants, flowers, birds. It seems an invitation to a thoughtless animal, subhuman existence. Didn't we evolve from that into something superior, a kind of creature capable of thought, reflection, foresight? Aren't we proposing the vagabond or gypsy as the ideal, instead of the thoughtful, forward-looking, prudent human being using his or her sense and intelligence to prepare for the future? Obviously, for one thing, this beautiful discourse of Jesus is dramatic, sweeping, poetic, a way of making an important point, hardly a literal invitation to quit our jobs, sit on the back porch, and let the Lord take care of things. Elsewhere, it is clear our Lord commends our ability to plan, think, respond. But this text is a reminder that our planning is limited, albeit absolutely necessary. We cannot omit it. But, along with our planning, there must be in our hearts and minds this confidence that we are in the hands of God, that our worries and anxieties are limited, that God can do more, can be trusted. Even psychologically, it is better for us to act with confidence than to be crippled or paralyzed by fear and worry.

"Do not be anxious about tomorrow, for tomorrow will be anxious for itself. Let the day's own trouble be sufficient for the day" (Matt 6:34).

June 21

The present, the past, the future—how do we balance them? It almost seems to be the primary question on the practical level in trying to live a Christian life. Do we live primarily in hope for what is to come? For something better, afterlife, for the coming of Christ? How do we do that without neglecting the present, the grace and opportunities that are all around us? The dangers of living in the past probably seem more evident: We all run into or are guilty ourselves of the attitude that finds all the good that ever happened in the past, our own or that of our society, our world, our Church. It seems fairly clear how unproductive, stagnating it is to live in that sort of sentiment.

But the past has its good uses; to put it very minimally, it is necessary for the present and for the future, at least for the Christian. Christian life in almost any Christian body is built to a large degree (1) around hearing and recalling the words of the Lord, and (2) recalling his suffering, death, and resurrection by eating a meal in memory of him. "Do this as often as you do it in memory of me." At Mass we recall the past not to sentimentally escape the present and live in a never-never land but (1) to be thankful for and mindful of all that God has done for us, even all the good our parents, teachers, friends have done for us. Not to recall this would be the sign of an ungrateful, self-centered heart. (2) And we recall the past to be challenged by it, to be urged to live up to what the Lord in his teaching and life has told us is our ideal and what we have seen of it in those people who have affected us.

We recall the life and death of Jesus to learn ourselves to live in that same unselfish mode, to learn through his grace (present in each such recall) how to continue his unselfish love in and for the world around us.

June 22

I'm sure some of my readers have felt a little cheated that more cheerleading for faith healing hasn't taken place in these pages. I have seldom suggested storming heaven as the solution to a particular problem of human life. More often I have urged some way of seeing the situation in the context of a Christian life modeled after that of Jesus, who went through our worst moments and an awful death. My understanding and belief is that he was mostly concerned to show us how to live life with its pains and problems and how to work with our hands and brains for solutions. His one extraordinary attempt at having a divine solution free him from human conditions (praying before his death in the garden) didn't work; I mean, God did not take the cup away from him but left it for him to drain, did not send a troop of helpful angels. What I've written about is what someone has called "faith acceptance" rather than "faith healing." Prayer is not an alternative to our work and effort but its support and supplement.

A very practical example of what I say came to my attention recently. Bob Davis, a minister and former All-American football player, has been diagnosed as having Alzheimer's disease. He says: "The greatest fear I have is what this disease does to your personality. It can make you angry, ugly, obscene, paranoid, cursing, and very difficult to handle before you become comatose. . . . Pray that I in no way inadvertently disgrace the Lord, this church, or the people whom I love. Pray for Betty (his wife) as I turn guardianship over to her. . . . Please remember me the way I was." As the statement shows, Bob and Betty have not simply resigned themselves to the disease; they do pray that it be limited, but in response to urgings to pray for a miracle Betty says: "This hasn't turned out to be a story of faith healing. It's a story of faith acceptance. Our learning to accept God's will is just as great a miracle."

Let us most often pray that we be strong enough to accept what cannot be escaped, to accept the real crosses that are part of our life.

June 23

When Christians make a big point about the humility and patience of Christ and argue that this must be part of following him, they are often reminded by their brothers and sisters that though that is all fine and commendable, power is a reality of our world. Power in this context is usually closely related to being able to dominate, rule, enforce one's will or designs, to be effective, to be known as a strong person (or nation) whom no one can take lightly. Undoubtedly to some degree our life in business, education, politics, involves some recognition of the reality of power. It presents a challenge to a Christian's ideals to use it properly, to be involved in its pursuit or attainment. Like money, it is one of the goods of our world, a *good* thing, and like all good things open to corruption or misuse. We probably need to spend more time considering its potential for evil than we do. Traditionally, Christians have been more inclined, it seems, to see all the dangers in sex.

There is another view of power offered to us in the life and teachings of Jesus. Jesus warns us against the kind of power that rejoices in lording it over others; the heathens do that, he says. Your power is the power to love and to serve (Mark 10:42-44). The power Jesus passes on to his disciples is a power, like his own, to be patient and endlessly loving, to bear with insult and deprivation. How difficult this is can be seen in the sad examples of the hunger and battle for the other kind of power in the Church and among believers. Our one-dimensional view of power needs to be countered by the kind of power that Jesus exercised, even from the cross. Only from it and in the midst of suffering was he able to draw all things to himself (John 12:33).

Popes John XXIII and John Paul I made good efforts to help rid the papacy of some of the symbols of earthly power inherited from the Roman Empire, such as the papal tiara. We can remove a great weight from our foreheads, too, by curbing the lust for power.

June 24

In almost any circle of acquaintances or friends you'll find someone who thinks, plans, and works to punctuate ordinary human life with something different, pleasant, relaxing, even exciting, for others. A birthday, an anniversary, an accomplishment, or simply a long string of dull days and hard work provide such a person with the excuse for a celebration. The size and magnitude vary and are probably secondary. What's important is the time and effort spent on bringing out more clearly the significance of some event or in appreciating someone or some achievement or in just celebrating friendship, love, life.

An ancient Greek philosopher (400 B.C.), Democritus by name, said, "Life without festivals is a long road without inns." Maybe we could say, life without an occasional celebration is like a long trip through a flat and dreary landscape without even a coffee break. Routine, sameness, dull work, stagnant custom, all make for a heaviness of spirit. Before we reach eternal life of unending joy and freedom from not only suffering but from boredom and lethargy, there is a lot we can do here and now to provide some glimpses, some taste, of better things to come.

It means we shouldn't underestimate all the factors that can go toward making human life more beautiful, more satisfying, more radiant. Just as art, music, theater, the great accomplishments of human beings in and through their bodies, mirror some of God's greatness and beauty, so the more ordinary little things that go to enliven human existence and raise our spirits do the same. If God is to be any sort of refreshment for us, it will largely be through our efforts to celebrate, feast, have a good time, and to make that possible for others. There are so many ways in which we can start doing this for others, for the world around us: all the way from a surprise phone call, good food, an invitation, a gift, sharing a word or two, a bit of humor, or some music. If we're too busy and serious for this, that is really too bad, really too, too bad.

June 25

One famous critic of Christianity (Friedrich Nietzsche) complained that Christianity has, over the centuries, oppressed human beings by continually opposing any kind of pride, satisfaction, joy, in one's accomplishments or gifts. It has taught a morality suited to slaves, he said, valuing only qualities like submissiveness, obedience, humility, and patience. He may have a point. Beginning with interpretations of the sin of the first parents, Christian thought has emphasized so often how prone we are to lifting ourselves beyond our merits and putting ourselves in God's place. And, human history shows we may need the warning.

But, like a good teacher, the Church shouldn't simply be negative, concerned only with repression of instinct, with "don'ts" and "watch outs" and "be carefuls." There is a very legitimate and necessary way in which we all need some pride. What else enables us to cut down on beer and burgers for the sake of our waist and well being if not, at least partially, a decent kind of pride in our appearance. What else motivates us to do our work well, to pump iron or proofread a paper or repair the porch?

No matter what great efforts we make or how we realize that self can be *the* enemy, it remains true that some decent self-regard, self-concern, pride, enters into much of the good we do. As the same Nietzsche said elsewhere, we do not even deny ourselves unless we have enough love for ourselves to believe that denying ourselves will gain something better for us, for example, a likeness to Christ, a closeness to God.

Let's try today to sort out a bit in our mind the right kind of pride from the wrong kind. We need the former.

June 26

History, for many people, is synonymous with boredom. "So what," they say, "let's get on with living." But for Christians it can't be dismissed quite as easily; we have to accept and use some of it, just like most of us utilize an occasional memory or two. That's always a bit of someone's history.

Believers look at history—for instance, "do this in remembrance of me"—to recall what God has done among the people and in and through Jesus Christ. In him, in that overturning of death and suffering, which he gained by his resurrection, we have an assurance for our belief and trust, our hope. Even in our own lives there are good events and happenings that we need to recall to bolster more deeply our faith and trust in the Lord.

Hope, faith, trust, confidence, must have some foundation, some basis. We find that basis in the life and death and, even more especially, in the resurrection of Jesus. Death and the powers that brought it about do not have the final words. His life and resurrection give us hope.

A great part of that hope is the encouragement it gives us to live, to make decisions or plans, to work, to endure, to struggle, because in Jesus we have pictured the fulfillment, the joy, that makes all our effort worthwhile. We know we are not just beating the air or occupying dull moments; by energetic work and decisions we are giving flesh to our hope, acting out our trust that it will all have its fulfillment. The history of Jesus and often our own history teach us hope.

June 27

Speaking of two friends recently divorced, a TV comedian says, "They shoulda stuck it out in the trenches, dodgin' that shrapnel with the rest of us that believe in true love."

Well, that sounds like strong encouragement to monogamy and fidelity to marriage vows. That may be a pleasant enough change in the media. But we all know that sometimes it isn't just shrapnel, bad as that may be, that hits the people in the trenches; it's more like obliteration bombing. There are marriages that just cannot be continued, relationships that strain the best of wills. No matter how much we believe in or even preach love and peace, the fact is that in our world there are going to be conflicts and misunderstandings that are not simply remediable by a few conferences with a counselor, confession, or prayer. With the variety of human beings that exists, there are some inevitable frictions, unpleasantness. If it isn't bombing or shrapnel, it's not all peaches and cream either.

Any love or friendship that survives must do it in the face of some disagreements (if there is also honesty) and hence the possibility of some bruised egos. When I hear someone spoken of as having a thin skin I often wonder if skins come in any other thickness, really. Some may not jump to show that they've been offended, but I wonder if we don't all have thin skins. It all means that married love and friendship are going to have to endure some differences, some arguments even, unless one party has simply become the doormat of the other. (This is obviously not applicable to truly impossible and life-threatening conflicts.) Our hope and trust, based on some good experience, one hopes, in the possibility of "true love," should help us stick it out in those trenches.

June 28

One of the most famous prayers is that which St. Augustine confesses was his at one time: Lord, make me chaste, but not just yet. Whether or not our prayers express it as honestly as Augustine's, our most heartfelt ones spring from a similar split in ourselves or from some need, something that is not yet.

Some are tempted to look down on our prayers of asking. They say such prayers are self-centered, not as high-minded as thanking or praising God. Or we seem to be treating God like an errand boy or a softhearted grandpa or an always on-duty mechanic. We call on God in prayer to make adjustments or repairs in the world's machinery, to take over the wheel from a reckless driver, call off a test or an interview, halt a flood that threatens Smithville, save us from the inconvenience of a strike or highway repairs.

But there is great encouragement to the prayer of asking from the Lord himself. Jesus even illustrates an *unanswered* prayer of petition for us. He prayed in the garden before his crucifixion that if possible he could pass it up; the answer, as we know, was no. Praying and the experience of being answered or not answered can all teach us to pray better. We learn that we may not really need that Harley-Davidson. We may move from praying for the good weather, good skiing, and a salary increase to asking for generosity, determination, or good humor. We really don't need to draw up in advance a list of permissible items to pray for: regular, trusting prayer will sort out for us what is silly from what is serious.

But will we ever be free from the necessity of asking for help in our weaknesses or for more self-control or courage or for the needs of hurting friends? While hoping to be more grateful and less self-concerned, we cannot ignore our defects and the needs of the present. We haven't yet arrived; till we cross the border, prayer, asking, is the language of the country we're in.

Someone has summed up country-western lyrics by saying they're all about "cheatin', drinkin', and prayin'." If we add a few more like lyin', gougin', and sufferin', we have a good summary of why we need the prayin'. Prayer of petition rises out of our sense of dependency, rises directly from real disappointment and the division in and around us. The Christian faced with helplessness before global problems like war and hunger, with personal stupidities, and with the desire to help loved ones, can and should always turn to prayer. And that even as we do all we can. Where our hands and arms are too weak, where our eyes and concern cannot follow, the love and power of God can. To pray means to believe that.

June 29

As we grow older, there is the temptation to become very cautious and careful. The antics and rashness of the young circling us on their skateboards or whizzing by on their motorcycles really shake us up. But like so many other qualities of the young, that daring or rashness has positive importance and is a part of faith and trust.

Besides being famous for denying that he ever knew Jesus, Peter in the New Testament is pictured as a very impulsive man. His faith and trust in Jesus, whatever other limitations it may have had at times, at least pushed him to risk, to jump out of the boat, to go beyond what common sense and self-interest would dictate.

We limit what God's grace can do in our lives by being too cozy, too cautious, too calculating. If we tend to be cautious in the life of the body, we often tend to be even more so in the life of faith. Rare as a Michael Jordan or a Mary Lou Retton are, there seem to be more of them than there are of Mother Teresas or Dorothy Days. We are more likely to risk our bodies and bones in the aerobics class than our pride and talent in responsibility for a class in religious instruction. We're all a bit like the little girl in the comic strip who is warned that everyone has to eventually leave home, travel, and "even live in hotels." She responds, "I'll turn the TV up loud, crawl into a beanbag with a bowl of ice cream and not think about it."

There's some, or even a lot, of this same inertia and willful avoidance in all of us. The recklessness and headlong approach of someone like Peter, the carefree daring of the young, still represents a kind of openness to God, a kind of trust that we need to value.

As someone has written, "Peter leaps before he looks, but that is still better wisdom than that of the person who looks for so long that he or she never leaps." Peter's daring and trust were met by the power and help of the Lord. Why wouldn't ours be met, too?

June 30

"The most staggering statement to be found in human literature" is how one commentator describes the passage in

John's Gospel where Jesus answers Philip's request to see the Father with "After I have been with you all this time, you still do not know me? Whoever has seen me has seen the Father" (John 14:9). Depending on their preoccupations, commentators have undoubtedly called many a scriptural statement staggering, but this one does seem to have an edge. It points to a particularly outrageous Christian claim: that to know who God is, what God is like, we need only look at a human being, Jesus Christ. What we see in him corrects and improves upon anything our reason can tell us of God.

We could, of course, turn this to selfish use and see in Jesus' wrath in cleansing the Temple or his rebuke to Peter a justification for our own impatience and anger. But, more positively, this truth means that in Jesus we see God sharing our suffering, our fear of pain and death, our radical loneliness, our sense of never being totally comprehended, our sense of abandonment at times. In the picture we have of Jesus, we are consoled with the assurance that God has gone through all this and does share it now with us.

Finally, because the Jesus who manifests the Father is also fully human, reflection on his life and death can help counter our tendency to think we especially have been singled out by an unfair God or by others for persecution and suffering. Jesus, who shows us God, also represents us before God. As every man and woman, he illustrates that the pains of our lot are part of being human and that the grace of God can transform them.

July 1

Sometimes we expect too much from our faith. Whew, that sounds like a real overstatement in itself! How can one expect too much from it? Well, I'm thinking of those of us who are tempted to think that because we love God, believe and trust in God, we should be able to breeze through all of life's pains, difficulties, quite easily, unlike those without faith. We rebuke ourselves for being down and depressed and even make it worse by feeling guilty, sensing that we are this way because there is something lacking in our faith, love and relation to God. Possibly—though I'm in no position to say—there does come a time in our life or our relation to God when that triumphs over all the pain and peril of everyday life but . . .

At least, in the meantime—and maybe longer—I'm inclined to think we have to expect God's help to come to us through very human, ordinary means. We should not bypass what is available to help us through difficulty, or blame ourselves for not being sufficiently "spiritual" if it doesn't all come simply in answer to prayer but comes because Helen called or Mike gave me a hug.

I remember a student saying once with more insight than he probably realized, "I'm so depressed, I'm either going to buy a new jacket or see a priest." Admittedly, shopping is not always an alternative for every member of the human race, but why not use some of these lesser consolations to keep ourselves in a mood more presentable to others around us who have to endure us in any case? Seeing a priest, a counselor, a friend, are, of course, all good approaches. My point here is not so much to help the big malls out by pushing shopping, but to encourage us to use the little, easily available means to overcome our low spirits, our otherwise insufferable moodiness. After all, why shouldn't we expect God to come through them as through a sort of sacrament?

July 2

People who have encouraged me with this book or at least heard I was writing it have almost invariably suggested, and strongly, "How about a series of reflections on hope." "Something hopeful is what people need." And, "I find hope sorely needed. So many people don't see that much to look forward to these days—the economy, national debt, poverty, racial unrest, cancer . . ." And one of them goes on to say well that to have hope requires some faith.

We so often distinguish faith, hope, and love, but basically they're very much intertwined. We hope and love, one might say, because we have faith, because we believe that God has loved the world enough to send God's Son to deliver us from all the dangers that threaten us and make us so fearful or despairing. Because God has done that and has raised Jesus from suffering and death to a new and eternal life we believe that linked to the same Son by faith and baptism, we, too, are on the way to a like destiny. We have, in other words, every reason for hope. "Think of him who submitted to such opposition from sinners: that will help you not to lose heart and grow faint" (Heb 12:3).

Yet it remains true that our hope is battered so often by the worries, dangers, fears that threaten us. As other pieces in this book make clear, I do not believe that Jesus delivers us from that kind of reality, but he does make it possible for us to go through all that with his help and with hope. Hope and faith do not take away the realities of the world we live in; on the contrary, "Faith gives substance to our hopes, and makes us certain of realities we do not see" (Heb 11:1). "We do not see" or feel, or touch, necessarily.

If these unseen realities—so much more "unreal" to our human eyes than cancer, the office, the car, refugees, poverty, golf, and money—are to be substantial enough to help us through agony and anguish, God must strengthen us, and we must open ourselves more to God's power. How? By prayer, reflection (some time spent letting this sink in), and by trying to act from our faith and hope. The first member of our new race has gone before us to give us hope! Alleluia.

July 3

I wonder if the separations and losses of ordinary life are not merely disappearances, but rather, part of our education, a preparation for death, for more farewells.

These separations can be more or less acute. A few years ago I saw a very moving American film, *Running on Empty*. In it a couple and their two boys are constantly on the move, pulling up stakes to go elsewhere because the parents years earlier were involved in an anti-war demonstration that had resulted in death or serious injury to an innocent person. Part of their strategy for surviving is that they stick together very closely. The older son, high school age, shows great musical talent and has numerous opportunities as well as love coming his way. The parents, sticking to their pattern, are unwilling to let him pursue either of these. But finally they see it must be: He must be allowed to go his own way. It is a heartrending scene but one that is probably only a tad more acute and difficult than it is for any parent to allow the children they have raised for seventeen, eighteen years to leave and be on their own, "independent," as we say.

As we move through life we see friends and family move away, disappear, die. Those who live to a very old age often have fewer and fewer of their family and friends around, are more and more "independent" at a time when physically and otherwise they are more and more dependent. Much of this, of course, consists in our letting those we have loved and even nurtured—children, students—go and become themselves, cease being our dependents, much less just our consolation, or worse, our possessions. Somehow we need to combine a lasting love for them with the willingness to see that love take a different character as they move on and life changes. In a way, it's practice for leaving this world. As some have pointed out, by the time we're near the age when death is more likely, we often have less left to hold on to. It has been made easier.

July 4

So often for Christians in any Church with a fairly well-organized structure or in one where authority carries great power, freedom is seen as a secular quality, or even as a threat to unity and order. Yet we insult the spirit of the first Christians and of much Christian tradition if we look so suspiciously at freedom. Rather, as part of a truly Christian spirit, we should aim for a more appreciative evaluation of freedom. Much of Christ's mission and teaching can be seen as an effort to free people from domination by constricting human rules, to free us from the burden of possessions, the phony demands of merely human civilization and culture.

In a section of one of his letters (2 Cor 3), Paul writes of the importance of the Spirit, of the interior, over against simply written laws and external observances. Unlike these, he says, "the Spirit gives life" (3:6), and further on, ". . . and where the Spirit of the Lord is, there is liberty" (3:17). The goal of a Christian life lived under the influence of the Holy Spirit, open to his power in prayer and longing, is freedom. Not a childish right to smash and make a mess (our idea of freedom often seems to be stuck at that level) but an ease in following what is good and in serving God, unencumbered by passing styles or fads, concepts of what is "proper." While this is the goal and may seem a long way off to us, still, elements of it should be breaking through here and now, shouldn't they? Truly "spiritual" persons are so influenced by the Holy Spirit (hence, "spiritual") that they feel remarkably free in all they do, not held back. It's like the famous words of St. Augustine, "love and do what you will." If we are driven by the Spirit, the Spirit of love, our actions, flowing from such a pure source, will be all in harmony with God's ways.

Pope Paul VI (in 1969) spoke words that as yet remain unrealized. Speaking of the Church of the future and the Spirit, he said: "We shall have a period of greater freedom in the life of the Church and of her individual members. It will be a period of fewer legal obligations and fewer interior restraints. . . . There will be promoted the sense of that Christian freedom which pervaded the first generation of Christians."

If we do not even value the ideal, how will we ever move toward that freedom? It would be a great expansion of our hearts and selves if we could learn to think more of our life in Christ and the Church not as a matter of more rules but of being guided by the Spirit toward freedom.

July 5

The word "grace" and its related form "gracious" serve such a host of purposes in our language that it makes the religious use of the word very difficult. For many, the word seems remarkably formless, without shape. In ordinary language we talk about someone's grace in dancing or in how they respond to compliments or rebukes. We speak of someone as being gracious in an acceptance speech, of what a gracious host someone is. In religious use the word seems to most of us very hard to pin down, to find what it corresponds to in reality or experience. It seems very vague: We talk about God's grace but seem to have a hard time imagining what that is. Theology has, when it has tried to pin grace down, pinned it down so brutally that it became something less than it should be, something as lively as a mounted butterfly. It ended up sounding like something that one could find on a shelf in a drugstore and ask for in pounds and ounces. It's been called sanctifying grace, actual grace, prevenient grace—and worse.

We're probably safest in taking grace as God's freely given, unearned love for us. Most theology would be quite reluctant today to speak of that in quantitative terms as if it were a thing anymore than we would speak that way of a mother's or father's love.

Like a parent's love, too, God's love arouses us, asks us to do something, to be responsive, to live up to that love, to return it. And it enables us to do that. It energizes us, inspires us, strengthens us and most often not in a manner that is recordable on a thermometer or on the Richter scale. Grace is primarily what God does for us and toward us, God's love. But not only this; it is the encouragement, the ability itself, to respond to that love in action; it powerfully moves us to do God's work. It is what God does in us *with* us.

July 6

In an earlier book of mine of more developed essays, a friend noticed the lack of any treatment of patience. Since he had known the author for quite a few years, he was not too surprised but maybe, rather, impressed with the honesty. Patience is something I feel I have learned so little of that I am not entitled to write or speak of it.

But I may have something to say to others who feel likewise that it is a very difficult virtue. Patience is related in its roots to a Latin word meaning to suffer. In ordinary usage we often tend to make it something a bit more domesticated. Patience means a willingness to wait, to be understanding of others who are slow. I think of patience in terms of how I feel when I wait thirty-five minutes for someone who doesn't appear for an appointment. After the first ten or fifteen minutes, my patience is so shot that I am generally more willing not to have the person appear at all than to appear then. I feel it will be hard to greet his arrival in a convincingly pleasant way. Obviously, I lack patience in this sense.

And this, it seems to me, is almost equivalent to saying I lack patience in any sense of the word. Patience is a mild enough sounding word for a genuine part of the following of Christ. Our following of Christ inevitably involves endurance, putting up with some insults to ourselves, our time, our efforts, some lack of appreciation. It is very, very hard. Some of us only learn it or have it in fits and starts. It is not some consistent quality that can be expected or presumed. We only learn something so difficult in a partial and unsatisfactory way. When we've been through the situations demanding patience or suffering, there seems always to be the necessity of asking forgiveness and understanding of the Lord for the way we have failed to practice it. Maybe the last word is that besides trusting in the patience of God in our regard, we also need some patience with ourselves.

July 7

"There is no greater sorrow than to remember happy times in the midst of present misery." That sentiment occurs in the literature of various peoples. Of course, at times it's just what we need to lift us up a bit from our present swamp, to be able to recall that there were better times and they could come again. But as the quotation means to say, it may also be a very bitter thing to remember great contentment when you're touching rock bottom. If misery and discouragement can bring us to long more for and to expect more from the Lord, then we may find Psalm 42 echoing our thoughts. The opening words are famous and could well be a regular refrain for many of us: "As the deer longs for running waters, so my soul longs for you, O God."

The writer apparently is the target of genuine enemies and in such miserable straits that he feels God, too, has forgotten him. "Where is your God?" they seem to say (v. 4). We may have occasional or even frequent days of the same sort. Getting to know this psalm and praying it often can help us use our misery to sharpen our desire for God and the good we know God can deliver. We need, in the midst of pain and desolation, to have recalled for us the faith and trust that may have shone so brightly at other times. "Why are you so downcast, O my soul? Why do you sigh within me? Hope in God! For I shall again be thanking him, in the presence of my savior and my God" (v. 6).

As the psalm goes on, the writer is like all of us in his expression of conflicting thoughts. One moment: "By day the Lord bestows his grace . . ." and then: "Why do you forget me?" We experience the same battle within ourselves at times. Faith, trust, and hope are not easily kept at a high pitch or free from attacks of despair, faintheartedness, and desolation. If we conclude with the author, then we're on the way back: "Hope in God! For I shall again be thanking him, in the presence of my savior and my God."

July 8

I've tried to avoid using the word spiritual in this book even though a bookstore—if I'm lucky enough to have one stock this book—might put it in the category of "spiritual books." (I'm afraid that more likely it will end up in some contemporary category like "new age" or "inspiration.") There's too much suggestion in the word "spiritual" that religion, Christianity, has to do with something completely other than the body, the flesh, the material world. But St. John, for instance, begins his Gospel by telling us that the Word of God became flesh, took on human form and life. Why should we, then, suggest that the human or bodily is inessential or, worse yet, bad? We do that, though, when we say that something or someone is spiritual and something else is carnal, fleshly, merely material.

Lurking in that language is the unfortunate attitude that there are two elements in our nature, body and spirit (soul), and that the former is evil, the latter good. Christianity has fought against and condemned that attitude frequently, but it has certainly persisted.

Part of it can be blamed on our misunderstanding of terms like those St. Paul uses in Romans 8. He says, "You are not in the flesh." In its most obvious meaning, it would be surprising that with all our perspiration, concern about losing a few pounds, and about what's for dinner we actually were not "in the flesh." But the point is that "in the flesh" for Paul means to be living by merely human standards, as if we were completely on our own. It refers to a way of living where the dominant forces in our life are greed, arrogance, self-sufficiency, pride, and aggressive behavior. Life "in the spirit," on the contrary, means living under the influence of God, of the Holy Spirit, living a life where all is dictated by concern for God's praise, where we are led by the Spirit in love, respect, selflessness.

Once again, the Lord and the New Testament in their teaching are more concerned to rebuke our self-centeredness, our imagined self-sufficiency than "the flesh," as we usually understand it. Nor does Scripture commend a life that rejects the body, a "spiritual" life in that sense, but a life where the Holy Spirit is our guide, consolation, and motivating power.

July 9

The famous psychoanalyst Sigmund Freud had several theories about religion. One seemed to be that religion was simply wishful thinking, people imagining that there was a good father-like God who would make up for this world's injustices and suffering by giving good people eternal happiness. Freud seemed to think that because the religious idea of a god and an afterlife was so much like what we would wish things to be, it must be wrong. Too good to be true. (We might ask, of course, why it would be that our best desires could not be fulfilled? Are our fears and a belief that all is bad and will continue that way more worthy, more true?)

Our wishes can be based too much on little things we happen to like. We may imagine eternal life as endless rounds of golf; a child may think of it as unlimited Dairy Queen; or someone else may imagine it as perpetually satisfying music. Obviously, all of these are limited. Possibly each a bit of the truth.

What should get more emphasis is *hope,* rather than wishing. Wishing is based on something we know or have experienced, anything from love to joy and achievement. Our wishing can show less pleasant faces, too, as when we wish, for instance, that all those who have done us wrong be punished or when we imagine God too much in our own image with all its pettiness and grasping.

Hope really is broader. Hope is based more on God's faithfulness and promises than on our desires and needs. Because it is based on the Other, who is so much greater than we are and is beyond our comprehension, it means our expectation is all the more justified, even if we can't imagine what form it will take. Hope is more open than wishing.

Hope says: Lord, I know you have been faithful to those who have loved you and trusted you, above all, to your Son Jesus. Because of that we believe and trust that our lives, with all their worries and imponderable problems, will be resolved and brought to fulfillment according to your wisdom, love, and foresight. Help us to hope and trust even as we struggle and work.

July 10

Movies and magazines devoted to the foibles and off-screen behavior of "stars," TV talk shows with famous personalities, biographies of the "great," the attention and time given to public figures all demonstrate our fascination with bigger-than-life people. No one wants to simply play a few parts in the local suburban theater; no, everyone seems to aim for the wider screen or Broadway. Who wants to play hockey on a rink in Millville when there's all that fame and money in the same game with the Oilers? We admire tycoons, stars, sensations, people gilded by fame in almost any way. In our most generous moments we admire peacemakers, great witnesses to the truth or justice, martyrs for the poor and oppressed, generous philanthropists, some musical genius. But our admiration or at least our interest at times seems satisfied to find the simply notorious. Our thirst for the details covers everyone from Lee Iacocca to Jimmy Connors, Lech Walesa, Marilyn Monroe, Ollie North, and Jeffrey Dahmer.

The temptation is to see our own unsung, quiet lives as of less value, as disappointment, even wastes. Who cares if I am an insurance salesman and father, an efficient administrator of the hospital, an effective teacher? How few people I affect; how few relatively know me. I'm not on the cover of *People* magazine.

Once we remove some of the clearly superficial preoccupation with glamor and the fast life, we're left with the problem of balancing ideals, hopes, expectations, and what is. At the time of the Reformation there was need in religion for people to learn that one could be religious, be a Christian star even, not simply in a monastery or convent but in the circumstances of married life and secular occupations. We have learned a lot of that, but there is still often the need to remind ourselves that our life here and now, doing our job, is usually what God expects of us. Rather than letting the secular world go to the devil, John Calvin, the great Protestant Reformer, taught what was needed: that most of us will live our Christian lives in the context of the factory, the bureau, the stock market, the shop or business, the office, and that there is no reason to be apologetic about it. Rather, we should be at peace in doing what we are asked to do by our life's circumstances. Calvin said it well: "Every individual's line of life is a post assigned him by the Lord that he may not wander about in uncertainty all his days. . . . It lessens considerably our cares, labors, troubles and other burdens when we know that in all these things God is with us as our guide. . . . There is no employment so lowly and ordinary, if it is our vocation, which is not truly respectable and even highly important in the sight of God."

July 11

In his *Rule for Monasteries* St. Benedict urges his monks to spend three hours and more a day on what we might call "spiritual reading." The idea is that most of it should be a reflective, prayerful reading of Scripture. The monk should not just read or study as a scholar might but open himself to its content, and hope to be formed by it, all the while responding in prayer.

Benedict entered the monastery scene after religious life had already begun among Christians. As found in the near East and in Ireland, it tended to extreme emphasis on physical deprivation and endurance. Benedict put the emphasis on obedience to the abbot, life in community, work, and prayer. In doing all this, he became known for his moderation. His form of religious life in monasteries in a short time became the standard in Western Christianity. It seemed to gain followers because of its balance, moderation, and flexibility.

That first paragraph about three or more hours of reflective reading per day must strike the ordinary modern reader as anything but moderate. Three hours a day! In appreciating this demand one would have to look at many other factors and the context. But for now, what does it say to us? What reaction should it have in us besides amazement? Besides members of monasteries, many laypeople today use this *Rule* of Benedict as a guide in their attendance at the "school of the Lord's service," as Benedict calls it.

Three hours a day tells us, who may find it so incomprehensible, that such prayer is more important than we generally realize. To sustain and continue the life of the monastery, Benedict realized that his monks needed a profound faith, trust, belief in the Christ they came to serve, something not to be taken for granted. It had to be daily nourished by the Eucharist, common life, and prayer, *and* this kind of more personalized reflection. We should make some definite effort, tied down if possible to time and place in our lives, to assure that each day allows direct contact with the word of God and the strength and encouragement it gives. We need it at least as much if not more than these monks.

July 12

We only doubt about persons and things that are very important to us. What do I care if someone I've only met casually really likes me or not? Doubt is a sign that we take something seriously. If we take our faith and confidence in Jesus and his teaching seriously, we are sure to have doubts, questions, problems. The alternative often is to hedge our belief or faith around with artificial protection so that we allow no questioning, no doubts. Eventually, this means that there is no faith left. We often insulate our faith against doubt and questions by simply parroting over and over again phrases we've read in a textbook or heard without ever attempting to make them our own or put them in our own words. It's a way of trying to measure or weigh faith like a bag of peanuts, or we try to squeeze it into a package. Faith and trust in God is never that simple, cannot be reduced to our size in that way.

Christian faith requires that we face questions, to the extent of our time and ability, and not just try to push them off or repress them. Just as a love relationship does not exclude doubt or questions but survives in spite of them—that's what makes our trust in someone else so great; that without knowing all the possibilities in that person we still trust him or her. Faith means leaving some matters up to the goodness and trustworthiness of the other. That's what we like in our friends; not having to justify and explain ourselves all the time because we know they have sufficient knowledge of us to expect certain behavior without knowing in advance what it will be. They trust us. Our faith in Jesus, too, is such. We know from past experience and trial, from his word and life, that he is to be trusted. We know there are and will be questions, sometimes terrifying ones about life and what happens in it. But beyond all that, we trust that he who rose from the dead and loves us will also bring us through to happiness.

July 13

At the small college where I teach it is still possible to know by name a great number of those who teach or study there. Even if one cannot know everyone, still, nearly all the students will know many of the professors. And because of the size and special efforts that are made, incoming students do get to know at least one professor well and very likely others. While living in a large city recently I was struck by what a luxury this situation is and, also, how desirable it is, how much most of us long to be known by name. In any large city there are large universities with huge campuses or many campuses spread all over an urban area. As I saw students rushing in and out of buildings apparently knowing very few people, it occurred to me how fortunate the students at my small college are to know a good number of students and many professors too in a social way, by name. As they and their parents could tell you, they pay for it. It is necessarily more expensive than a public institution. There should be some such advantages. And we're thankful they are available.

But even if the same situation cannot easily be duplicated on a campus of forty or fifty thousand students or in a corporation employing hundreds or thousands of people, the need to be known, to be recognized, to be more than a number, is always there. The same is undoubtedly true in a large factory or apartment complex. We all want to be known for ourselves, even loved and appreciated by someone.

All this underlines the fact that we make real the Lord's command to love our neighbors by taking some time to know their names, to greet them, to risk friendship and acquaintance, the entry of new people into our lives. There is no way to overestimate the importance and value of our effort to identify and know others as the individuals they are, especially in a world where so many of us are merely numbers or interchangeable "occupants" to others around us. Recognizing John or Kathy, Ted or Beth, by name hints, at least, at the loving God for whom there are no strangers.

July 14

I've usually felt a bit apologetic about saying that I thought one could envision eternal life as a perpetual brunch on the beautiful hills of Sausalito overlooking San Francisco Bay. Camellias, rhododendrons, and azaleas blooming all around, an ideal temperature, a sunny day, carefree pleasant company, not to mention the menu—that would be getting a bit too materialistic. But recently I've been emboldened to reaffirm my intuition about this and to stick with it. (I'm sure, allowing for different geography and experiences, we could all come up with another location.)

Old Testament writings frequently speak of what the Messiah will bring about in terms of a banquet or supper of unlimited and choice food in an atmosphere of rejoicing people united in love and friendship. "On this mountain [Sausalito, see!] the Lord of hosts will make for all people a feast of fat things . . . will swallow up death for ever, and the Lord God will wipe away tears from all faces" (Isa 25:6-9). Elsewhere the prophet Baruch speaks of the age of the Messiah as a time of free flowing wine (29:5). Jesus likewise speaks of the banquet to which all are invited, in fact, a wedding banquet.

While all this—the mountain, the free-flowing wine, Sausalito—is an attempt to catch in our limited words (and, therefore, likely to be very human) the goal God has for us, still, it seems to be the best that Scripture could come up with, too. We shouldn't despise it or too easily discard it. It reminds us of the goal toward which we all must work: unity and peace among peoples, a just sharing of the world's goods and plenty for all, happiness rooted in love. The Eucharist, the Lord's Supper, is meant to picture this, no matter how poorly here and now, and encourage us in our efforts to make that situation ever more likely, even before the end of all things. Both our participation in the Mass and our meals with others should have more and more festivity and joy, genuine good will and respect for those who eat with us or will some day.

July 15

"Prayer is just talking to yourself." For nonbelievers or those who have serious doubts about prayer, that is sort of the maximum value they give it. For Christians, that is really its minimal value. The Christian believes that Someone is listening. But, even granting that, talking to oneself about what matters most, about people we love, even about those who bug us, has some value. And it may be a good beginning for prayer and provide the subject matter of genuine prayer too. If we wonder what we should pray about at times, all these concerns that tend to preoccupy us and cause us worry can also serve as subject matter for prayer. At the very least, this kind of prayer is often a matter of asking something, and Jesus himself is not disdainful of such prayer. He tells us to be insistent and persistent, to keep it up. Even if what we're sure we need—a Lamberghini, a promotion, quieter neighbors, a new roommate, a better disposition—even if this is not immediately or ever realized, something important is happening.

Just by the fact of persistent prayer, we open ourselves to our deeper, often unspoken needs and to the recognition that Someone else is involved. We are expanding our narrow selves.

If we keep at it, we may very well be answered in ways we could not ever have guessed or wanted, but ways that are the reward of our trust in prayer and in the one to whom we have opened ourselves. Understanding what we want, what we get and how we get it is not always necessary. "Everyone who asks, receives," in some sense, in some way, at some time.

July 16

"Leave it alone, it's okay the way it is." We've all heard or expressed similar sentiments about an object or a machine or some situation we consider good the way it is. Leave it alone, let it stay the way it is. It sounds good. But it's just not true! If we leave things alone, they fall to pieces! Leave that lawn alone, don't mow or weed it and it becomes a jungle. Leave that white fence post out in the yard alone and it becomes black or at least gray, splintered. The beauty of a Notre Dame Cathedral or any other great piece of art is in the same situation. Leave it to the ravages of pollution and abuse and it will fall apart. Even for great historical monuments there has to be a kind of maintenance somewhere between neglect and distortion.

Our relations to God and to each other are similar. Without care, they grow weak and routine. If we're not changing, going forward, we're going backward in these matters. There is no standing still. Jesus left his followers the Holy Spirit not simply to preserve in some wooden fashion what he had taught but to renew, enliven, and change them. The refrain in the Church's prayer to the Holy Spirit is always, Come, Holy Spirit, renew the face of the earth, renew our hearts.

Through the gift of Jesus the Holy Spirit is available to us in prayer. The Spirit comes to help us avoid the awful situation of living in a rut, living a stale, numb existence, which eventually allows everything to go to pieces. Is there anything worse than just being bored, feeling there is no life in our life? We pray to the Holy Spirit not so much to change anything in God but that the Spirit change us, recharge us. Every prayer is, in a sense, an act of hope; otherwise, why pray? If everything is perfect the way it is, why ask for the Spirit? To pray to the Holy Spirit means to recognize our need for repairs, for change, for growth, our need to walk more closely the path of the Lord. We pray appropriately to the Holy Spirit in one of the hymns for Pentecost, "to bend our stubborn heart and will; to melt the frozen, warm the chill."

July 17

Often over the past few centuries, the differences between Catholics and Protestants has been put very neatly: Protestants believe we are saved by grace; Catholics believe we are saved by good works. That's a lot more than a simplification; it's basically an insult to both parties. But it took some cooling off after the Reformation for both parties to get a better view. Today all of us benefit from a more balanced view. It is expressed in the farewell words of Jesus as given by John: "I am the real vine, and my father is the gardener. . . . I am the vine, and you the branches. He who dwells in me, as I dwell in him, bears much fruit; for apart from me you can do nothing" (John 15:1-5). All Christian belief is rooted in the conviction that only in and through our union with Christ, our dwelling in him or he in us, are we able to honor God and love others. In that conviction is rooted our need for prayer and our sharing in the sacraments. "For apart from me you can do nothing."

Opposing what they saw in Catholic practice—the attitude that we were somehow to impress God by accumulating good deeds—the Protestant Reformers insisted that nothing of good is possible without our being moved by God. God's love for us is there *before* we do anything. God does not love us because we're so irresistible. Catholics were suspicious that the Protestant view would end up meaning that God does everything and what we do or don't do is a meaningless game.

The reality, which seems to be another great point of convergence today among Protestant and Catholics, is that faith and trust in God—what he does in us—and our deeds of love are part of the same package. Good works, love, are the result of God's love given to us, a picking up on the impetus given us by God through Jesus Christ. "For apart from me you can do nothing." And Luther wrote, "To this we must add that if good works do not follow, our faith is false and not true." As branches of Christ the vine we have every reason to expect to be fruitful.

July 18

"He showed no mercy" is the use of the word "mercy" we're familiar with in ordinary language. We don't say in ordinary daily English that he showed a great deal of mercy or he is merciful. It all smacks, probably, a bit too much of the lord of the manor offering some day-old bread to his starving tenants. We don't, in other words, seem to find much positive use for mercy in our talk or conversation. But we do use it regularly in Mass: Lord, Christ, have mercy. We find it in our English translations of Scripture. In some of the prayers of the Mass we speak of the "Father of mercy"; for example, "You show your almighty power in your mercy," "God of mercy and love."

Yet the word deserves to be distinguished, as it is in that last phrase, from "love." And it deserves a stronger meaning than whatever little meaning it has in ordinary language. In the Bible it is a very important word used to describe God's attitude toward us and the consequent attitude on our part towards our neighbors.

What is most important for our following of Christ is the recognition that mercy is that aspect of God that assures us that God cares for us unflaggingly and will go to any lengths to help, forgive, heal us. Obviously this has all been shown most outstandingly for us in the coming into our life and world of the Son, the very picture of mercy. It is not simply a mercy that from on high offers help and consolation but one that enters into the conditions of human life and endures them along with us.

Mercy sets up in us the obligation to show the same mercy, the same loving care and eagerness to help and forgive that has been shown us. In fact, the Gospel writers present Christ as saying in place of the earlier words in Scripture, "Be holy as I am holy" (Lev 19:2), "Be merciful as your Father also is merciful" (Luke 6:36).

"Be merciful as I am merciful" is difficult enough! But let us at least see that as a mark of our following of Christ: compassion, consideration, a willingness to help.

July 19

The owner of a small cafe was once asked, "How do you keep so happy? You always have a smile on your face. Don't you ever have a bad day?" She replied, "Of course I do, but

I don't let it show." I suppose some would see this as hypocrisy; instead of letting her "real" feelings show, this woman is putting on a front. Isn't it just as likely that she shows a kind of selflessness that most of us can't match? I don't think we can completely discount this person's effort by saying it's good for business. We've all met enough grouchy salespersons and proprietors to know that money may not be a sufficient motive for congeniality. We can see here a kind of extraordinary consideration for others, an unwillingness to bring them down, to spread our own unhappiness. Concern for others can help us keep our bad moods to ourselves, avoid spreading the gloom. Certainly a wonderful way to go if it works for us. But my guess is that many of us are victims of depression, bad moods, vaguely lonely feelings, self-pity about which we seem to be able to do little.

To pray in this situation with our sense of desolation, pain, boredom, misery, indifference is certainly appropriate. We often do our best praying, unsatisfying as it may seem at the time, in such moments. We pray from the heart, from a heart breaking with sadness or hopelessness. "My God, why have you forsaken me?"

But often there is more we can and should do. For example, we could think of the problems of our friends, so much worse than ours: of Dave who hates his job, of Jill who faces an ugly seminar, or of Tom, just told of a serious illness. We can call or write someone else in need of a good word. Do some gardening, putter around the car or house, play a game. Listen to music that helps us forget ourselves: some old favorite, something moving, consoling, soothing, or exciting. Think of how well dear friends and relatives, now dead, went through even more difficult and boring times, lived through years of devotion and faithfulness with little reward. All this is preferable to our tendency to eat and drink more to console ourselves.

Christians occasionally have the temptation to think that God alone in some direct sense should be the solution to such problems as depression, moodiness, pain. But who are we to demand: "I want my consolation served only by the manager or, at least, by the head waiter?" Christians also need counselors, therapy, drugs, medical help. In the more modest and everyday conditions of sorrow or dissatisfaction, we need to avail ourselves of the homely, near-at-hand helps rather than demand some special intervention by God. In answering our prayers, God will ordinarily work through the instrumentality of others and the resources of the world around us.

July 20

Perhaps parents could learn something from God. That's undoubtedly understating it; like anyone of us, they could learn *everything* from God. But I'm thinking of a most basic matter: learning from the pattern of God's relationship with free creatures called humans; learning from that how to treat our own children or those for whom we have some responsibility. From the whole story we have in Scripture, it seems plain that God gave human creatures minds and the ability to choose and respond. (We can debate elsewhere how much of this always exists, but the teachings of Christ are based on the presumption that we have some freedom, some ability to say yes or no, to be guilty or congratulated.)

Part of that relationship is that God entrusts a great deal of the universe to our management. God's intervention is something we can ask for, but generally we expect that the usual qualities of our world are fairly consistent. No matter how loved we are by God, there seems to be no way of translating that into protection against injury, illness of some sort or another, of arthritis or rheumatism accompanying old age. Our salvation is to be worked out within the limits and confines of the world we have, and a great deal is left up to us. We can get rid of slavery, racial discrimination, war and poverty only if we want to and work to do so.

God is apparently not like some of us nervous elders or parents who are afraid to risk letting the young, our children or charges go their way, make their own mistakes. We worry if they will go to Mass or pray while they're away at college, if they will steer clear of dangerous relationships, if they will do well. At times we even make the business of how others raise their children our business.

But isn't letting others be, letting them go about being what they should be after we have done our best to suggest and model for them what we believe is right, isn't this letting go the greatest and most important thing we do for them? What else shows our respect, love, and trust more than this? What else shows our confidence in God, too, who has guided us, and to whom we trust those God also loves and loves more effectively than we can.

July 21

So many long-awaited experiences or achievements come as a letdown when they are finally realized. Dairy Queen eventually leaves even a child sated and looking for something more. The exhilarating long ski run may eventually pale. Our imagination builds up expectations that can never be met adequately or for long.

Yet Christian life is built on a hope that more can be done or will happen than we can imagine. St. Paul speaks of God, "who is able to do immeasurably more than all we can ask or conceive, by the power which is at work among us" (Eph 3:20-21). Such lines encourage us with the expectation that what God will do is by no means limited or even suggested well by what we can imagine or think.

While it is profoundly necessary that we do all we can to understand and even justify our belief for ourselves and for others by education, study, and the like, it remains equally true that we realize we are in no position to limit what God's love toward us and our world can do. There is always an element of the unknown, the incomprehensible, in Christian life that goes beyond our powers to conceive, leaving God free to do and achieve way beyond our bargain basement level of thought.

Our lives can, for this reason, be filled with hope and trust that even though the steps ahead look dark and even hopeless, God's possible "outs" for us are not limited by what we would dream up. After using our minds, our education, the advice and counsel of friends and specialists, we still need to put our life and activity in God's hands. In a way beyond our comprehension, "He has the whole world in his hands" and can contrive a happier ending than we or Disney could ever imagine.

July 22

One cheap substitute or simulation of maturity is to put on the appearance of boredom with practically everything. To some young people and to a good number of older people it seems to be more sophisticated than betraying enthusiasm or delight.

It probably wouldn't be so bad if it were only a pose, but if it's deeper, we should be worried. Our growth in Christ and, therefore, in appreciation of the world and persons through which God chooses to be revealed should bring with it an *increase* in interest, a sustained enthusiasm despite the moments when that may be crushed. As we learn more and more that all that surrounds us is a gift, it becomes more apparent that our life, time, and talents are really inadequate to appropriately appreciate it. All the more reason to put all we can into what is around and before us.

As I've urged before in these pages, the young—from two to twenty-two—can show us a lot in this regard. Witness their enthusiasm and excitement. Forget what it may be about; we don't have to share the objects: Madonna or football or cute movie stars. The point is the capacity and power to be so enthusiastic, unabashed, breathless. Besides being reluctant to put a wet blanket on their excitement, we should be careful about restraining our own too soon and too completely. They have the right view: Life, the world, friends, what is happening around them, are all new and fresh. It's only we who become old and worn-out.

The world around us should not be taken for granted; it is a gift; why should we deserve any of it? Look at our experiences, friends, events, more often in terms of how we feel; otherwise the feelings probably atrophy. Try to be present to what is happening, to those around us, to this moment; they will never return again in just this way. God gives all this to us; why dismiss it or act as if we're waiting for something better? The goodness, freshness, vitality, beauty, of what is before us only reveals itself if we enter into it wholeheartedly without always looking before and after.

July 23

Like families and governments, the community of believers (the Church) seems stretched between two opposed tendencies. Call them uniformity and diversity or discipline and freedom. One approach is concerned to keep individual tendencies in line with the essential direction of the whole group. The other values very highly some scope for the variety of individuals and their likes and aspirations. Much of the political history of the world is probably concerned with varying approaches to balancing the two. Without some unified direction a movement may fall apart or accomplish nothing. Without attention to individual needs, freedom is quashed, and we lose many a possible contribution.

The greatest temptation for the Catholic Church in recent centuries has been toward uniformity. For centuries one language was used in much of the Catholic Church at the expense of comprehension and participation. There was an Index of prohibited books and an Inquisition to severely limit new ideas. Bishops, clergy, and theologians were expected to echo the popes in much the same way that *Pravda* had to echo Stalin or Khrushchev.

In our era of more and more worldwide sameness (someone has pointed out that shopping malls all over the United States are practically interchangeable), variety needs more celebration than suppression. In daily life, rather than being irritated by diversity, we should be gladdened for those bits of individuality and variety that may still persist in native customs and eccentric individuals. Variety is one way to suggest, at least, the infinity of God. If the Creator put so much variety into the universe, in types of animals, and plants, for instance, we should be concerned, too, to nurture variety and rejoice in it.

To me the charm and attraction of large cities (whatever their drawbacks) is just this diversity in people and in all that is available, from cheese to services. A student of the medieval period has written that the ordinary villager in a small medieval town never saw more than a hundred different people in his or her whole lifetime. Part of the expansion and change in human life and culture over the centuries has been to introduce more and more people to more and more of the diversity of life and creation. Our faith, too, should be happy with diversity and with the many possibilities available to human beings today rather than hankering after the time when everyone thought the same because they were stimulated to think so little by reason of the sameness of their lives.

July 24

The unique contribution the following of Christ has to make to the world is hope. Much of the world around us doesn't provide a basis for hope when it tells us that everything happens either by chance or by some rigid natural laws, which, as often as not, are leading the universe to extinction and each of us to nothing but the grave.

On the contrary, the opening call of Christ in the Gospels is to change, to a renewal, and that remains the core of Christian belief. We see it in the Body and Blood of Christ, in the Mass, probably more than we realize. Historical evidence shows that Christians from the earliest times believed that the Lord became present in the bread and wine at the Eucharist. And that has remained the belief of most Christian bodies ever since. That change in the bread and wine is, to put it in very human terms, the specialty of the Holy Spirit. The additional prayers for the Canon of the Mass, which were restored to our use after Vatican II, state this: "And so, Father, we bring you these gifts. We ask you to make them holy by the power of your Spirit, that they may become the body and blood of your Son, our Lord Jesus Christ, at whose command we celebrate this eucharist" (Eucharistic Prayer III).

The Holy Spirit is called upon to change the bread and wine into the Body and Blood of Christ. But an important part of that same belief is that the Holy Spirit changes not only the bread and wine but us who receive the Body and Blood of Christ, too. We, too, are changed into the Body of Christ. St. Augustine says that we become what we receive. That is probably the most essential point: We receive the Body and Blood of Christ not just as some cozy reward for being such nice people or to provide us with a few minutes of private consolation in the midst of a cruel and unfeeling world. We receive the Body and Blood in order to become truly the body of Christ in this world. We shouldn't limit our use of the Body of Christ to the wafer or piece of bread; that, in a sense, is the instrument to form all those who receive it into one body with Christ as head, to bring about a real change in us. To change us from simply self-seeking, self-centered individuals into the body of Christ, where we seek the good of one another and are able in Jesus our head to truly honor God with a transformed, changed life, a life charged with love and generosity.

July 25

Order, routine, and stability are the enemies of love. There! That should be provocative enough. Most of us value all of them sufficiently to be unhappy with the idea that we cannot have order and love at the same time. Think of some examples. What's messier and less predictable than the requirements of love for a baby or a child? Dirty diapers and messy meals, hours that hardly prepare one for work the next day, illnesses and inexplicable crying. Or take the romantic love of the teens and beyond: being torn between two or three equally attractive but incompatible loves; tears and reproaches about insensitivity and forgetfulness. Or married love: It's easily unorganized and unpredictable despite the promises given (that's where the faith and trust come in).

Conceivably in eternal life, love and passion are reconciled forevermore with order and stability, but here and now we have to put up with a lot of loose ends. Love means encroachments on "our" time, inconvenient hours and interruptions (those phone calls in the middle of the night, dropping everything to respond to a crisis, agreeing to some activity that would never have entered our head otherwise). Love is unsettling. Unsettling is an understatement: Think of the Lord of love who found himself crucified for it.

Help us, Lord, to risk loving, to continue loving, to try it, despite the unsettling results we may foresee, the likelihood of change and inconvenience. All that is so little, nothing compared to the good that love can do for lover and loved. It can open and reveal new possibilities in both, can put zest and excitement into an otherwise dull and humdrum life. Pour your love into us so that we can keep pouring it out, giving, trying, risking, not being defeated or discouraged by false starts and failures. Giving everything to love is the only way to make our lives worth living.

Order, routine, and stability may not actually be enemies of love, but they come way after it in terms of importance.

July 26

Our experience of the bleakness and even darkness of our human lives, painful as it may be, is part of the necessary background for our appreciation of our God, who is light, love, and deliverance. Our sense of discouragement and total loneliness, even of despair and hopelessness, of the awful cruelty and insanity of human behavior, is the unavoidably necessary setting for an adequate appreciation of what a Savior is. From them we learn what it means to say with Psalm (26) 27, "The Lord is my light and my salvation; whom should I fear? The Lord is my life's refuge; of whom should I be afraid?" (v. 1).

We don't have to *look for* the experience of emptiness, of despair, of hopelessness, because that kind of trial seems to come to us all sometime or other. It is a, maybe *the*, form of the cross built into human existence. Our sunny days may sometimes or even often be overcast. Our hope and joy will be tried and even torn and shredded. My hope is that we can prepare for such storms and agonies in our better moments by asking for more profound faith and confidence, by trying to exercise them in lesser difficulties, in smaller disappointments.

In the meantime, we are not helpless. We can be aware of the reality of this trial and be understanding of those around who are "walking in the valley of darkness" (Ps [22] 23:4), be ready to comfort, to be available when needed. And conceivably we can give of our own hope and confidence, our faith, but with sensitivity. None of that "buck up, my friend," "cheer up," "why so gloomy," "go to a movie," "did you hear the one about . . ."

Our witness to faith and confidence needs to take into consideration the condition of those around us while being true to itself. It calls for delicacy and tact, true concern for the other. We only recognize light because we have some experience of darkness; others must be allowed the same before they can say, "My light and my salvation."

July 27

"Love is its own reward." For all I know, the idea has a thousand other expressions. In this book I've tried to encourage hope and trust, both of which are to a great degree oriented to what is yet to come. That may have suggested to some that we are always thinking about what the future will bring, what results there will be from what we do now, and in the process, shortchanging the present. This expression, "love is its own reward," should help us give the present more value.

To say that love is its own reward means that the very fact of loving, of offering love, brings with it reward or joy, a kind of satisfaction. We do not need to look beyond it for something better in the case of genuine love. Love itself is happiness.

No matter how much our belief involves hope for the future, even for the world to come, it would be an insult to love to always be thinking that beyond the good will, affection, service, or even passion that I bring to this relationship, I should be looking over his or her shoulder to something more, something beyond, some reward for being such a gift to my neighbor!

The beyond, the something more, will take care of itself, if we give all to love here and now. It's only appropriate that we give our relationships here and now full attention and not look on them as stepping-stones to something else. We know how little any of us likes to be thought of simply as a useful contact; we like to be valued for ourselves.

If love is from God and we try to share it and pass it on, there is no reason to undervalue it by looking beyond it. Love in this moment is worth our whole attention, our whole strength, our whole heart, our whole mind.

July 28

It's a familiar thought in our culture and our religion, too, that we humans are so frail but that we do not like to think about it too much. Or if we do, it's in an impersonal manner that really doesn't affect us. But illness, whether something pretty serious and potentially lethal, or a cold, the flu, an athletic injury has great power to make us sense what frailty means. When we're hit with even the least of these and our ordinary schedule is impossible or rendered miserable, we realize how fragile our whole existence is. If a microbe or a little sprain can do so much damage to our joy, our self-confidence, our good spirits—whew!

Even if we somehow determine beforehand that we're going to avoid sick people, be very careful about sanitation, be faithful to diet, jogging, and aerobics, we still find that there are chinks in our armor. And there are freak accidents out of our control. If, while we're jogging, someone runs into us, a car door opens and bangs our leg, what could we have done to avoid it?

Once we're well into our illness—the body aches, we feel tired, unable to shake the stuffed-up feeling—all our good intentions about being cheerful, helpful, active, and generous are dashed. As far as we're concerned, it easily appears that nothing else is going on in the universe now that really matters. Our concern is all turned in on ourselves. We may even resent the good health and good cheer of others, of those who have taken no precautions and yet are bouncy and sound while we drag ourselves around and fill baskets with used tissue.

It certainly sounds bad, and I can't say much good for it myself. But learning or sensing our weakness, our dependency on others and on God is not at all bad. It can help us develop a more realistic and profound trust in God, a sense that we are in God's hands always.

And, finally, all this can deepen our sympathy and concern, our understanding, for those who share this kind of illness or disability and even more for those whose lives are spent constantly in disability, pain, handicap. Help me, Lord, to use my health and vigor not just for my own enjoyment but as a gift to serve those around me. Let me be pleasant and friendly if possible, but always ready to help.

July 29

While Jesus was miraculously multiplying loaves and fishes for tired, hungry people—as is described several times in the Gospels (Matt 14:13-21), there really was no reason why he couldn't have also done the distribution miraculously. Couldn't the bread and fish just as well have been given to each individual present? Why limit the miracle to the increasing of the available food, why not add the distribution? But, in fact, Jesus leaves that task to others. While the miracle of the multiplication of the food tells us very clearly of God's love for the people, the fact that the Lord calls upon his disciples to do the distribution tells us something else.

Doesn't it tell us that God's love for us and goodness to us is ordinarily going to become apparent through the instrumentality, the cooperation, of other human beings? In fact, it may have reference to the huge problems that continually dog our world of unequal distribution of resources and supplies. Why don't famine-stricken people in Africa or Asia have a better deal? Because the affluent have not learned to share the surpluses that are often theirs.

One way to make the oh-so-familiar words about how God loves us come alive might be for us to look more often for the signs of how others are channeling God's love and compassion to us in ordinary life. Instead of our all-too-frequent tendency to judge others, we could substitute a determination to see the signs of God's love and goodness that they give. In one we see faithfulness and perseverance mirrored, in another gentleness or patience, in others good spirits or thoughtfulness, in others directness or sensitivity, honesty or simplicity. Draw up your own list.

July 30

One of Sigmund Freud's objections to religion is that it represents a sort of widespread mental illness. In this view people "afflicted" with religion are that way because they cannot face reality. The reality, according to Freud, is that we are alone in this very difficult, threatening world and must take care of ourselves, do whatever we can to make it livable. There is no one out there who is going to help us. People who are not "realistic" refuse to face the fact of our isolation and console themselves by imagining that there is some superior, invisible being on whom they can depend, a father-god who will take care of them and defeat the evil forces around them. This God will finally make up for this world's pain in a better and happy world to come.

To stand alone, bravely battling the elements and enemies, withstanding strong forces and ogres of various kinds, is an ideal we see in literature, film, and art. We call such people strong, independent, self-reliant. The great American West is built around such strong, silent characters.

Dependence and independence definitely are not simple matters. We expect children to become independent, capable of taking care of themselves. We hope to be able to leave our parents' home and start our own family, career, life, without having to run back for help all the time. If people in their forties are still asking Mom or Dad whether they can have some more popcorn or go out, we see this as a kind of sick dependence. Yet while we're growing up, there is a legitimate dependence on parents: for food, instruction, protection, guidance. Even the hero of the Wild West may have to depend on others for forage for his horse and a hideout from the bad guys. Throughout our lives there is a mixture of dependence and independence. There is a right kind of dependence and an unrealistic kind.

To be dependent on God from whom we come, without whom we and our world would not exist, who has a goal for it and can do more than we could ever imagine—this is simply reasonable, recognizing what really is. To accept that we do not create ourselves or have the final word is truly realistic. We rejoice in this dependence and expect the most from it when we express our hope and trust in God who embraces the whole world. Every kind of prayer is a recognition of our dependence.

July 31

Outstanding horror stories in our times such as that of Hitler or Jim Jones have warned most of humankind off from any kind of unthinking obedience to someone claiming to speak for God or for some other unquestionable authority. Even in the ranks of the authoritarian nations of the world, it has become common to have that authority challenged. It's more and more difficult to keep the lid on the boiling ideas and aspirations of ordinary human beings.

And it seems only appropriate, as we learn through education and leisure that we be responsible for our own decisions rather than leaving them up to various lords. Where education and respect for the human person have made an impact, people are inclined to challenge authorities who justify themselves with "God told me" or "This is God's will for you." After a couple of centuries of representative government in many parts of the world, Pius XII in the fifties stated that democracy was the most fitting form of government for people with any ability to think for themselves.

As absolute obedience to those claiming to speak for God has lost ground, obedience has gained ground in another sense. Along with an increased awareness that our salvation is inseparable from that of the rest of humankind has come more willingness to hear the voice of God in the legitimate aspirations and needs of our fellow human beings.

If the word "obedience" is used today, it may well refer not to some remote authoritarian figure but to our response to the wretchedness of the poor, the oppressed, the powerless of our world—our sensitivity to what God may be asking of us in all the circumstances of our life, in our work, our family life. The life of our community asks of us what we can rightly call obedience, a realistic response to hurting human beings. Through faithful sensitivity to our surroundings and those with whom we are linked, we are formed into servants like the Lord. It may be a slow process, but we know that in the needs of others we have the clearest indications of what we should do next. The ability to respond to what we have promised, to who we are, to all with whom we share this planet and life, to our environment, is obedience finally to the Creator of it all.

August 1

I heard someone once say "I can't imagine myself living long enough to become as generous as Bill or as thoughtful as Mandy. There must be another life or world where I will become that generous, that thoughtful." Possibly another reason for hope, for trust.

It is also another bit of the liberating teaching of Christ. If we are observant enough, if we see the demands that the following of Christ makes on us, we all have plenty of reason in ever-new examples before us to realize how unfinished we always are. When we think we've made it in some area—for example, I no longer blow up at other people—there comes an explosion that puts the local police on red alert.

The great example of so many others and the disappointing eruptions and failures in our own life all point to essential reasons for more trust and confidence. We are not meant to become such that we no longer need a Savior: Jesus says that we are only capable of being his followers insofar as we recognize that we need him, the physician, the healer, the forgiver.

Our failures, our sins, our inconsistencies, our lagging so far behind Mandy and Bill are all good reasons for trusting more to the Lord and Savior of us all. They are all good reasons for realizing that our holiness, our "perfection" if we want to use that term, our completion as his followers, is not something simply up to our straining and struggling.

Our acceptance of the Lord, our receptivity to what he can do, allows God to begin now in us the work that can only reach its total fulfillment beyond this life and, in a way, beyond our strength.

August 2

As I write these notes I am conscious of two contrary pulls. One, probably the predominate, is to help the reader with some motivation, some joy, some confidence and hope in the midst of what can be a very demanding life, or even a terrifying one. The other pull tells me that we cannot hide from or turn our backs on the suffering, problem-filled world around us. We've had quite enough in recent and past Christian history of a "spirituality" that is just that: something having little or nothing to do with the material world around us, a refuge from reality, a matter of finding a place of quiet and consolation for me with "my" God. Such an approach can mean, in effect, that slavery, persecution, problems with drugs and violence, are none of my business as long as I can have the consolation of being with Jesus.

But it becomes increasingly clear that following Jesus requires participation in the suffering of our fellow human beings, and concern about the quality of life in this world around us. "The Christian needs to have more, not less, exposed nerves than others to see the world with honesty enough to grasp its appalling cruelties" (Leech).

As the popularity of me-and-Jesus books in the drugstore and all sorts of me-centered literature illustrates, there is a great demand for being just comfortable, not disturbed by all these awful things. But somehow, what has to be done is (1) to face the pains and problems of the world around us in such a way that we do what is appropriate to remedy them; and (2) to retain in the midst of all this a rock-bottom confidence in the Lord, who puts in our hands his mission and supports us in what we do. What we try to do is the Lord's work, and he has begun it, continues it in us, and, as we know from his resurrection, will complete it.

August 3

Hearing people exclaim that they are saved, or simply reading statements to that effect in Scripture, many of us often wonder where we missed out. We don't seem saved from worry, difficulties, suffering, disappointment. We don't seem much different, in fact, from people who have no idea of such salvation or who would deny they're involved or who even scorn it. And often enough some of the louder proponents of "we're saved" seem to use it only to set themselves aside as judges of the rest of humankind.

According to St. Paul (Rom 6), we have died with Christ and risen with him, and the reality is twofold. (1) Jesus, the Savior, has come and does affect all those who open to him by faith and baptism. In us, no matter how dreary the days and life itself at times, is the power and presence of the Lord. Or put another way, we have been grafted on him, the true vine, into his body and share the same life and vitality. We don't have to *feel* it for it to be real, much as we'd all like to be carried along by a great swell of excitement as we face another day of tough work, difficult people, or simply boring routine. (2) Yet there is something lacking; there is more to come. We have not arrived at the final moment of our salvation. Like Christ, we must move through the changing moments of life and finally through life's end. Our world, too, must move through much development before his influence and power are fully realized. It isn't any simple lack of faith that prevents us from seeing our salvation; it is not totally here yet.

Opening ourselves more, surrendering ourselves more to the power and presence of the Lord, growing in faith, hope, trust, can release the power of the Lord in us. Most of us don't need a lot of creeds listing propositions about God and ourselves. We need a type of belief that we can call on in the difficult moments, which tells us the Lord is risen and he lives within us, in me; he is at work even now.

August 4

One form of seriousness about religion, about God, our life in Christ, is to assume what is basically a pose, no matter how unconsciously we seem to do it. It consists in determining that everything in Christian life and practice is of equal importance and that I am going to try, usually with a rigid jaw and a rather grim look, to treat it all very conscientiously. It has an appealing simplicity about it. But the trouble is that like human life, Christian life is not that simple. Everything in Christian belief and practice is not of the same importance. In times or places where Christian belief is attacked, the temptation is to act as if every single element were of equal importance. People under constant pressure from an anti-Christian government tend to hang on to every bit of custom and tradition. We need to be more confident in our belief than that. We need to realize that grace before every meal is not on the same level as our obligation to worship in the Christian community. The Nine First Fridays cannot be on the same level as something founded in Scripture like the celebration of Christ's suffering, death, and resurrection.

Not every matter in our religion that has its salespersons is on the same level of importance. One can have a perfectly acceptable devotion to the example and place of Mary without having anything to do with devotion to her image at such and such a place or with so many Saturdays of prayer. Christians need to know the Scriptures, especially the Gospels better in order to have some norms for judging what is often put before them.

Too, our efforts to bring all Christians together require that we not put up irrational barriers to common belief and worship by interjecting some little peculiarity of Christian devotion as if it were at the heart of Christianity. Such insistence is a bit like requiring not only that our friends and ourselves have much in common, but that we all wear the same hair style.

A great theologian of our century, Karl Rahner, has said that it would probably be better if Catholics sometimes knew less about certain details even of the catechism and would really concentrate on the decisive questions in a profound way, questions regarding God, Jesus Christ, his loving grace, sin and forgiveness, love of God and neighbor and prayer. We could simplify our lives as Christians by periodically doing some evaluation in terms of some such a list (based on the great themes of Christ's teaching) rather than in terms of the pitch of some narrow view. Truths and practices of Christian religion are of varying importance in terms of how close they stand to the heart of Christian belief.

August 5

While faith, hope and love, are all gifts of God, something we cannot produce ourselves, still they don't survive without some care, even work, on our part. For the Christian this means prayer where we exercise faith, hope, and love. And it means the sacraments and Scripture through which they are strengthened. Romans 15:4 tells us: "All the ancient Scriptures were written for our own instruction, in order that through the encouragement they give us we may maintain our hope with fortitude."

"Instruction . . . encouragement . . . maintain . . . hope . . . fortitude." Our hope, a gift from God given to those who are open and aware of their need for God (that's what "blessed are the poor" refers to), needs instruction from the example of the great "hopers" who have gone before us. All of us probably have benefited from some friend or family member who has illustrated hope and trust in trying circumstances or has seen it justified in their lives. Scripture tells us, for example, of people like the psalmist, who trusted in God and was brought through tough circumstances. Above all it tells us of Jesus, whose faith and hope eventually led to new life, the resurrection. Such Scripture provides strength for our hearts and minds. It offers the encouragement we need to hope and trust.

The instruction of Scripture will help us, Romans says, maintain our hope. One maintains something that already exists; if not maintained, it falls apart. Even though hope is not an object like a house or a car, still, that power in us requires something like maintenance—nourishment, care, attention—to continue to be powerful in our lives. Our hope, with some daily attention, will not be some wimpy quality but a source of strength. Our aim must be to have a firm hope that will survive even the worst that life and the world can do. This verse from Romans should encourage us to begin or continue the practice of some regular and prayerful reading of Scripture in order to "maintain our hope with fortitude."

August 6

"Unable to write, or even to speak clearly" and "helpless in his wheelchair" and "the last twenty years trapped by Lou Gehrig's disease" all describe Stephen W. Hawking. These words from the book jacket of *A Brief History of Time* (Bantam Books, 1988) also describe him: "Widely regarded as the most brilliant theoretical physicist since Einstein," "One of the great minds of the twentieth century." Now a man in his late forties, Stephen Hawking is a professor at Cambridge University. Before beginning work on his doctorate in physics he was diagnosed as suffering from ALS and told he had one or two years to live.

Some twenty years later his book has been a bestseller, and he continues with the help of an assistant, a synthesizer, and personal computer to communicate his insight and discoveries to an amazed world.

In the opening pages of his book, he says: "Apart from being unlucky enough to get ALS, or motor neuron disease, I have been fortunate in almost every other respect. The help and support I received from my wife, Jane, and my children, Robert, Lucy, and Timmy, have made it possible for me to lead a fairly normal life and to have a successful career. I was again fortunate in that I chose theoretical physics, because that is all in the mind. So my disability has not been a serious handicap. My scientific colleagues have without exception been most helpful" (p. vii).

From the drift of his theories about the universe and its origins, it seems clear that he has no belief in God or, at least, has no certitude about God. What strikes me in the paragraph quoted above and in other passages is the thankfulness he demonstrates about his life and opportunities. Admittedly, he does not use the word "thankful" or "gratitude" as one might if speaking of God, but feeling "fortunate" is close. It tells us that despite terrible disabilities, he totals up a list of things that have made him "fortunate"! Maybe you and I who most likely don't have ALS or anything approaching it could draw our own conclusions.

August 7

"We refuse compliments in order to hear them again." If you haven't heard that remark, you've at least noticed the practice. Someone says: "My, you do such beautiful work" or "That was a great job, Bill." The one complimented says: "Oh, no; naw." The other says: "Yes, you do; it was a great job." And we get a second or repeated compliment, a bonus. The conversation, so often duplicated, illustrates how self-congratulation and self-depreciation are mingled in us. We want to be both humble and self-satisfied. We think we should be humble but we are proud at least of some things we do or what we are.

And this self-seeking, self-concern, self-consciousness, self-love is ever present, unavoidable to some degree, and in a very basic sense, necessary and good. Without it, in fact, we could not even desire to be humble. After all, wanting to be humble or self-forgetting is something we desire because, in some sense, we expect it to be "rewarded by God," or to bring us to our best self.

Without self-love, self-concern, we would not accomplish some of our best deeds. There is a legitimate kind of pride that pushes us to do our best. Self-respect helps us do our work well, take care of our appearance, control our appetites, move away from the table. It's the necessary force behind much that makes us more lovable to others.

And unless we love ourselves in some proper sense, we can't love others either. Our Lord commands us to love our neighbor *as ourselves*; there is a basic sense in which we must love ourselves. As someone else has written, "Self-seeking, which is blamed for all our misdeeds, should often be credited with many of our virtues."

We need to distinguish in ourselves, in our actions and lives, between excessive self-love, self-centeredness, and a legitimate concern for self, a legitimate self-respect and love. A legitimate self-respect is a reflection in our behavior of the fact that we are loved by God who made us, as Genesis says, good.

August 8

As I hear of friends in various straits, I worry about my efforts here to be hopeful and encouraging. Am I dreaming, really unrealistic? One, I hear, "has a lot of trouble with the nerves in his feet; they are killing him and the doctors say they can't do anything about that. And now his left arm and shoulder has broken out in blisters. It looks terrible and it is very painful." Mary seems to be doing okay for now; "she is still getting radiation, after having had chemo treatment." And "son Chuck is deeply involved in a nasty divorce which is draining his and some of my financial resources." And so on, each of us could add to the day's litany of suffering and painful experiences even without watching the riots in Los Angeles on TV. I write and work on these reflections in the relative comfort of a year away from my usual teaching and responsibilities. A dream come true for many a person, I'm sure.

How will my reflections, my efforts to find motivation for hope, encouragement, even joy, in my, our, faith, how will this hold up for me in a tougher time? I hope what is here is more than words, more than rhetoric, more than dreams, imagination, operating in an unreal situation.

But in one sense what I am trying to do is something we all aim to do (the most any of us can do), have faith. We aim to strengthen it in good times with the hope that it will help us through the more difficult, even devastating times. One of the lessons I need to repeat to myself is that not all the future is ever in my own control, under my direction. It has to be built on hope and trust in the Lord and, possibly even more basically, on a surrender of my life and times into God's hands. The enigmatic words of Jesus to Peter after his resurrection have meaning for all of us: "When you were young you fastened your belt about you and walked where you chose: but when you are old you will stretch out your arms, and a stranger will bind you fast, and carry you where you have no wish to go" (John 21:18). Our passage through life must have more and more of a character of trusting, even joyful surrender to God who has loved us so much in the past. Why not in the future?

August 9

"Most people come to religion for what they can get. But we learn religion to learn selflessness—to be righteous regardless of whether we get rewards" (Mokyrai Cherlin). Whether or not we find "most people" too strong or not, there is obviously some truth to it. Some famous preachers and gurus certainly seem to have come to religion for "what they can get." We continually see examples of people running to some evangelist (sad that the word, meaning one who announces "good news" should become so disreputable), expecting him or her to fulfill the promise of health, wealth, happiness here and now. The promise often is that faith in Jesus will guarantee quick cures of maladies that others must slowly and painfully overcome with the help of medicine, time, and loving care. There is probably no preaching more contradictory of Jesus (who died in his early thirties generally despised by the local folk) than that which tells us that belief in him will bring those here-and-now blessings.

In one sense, of course, all of us come to religion for something: for salvation, for a way to handle our faults and sins, for instruction, for inspiration, for hope, for consolation. But Cherlin is correct; Jesus teaches us that the way to all that is through an emulation of his unselfishness, a participation in his self-giving. Those who lose their life for my sake, he says, will find it (Matt 10:39). The success and happiness of our world is bound up, in Christ's teaching, with the transformation of human beings by love and selflessness. But the following of Jesus *does not* promise each follower success, prosperity, perfect children, instant happiness. The reward of a Christian life here and now is to become another Christ, another human being who gives himself or herself to and for the good of the world.

Does the author quoted think of believers as coming to religion for the rewards of eternal life, of happiness with God? Jesus does not completely rule out our thinking of reward, yet it is certainly not central in his teaching. Eternal happiness is to be the inevitable by-product of a life well lived, of selflessness. We do best to live in the present, living here and now, this day, this hour, this job, after the style of Jesus himself. Our absolute hope, faith, and trust is that like him we, too, will rise from our death—including our death to self—to a new life with him forever.

August 10

Believers are often troubled by a crowd of questions that mean nothing to those who don't believe. Believers wonder if they really love God; if it isn't just a habit or the repetition of some words learned way back in childhood. They wonder if Jesus did cure all those people; if there is a God, in the face of so much awful news and suffering; if God is really loving. They wonder if there are genuine reasons for hope and trust.

These problems only arise for believers because they do have faith, they do believe. They take their belief seriously enough to question it. We never worry about the love of stranger for ourselves. Our doubts only arise in relation to someone close, someone we know loves us. Nor do our doubts concern some purely theoretical idea, the third law of thermodynamics; most of us don't agonize about the derivation of a word. If we don't occasionally have some anguish, doubt, uncertainty, struggle, about our faith and hope, it may be because they are not sufficiently mature.

Doubts and questions only testify to the seriousness and value of what or whom we doubt. Rather than despairing because of them—and we *can* do something about them through study and inquiry—we should be happy that we take our God and our relation to God so seriously; that it means that much. "Lord, I believe; help my unbelief" (Mark 9:24).

August 11

The media a couple of years ago were full of news about an earthquake in Armenia. Figures say somewhere near fifty thousand people were killed. What does human fulfillment mean in their case? Did these lives all reach their goals; were their right and just dreams all brought to completion? One certainly could have one's doubts. What meaning, what purpose, can we see in their deaths, in their lives? We speak of being nipped in the bud, cut off in the bloom of youth. Many of these, no matter what age, would have felt that way about their lives if they had known they were going to end this suddenly.

One exalted view of the whole matter claims to look at it scientifically. We must, in this view, see death, disaster, all as part of the inevitable price to be paid for evolutionary progress, for the development of our world and of human life. Our suffering simply "manures the soil of future harmony." The end result, a new humanity, is worth the price. We should forget our petty concerns and see the big picture.

Or, poets and others have told us we need to be happy with the thought that (1) we will live on in the memories of those who have loved us and not be forgotten; and (2) we will live on through our accomplishments, what we leave behind: a good family, a work of art or science or literature, a model life for others.

Woody Allen speaks for most of us, whether he shares Christian hope or not, when he says that he doesn't want to live on in his books or writing, but he just doesn't want to die, period. Christianity doesn't promise that, that we shall not die. But it does promise a lot more than the preceding two views. It says that we must share death with Christ and that, like him, we can expect to rise to new life by God's gift. Our only final and failproof fulfillment will be given by God in a new life. While we agonize about the awfulness of deaths from disasters, we need, at the same time, to recall that our fulfillment is not simply a matter of what we can do but of what God can do.

"Surely I haven't suffered simply that I, my crimes and my sufferings, may manure the soil of the future harmony for somebody else. I want to see with my own eyes the hind lie down with the lion and the victim rise up and embrace his murderer. I want to be there when every one suddenly understand what it has all been for" (Dostoyevski). That's God's promise to us.

August 12

We launch a boat with champagne; we shake hands on being introduced. We give neckties, chocolates, bouquets, and jewelry at Christmas time or for anniversaries. We may make the sign of the cross on entering the church. The best man carries the wedding couple's rings. Hindus bathe in the Ganges. And we all do many other similar things. All of these qualify as traditions, but not all of us partake in all of them.

Ideally, a tradition expresses a conviction or a belief that we still share even though the custom may be centuries old. Just because they often are old, traditions have a hard time in our fast-moving and questioning world. Does anyone remember when the first teenager questioned the importance of standing for an older person? How fast things change was illustrated when Studs Terkel teased a group of young people "for having no sense of tradition and for supposing that the history of music began with Bob Dylan. One of them asked, 'Bob who?'"

Christians celebrate a number of traditions continuously in order to maintain a relation to the earliest disciples of Jesus and to their belief in him. We celebrate the Lord's Supper because he told us to do it in memory of him.

While there are complaints to make about traditions, they go far toward giving our life meaning, order, and identity. We all begin our day with a crowd of traditions that may go all the way from praying to brushing our teeth to having something to eat to kissing the children good-bye. We should be grateful that we don't have to think up each day a new and appropriate procedure for beginning it. We'd never get to the job or probably even out of the bedroom!

"Good traditions are a way of giving a vote to the dead," G. K. Chesterton once wrote. They take into consideration the experience and knowledge of many others gone before us. He went on to say that tradition asks us not "to neglect a good man's opinion even if he is our father." We might spend a few moments thinking of the good and helpful traditions we live by and that we have, often, received from parents, the Church, teachers.

August 13

"God is truth" and along with this has often gone the conviction that we (Catholics, Christians) have both God and that truth in our pocket. We have it all figured out. The unfortunate consequence over the centuries has been a bloodcurdling willingness to kill and silence those who obviously don't accept this truth about which we are so sure. Christian (and other) history is filled with examples of the persecution and destruction of those who don't agree with us, and all this is seen as a service to the truth. Our century is by no means the first to hear religious leaders urging believers to kill.

But there has also been in our time a recovery of the biblical notion that God as truth means that God is faithful, *true* to God's word, unfailing in love. There is no division between what God says and what God does. God is not primarily the source of a number of enlightening statements but the constant and faithful one on whom we can depend or whom we can trust. In this sense God is true, God is truth.

Imitating and responding to this kind of God of truth makes demands on us and is more likely to leave others safe in life and limb. It requires that we, too, be faithful to our word and take seriously Jesus' condemnation of hypocrisy and of the willingness of religious leaders of his place and time to demand much of others and little of themselves. There is no danger in trying to make the ideals, the truth we see, and our actions one, as long as we honestly admit our failures. Ideals are nothing if we can fulfill them today. True ideals are not realized in such a way that we can file them under "completed projects."

Our ideals and our failures in regard to them need to be accompanied by trust in God's forgiving love. Having ideals we do not live up to is different from having ideals we never intend to approach. Luther once made well the point that the preacher must preach beyond where he himself is in his own following of Christ. All of us must hope and aim beyond where we are and resist the temptation to equate the ideal with its fulfillment, to believe we have realized it because we feel great about it. What we can justifiably feel great about is our trust in God, whose power alone can narrow the gap between ideal and real.

Lord, I believe, help my unbelief; I love, help my unlove; I trust, help my lack of trust.

August 14

Part of the necessary background for acceptance of Jesus Christ as Lord, Redeemer, Savior, is our recognition that something is always a bit off in us, in human life. "The good which I want to do, I fail to do; but what I do is the wrong which is against my will" (Rom 7:19). There is a reluctance on our part to live, to give ourselves on the model of the Lord—or, more basically, to allow God's love to work that forcefully in us. We are inclined to either deny there is anything wrong, to blame it on someone or something else, or to presume that we will take care of it ourselves with a bit more education or a more determined will.

But a necessary part of life is a recognition that we do need the Physician, that we rely on and can find our ultimate freedom from all that's wrong only through the power, the love of God for us, shown in Jesus Christ. Besides our tendency to think it's a matter of me saving me, there is also our tendency in darker moments to think that nothing finally can be done about it. We've seen ourselves fall back into the same patterns of neglect, dishonesty, unfaithfulness, selfishness so often that we easily incline to the theory that it's just one big vicious circle.

The essence of our faith in the Lord is a trust that God's power and love are stronger, more penetrating, more effective than either our efforts or our failures. To recognize this is not an additional cause for despair but for great happiness. In the end, it *doesn't* all depend on me gritting my teeth. To recognize happily (we hear in the Easter season "O happy fault which deserved such a redeemer!") our helplessness opens us to trust in the God who is more powerful than all our inertia and resistance. "In Christ Jesus the life-giving law of the Spirit has set you free from the law of sin and death" (Rom 8:2).

August 15

Two things seem certain as one looks ahead to the life of religion toward the end of this second thousand years after Christ. (1) Pseudo-prophets and people hoping to profit are going to announce that 1999 or 2000 is the end, the final day in human history, that somehow they have figured this out by reading the Bible. This distorted interpretation they will share with anyone who buys their books or tapes (and thereby, by the way, assure that they will have a good financial cushion to last them way beyond 2000!). (2) Others who deem themselves more practical and seem more responsible will be calling for the teaching of morals, the reintroduction of moral education built around some code, the Ten Commandments. About the first certainty you'll find more elsewhere in this book.

The second is more understandably attractive to reasonable people concerned about the state of the world. Almost anyone will tolerate religion if it is seen as supporting law and order, cutting down on law-enforcement costs. Possibly—I'm not all convinced—such teaching may have some value. Does it lessen murders in Washington, D.C. or muggings in Central Park or the subway? The solution is too superficial and unlikely to appeal to people who have no profound reason for wanting to live more honorably or in peace than that some commandment or law says they should. We don't steal, commit murder, swindle, because we've *forgotten* that they're wrong! Or never knew it!

What seems more basic is a combination of two other elements: (1) a vision or picture of what a human life should be, and (2) a character formed in accordance with that vision. The vision is given us in Jesus Christ, in his life of relentless love, which brought death. That vision is presented to us in the community of believers: through the Scriptures, the sacraments, and the life and love of others. Such a portrait can inspire in us aims and desires that go to make up a character willing to respond on the model of love illustrated by Jesus. Strengthened by the Lord, we can learn to trust in the power of love to change the world. A list of prohibitions and limitations does not change human behavior. However, God's grace allowed entry into human minds and hearts can form them after the mind and heart of Jesus, love made flesh.

August 16

In St. Luke's Gospel there is a surprising emphasis on the dangers of wealth and our desire for it. There is a contrast (Luke 16:1-13) between elusive or perishable wealth and that which lasts, or between the wealth of this world and the wealth that is real. By the wealth of this world the Gospel means the things we can't take with us: our BMWs, our RVs, our PCs, our IRAs and, of course, more happily, our outstanding bills and mortgages. What we can take with us are distinctively human qualities like love of family and friends, honesty, a sense of appreciation and gratitude, and many others. But as the Gospel complains, we are often not as wise and forward looking about these as, say, a golfer is about his or her game. The golfer takes lessons, practices, and reads books, while the genuinely human in us is often squeezed out by other concerns and left to a diet that is the religious equivalent of Ding Dongs and diet soft drinks.

This is not a suggestion that Christian life should or can be scientifically mapped out in ten easy lessons, that we can really put it into the form of four-year plans, but that we need to give more thought, more attention, to the elements that go to enrich the inner self. It means being sure that we put being someone, being human, being a friend, a father or mother, a worshiper, one who is grateful for life, ahead of having something or many things.

Some questions might sharpen the issue for us. What is there to me besides what I have? Do I look at career and vocation only in terms of income? Do I put my desire to have things ahead of my neighbor's needs, ahead of family responsibilities? What is there in me that is not subject to rust and rot? What really matters in my life and relationships? Do my relationships—with God and those around me—really matter enough for me to take time for them, to put them before other considerations? Do I value friends not simply for the company they work for but for their company?

A life genuinely humanized by Christ allows time for enjoyment, worship and prayer, play, appreciation. These activities build up traits that survive all the changes of this life and beyond it through the door of death.

August 17

For some centuries in Catholic piety it was common to put great attention on denying ourselves, to spend a heck of a lot of time and energy on the selves we were supposed to forget and let die like the grain of wheat. A lot of that is counterproductive. How can we lose the self if all we think about is how to lose, forget the self? Wouldn't it make more sense just to forget it?

We do that partially by putting our attention elsewhere, above all on the good and the needs of others. We all know how easily we forget the self, become unselfconscious when we are completely absorbed in an intense game, an intriguing movie or book, a beautiful concert or ballet. All that is necessary, of course, to our health, and instructive also for our Christian life. But some Christian "spirituality" has not helped us in this. Rather, it has made us a bit like the person walking in front of a long mirror or a series of reflecting windows who decides to be more conscious of how he or she walks; within a short time we become quite artificial and almost unable to act naturally. Too much self-consciousness.

There is a paradox that we will probably find our true self if we try more and more to forget it, not to put the attention on it. Christ's words about losing ourself in order to find it hardly are meant to rule out human effort, as we know from all that he taught. But the point is that human activity can become constricting, counterproductive if it means all the responsibility, the effort, is linked to me, to myself. An ancient Chinese writer Chuang Tzu says, "You never find happiness until you stop looking for it." Happiness, holiness, self-fulfillment, likeness to Christ are consequences of selfless living, loving service, self-forgetting.

If the attention is off the self and its importance, its ingenuity and virtue, we leave ourselves open to the influence of God's grace, open to a longer view than ours, a stronger arm than ours and a surer touch than ours.

August 18

"Let a woman in your life and . . . ." In the famous musical *My Fair Lady* these sexist lines occur in one of its many memorable songs. The man singing the song, of course, is detailing the changes made in the routine of a bachelor who enters at long last into a relationship, albeit somewhat unwillingly, with a woman. Broadening the point, we have probably all seen or experienced that same thing: how a friend, a new person in our life, brings changes, new demands on our time and capacities, unexpected consequences. A number of fine movies have made this point, and maybe you have seen one or the other of them: *Baghdad Cafe, Babette's Feast, Rainman.* A fortuitous appearing encounter leads to such transforming results. Egoism is diminished; backbiting and smallness are overcome; a bit of fresh air and light come into dark lives; feelings and aspirations are unleashed, and deadly routines and deadened lives are shaken.

If we haven't experienced this, we should open ourselves more to the possibility. Good friends and transforming relationships are not a simple matter of casual encounters or barhopping, but require some good will and selflessness. The point in all this is something intrinsic to the following of Christ: We meet God, we learn more about God and about ourselves through the kindness, the interest, of others, through allowing or preferring some change to living a too enclosed, too narrow life.

One other who is always available to us, not only in all these others, is the Lord Jesus. In a combination of sacraments and Scripture, Jesus can come into our lives and bring about changes. Above all, we meet the Savior in the midst of the community of other believers and in the Lord's Supper. And to make that more fruitful, it is open to all of us to deepen our relation with Christ through reflection on the Gospels and other works of the New Testament. "Let a man, woman, a child, a friend . . . let Christ into your life and . . ."

August 19

Christians are united, St. Paul says, by one baptism, one Lord, one hope. One way of describing the content of that one hope is as a share in the kingdom of God. What can that mean for most of us who don't live in kingdoms? Judging from the interest of the media in everything royalty do, we who live in a republic have a lot of romantic interest in kingdoms. But to understand kingdom as used in St. Paul and in the Gospels, we need a bit more realism.

The kingdom spoken of so often by Jesus in several of the Gospels is a condition (rather than a place requiring a passport) into which we enter here and now by giving God free "reign" in us, where we allow God's will and purpose to be first in our hearts and wills. Yet for many it has long been customary to think that the kingdom means the world to come, a situation in which we live with the Lord forever in happiness. This does not seem to be the primary meaning in the Gospels; it has a more immediate reference to what we do here and now. But the two differing ideas highlight a constant problem for Christians. Do we prepare best for the life to come, for eternity, by making the present crucially important, giving it everything, our energy, talents? Or do we prepare better by keeping our eyes on what is to come and regarding the present as more of a waiting period?

It seems to me that we Christians need to do more of the former. There is a suspicion around that we do not take this world seriously, that genuinely committed Christians do not really care what happens to it since it's not lasting in any case. But the kingdom to come and the world we live in are related. The life of the world to come grows out of the way in which we give ourselves generously, even joyously, to the present, to our world, to those around us. Insofar as we open ourselves now to the influence and power of God and grace, the kingdom comes and God's will is done on earth as it is in heaven.

August 20

When we think of the parable about the weeds and the wheat growing so closely entwined that the weeds have to be left to harvesttime for fear of destroying the wheat, we easily imagine that there is the wheat, wonderful you and me, and alongside it the weeds, those slobs, those good-for-nothings, those people who seem to have no morals. The world is divided into the good and the bad, the caring and the cruel, the cheaters and the charitable.

Yet just a bit more reflection makes us realize that the weeds and the wheat coexist within each one of us; that I can somehow manage to be both cruel and charitable, alternate between giving and grasping. Within us exist both the wheat and the weeds, the radishes and the ragweed, the willing and the wimpy. Our virtues and vices, as in a garden, are closely entangled. We have some real talent but along with it extreme pride in that talent. Our energy and vitality, our willingness to get things done, may easily be accompanied by impatience and hot temper. Or, even more extreme, we may be very generous to the poor or strangers and be real bears around home. We may be very ready to help a sick or elderly person but also specialize in backbiting. If we look carefully, we'll realize that the line between good and bad does not go between you and me or between Americans and Libyans but right down the middle of each of us.

Knowing that about ourselves is certainly reason for humility and, too, some patience. But better yet, let's apply it to others. Let's realize that they suffer from the same character split in their lives. We have good reason for being less severe with that son who is living with a girlfriend, a sister who has joined an odd religious sect, children who are involved in drugs, a friend who seems very tightfisted. Self-righteous separation from others and disdain of them is foreign to the teaching of Jesus. He himself carried it so far as to be accused of running around with bad company, and eventually he died between two thieves.

At times all of us are bad company for others and for ourselves. Both weeds and wheat exist within you and me. Like God, and with God's help, we need to be more forgiving of the prickly weeds we see in others.

August 21

Despite their banality, T-shirt slogans and bumper-stickers do, at times, seem to express if not "eternal truths," at least truth at some level in a catchy fashion. On the T-shirt on the man at the bar is the phrase "I'm in no shape to exercise." An apt and incisive expression of the tendency of all of us to put off all that is good for us, all that we should do, by telling ourselves we are not ready.

We just don't go from being in no shape to being in shape in one fell swoop. But we do hate that beginning, the effort, the work, and the sweat we foresee is coming. The future can exercise a great pull on us; it can also exercise a great deterring influence on us, frighten us. The unknown, the awful things our imaginations conjures up, all tell us to stay where we are, at the bar with our beer, rather than getting to the gym. The obvious truth, of course, is that we don't get in shape unless we start somewhere, even where we are, in possibly awful shape. Our imagination can help us to push toward a future goal by picturing it for us; we can picture a slender, trim body and the self-confidence and pride it might inspire in us. On the other hand, our imagination can picture the road to it as paved with suffering and impossible obstacles. It can picture the ideal and we can see where we are right now but, often, the temptation is to by-pass the more mundane and mixed area in between.

We move toward none of our goals except by taking some immediate steps, no matter how small and insignificant they may be. If we can and will throw off all our clothes like a St. Francis of Assisi and embrace absolute poverty today, okay. But for most of us, the ideals are going to come about through the more ordinary and less romantic-appearing ways of resolutions about small matters, chipping away day by day. Let's not let our grand and glorious ideal mesmerize us or cause us to despair but, instead, take now the first steps toward making it real.

August 22

Some time ago Protestant theologian James Luther Adams, now in his late eighties and widowed for ten years, was asked about how he dealt with loneliness. One of his suggestions about which he was quite forceful was to write letters to old friends.

In letters, he claimed, you could set down "things that are substantial and meaningful" in a way that is not possible through phone calls and even visits. That may not be the experience of all of us, but the suggestion seems to me to be, indeed, a very good one for a number of reasons. (1) Writing is a way of expressing more clearly and directly what one wants to say. As someone has said, I don't know what I mean until I see what I write. Writing forces us often to put our thoughts and feelings into clearer formulation, something we may not have time to do in ordinary oral communication. How often after a conversation have we said, I wish I had thought to say . . .

(2) Writing our thoughts and trying to be concerned about the reader is a good way to take our mind off our more immediate pains and worries or, at least, to relieve them by expressing them, if that is appropriate.

(3) Above all, I think the great thing about writing letters is the pleasure and surprise they can bring to the one who receives them. Often, in the experience of many of us, nothing has been more brightening to the day and our life than to receive an unanticipated letter from a dear one, an old friend, someone we think of often or have even almost forgotten. Even a few lines, a note, a postcard, give the one who receives it a sense of more worth: Someone has taken the time to write, to think of me. Those who *don't* write know exactly what I mean: What keeps us from writing often is the effort it takes, the fact that it requires taking a little time out of our ordinary round of activities. When we're young and busy this is all the more difficult—but probably, for that reason, all the more appreciated by the receiver. When we're older and there isn't all that much we have to do, why not write?

August 23

Will Campbell is a writer and preacher from the South. When asked about the Gospel where Jesus tells his disciples to give to Caesar what is his and to God what is God's (in answer to a question about paying taxes) Campbell got radical. "Where do you draw the line at what you will or won't do in regard to Caesar's, the government's, demands?" His response: "I think that when Jesus said, 'Give to Caesar what belongs to Caesar,' he was drawing on his tremendous sense of humor. He held up this worthless coin and said, 'Okay, then, give him a quarter.' In other words, give him nothing."

If he is right, this passage says a lot more about ordinary life than it does about religion and politics. Jesus says the only thing a committed Jew or Christian could say: Everything belongs to God; not partly to him and partly to the IRS, Donald Trump, or you or me. In Psalm 50 God says: "If I were hungry, I would not tell you, for the world and all that is in it are mine." We are all stewards, managers, of someone else's property and power.

Though God needs nothing from us, God has chosen to deputize us as governors, prime ministers, fathers and mothers, executives, kitchen supervisors, team captains, and bouncers. We are agents, entrusted with the management of some portion of creation. And God is very serious about it. Unlike an overanxious parent, God doesn't sit in the window, nervously watching, ready to jump in if we seem to be botching things. God doesn't even step in to stop the abuse of children, the torture of political opponents, or the ravages of Third World disease. That is *all* left up to us, the managers. We are responsible for the world, for each other, for the world's potential. The only proviso is that we recognize that they belong fundamentally to their Creator and under God to everyone. They are never at the absolute disposal of Exxon, IBM, Michael Jackson, the state, the U.S., or you and me.

No part of our life is unrelated to God. Politician or printer, accountant or attorney, our work and vocation have a relation to God and God's purposes. No element in human life can be exempt from honesty, for instance, or respect for others. We cannot welcome God into our family life and then exclude God from how we sell insurance or condos or run an election campaign. Recalling all this can help us come to our tasks with more respect for what we're doing, the world we are working on, and those with whom we work. You might say that though the world and all we use of it never absolutely belongs to us, our success as Christians depends absolutely on how we use it.

August 24

"There's no one dearer than the face in the mirror," expresses a down-home truth. What other passion in our life starts as early, even in the crib? And to what other love are we so faithful? As in so many other instances, the only way to overcome a love like this is to replace it with another.

Only under the magnetism of love for another can we turn from our conviction that everyone else is meant to serve us, to wait on and for us, to excuse us. Laws, rules, regulations, systems of morality, will not do it. For the Christian even to say that love for Christ is what will and can save us from self-love is possibly not quite accurate. For most of us that love for Christ needs the face of a friend, husband, wife, or an admired person. Most of us need to find Jesus in some individual who brings out the best in us, who helps us forget ourselves, who helps us learn generosity. To think, as some Christian piety seems to have taught, that the love of God and the love of others are opposed seems really off the mark. The love of self and of God—these are opposed. But the love of another is simply a way in which we love God, the source of that other, of all the good that attracts us to him or her.

Only another person can ordinarily move us to pass up a night out or the chance to really enjoy a bad mood. Only another person can help us escape from the narrow love of self into a stronger, wider love. In loving these others, we may in a sense lose ourselves, but only in order to find ourselves on a higher plane, to find a better self, one more like him who lost himself on a cross to find life in an entirely new way.

August 25

There is a danger that we do not go far enough with the presence of Christ (and of God) in the Eucharist. The danger is that in appreciating his presence there, in the bread and wine on the altar and received into ourselves, we stop there, forget, neglect to appreciate his presence elsewhere. We may neglect to see the Eucharist as a reminder that God is always to be found in such ordinary products of human labor and the earth as food and drink.

God is also present in the word we hear at Mass or the Lord's Supper. That word is living and powerful here and now, able to affect and transform us. God is present in the community of all those gathered for the celebration of the Lord's Supper. God is present in the human community in general, not just in believers but in all who live and breathe by God's ever-present power. God is present in all of our world, sustaining it and appearing in various ways to the eyes of faith.

Our emphasis on the presence of Christ in the Eucharist should not be at the expense of the other forms of his presence in our world. Rather, it should remind us, as we celebrate it in a very special way in church, that it is a focused moment of that presence but that God is present in all of our world.

> Where can I go from your spirit?
> > from your presence where can I flee?
> If I go up to the heavens, you are there;
> > if I sink to the nether world, you are present there.
> If I take the wings of the dawn,
> > if I settle at the farthest limits of the sea,
> Even there your hand shall guide me (Ps 139:7-10).

God's presence in the Eucharist does not have its full effect if we do not see God in our distasteful, irritating neighbor, the deprived and oppressed of another part of the world, the poor in our big cities. God's presence in the bread and wine is only partially appreciated if we do not see it in the sea, the heavens, the snow and sun, the beauty and power of nature. Our veneration of the Lord in the Eucharist by bows, genuflections, kneeling or standing, is false, play-acting, if we do not have a like reverence for the neighbor, the deprived and suffering, for the riches and powers of nature, for the environment.

August 26

If the prophets of the Bible had been the kind who could tell us in advance the winning horses at the race track or how the weather would be for our vacation in Montana or Aruba, they wouldn't have suffered rejection, persecution, and death as they did. But in the Bible a prophet is not one who foretells the future but someone who claims to speak on behalf of God, who tries to make clear what God wants. So often this means calling to our minds unpleasant truths and realities, uncovering the well-hidden or ignored defects of our world and society. The words of prophets are often, Abraham Heschel wrote, "stern, sour and stinging, but still rooted in love and concern for the hearers. If the prophet didn't love the world as God does he or she wouldn't bother to tell it that it might be going to hell." In order to be open to disturbing words, we need to broaden the concept of prophet so that it just doesn't refer to some ancient bearded Jewish fellow from the fifth century B.C. People who speak or proclaim to us any uncomfortable bit of insight can be called prophets; they may warn us about preparations for war or about the dangers of macho diplomacy, about the way we live, about how we pollute our lakes and environment; they may be trying to rouse us from sleep, to make us question a government's plans or policies. We usually call them agitators, troublemakers, activists.

Almost by definition prophets are intolerant. They think of ordinary matters as irrelevant; everything, everyone else seems impure or tainted to them. Again Abraham Heschel says: "To a person endowed with prophetic sight, everyone else seems blind; to a person whose ear claims to hear God's voice, everyone else appears deaf. No one is just; no knowing is strong enough; no trust is complete enough for them." We need to hear these people even if the message seems too shrill, too piercing, "pitched an octave too high." Even if we wouldn't want to have them back to dinner again.

We need to hear uncomfortable truths, be reminded of other sides to issues than those our comfortable middle class may be inclined to. We need to have our indifference and laziness shaken up, our certainties questioned, be forced to rethink matters. No one of us, the prophets included, has the whole picture. We're more likely to get a complete, wide, catholic viewpoint if we listen to a variety of uncomfortable voices, a variety of often angry and unsatisfied people.

We do this when we hear uncomfortable, strange words in Scripture, a sermon we find hard to swallow, when we listen to people who don't just confirm our prejudices or echo our sentiments. We all need their additional eyes, the further depth they bring to our vision, the better hearing they bring to us.

August 27

Our most difficult choices may not necessarily be between what is good and what is bad but between two or more good actions, plans, proposals. We feel that very pointedly when we are pulled in several directions by contrary suggestions, proposals, aims. Take Kate the college student who looks forward to skiing with friends over the Christmas holiday. That may seem the most obvious and wonderful thing to do. At the same time, her parents may consider it equally obvious that she should be home with the family. A college counselor or professor may also be suggesting that she use the time to prepare for the end of some course or a qualifying exam for graduate school. Or, keep the skiing plan in place and it can be complicated further by Kate's parents being divorced. Both think she should spend the vacation with them. Obviously in less than a page, this author is not going to offer a simple formula for these typical conflicts that all of us encounter, conflicts between a number of often very commendable options.

What do we do? How do we resolve the conflicts? Barring elaborate and probably unrealistic solutions to satisfy all parties, we must ourselves take some responsibility, even risk offense to someone or other and, in the process, achieve some peace of mind. Just as our life itself is so often made up of opposing but good aims, ideals, plans, so our solutions, too, may involve accepting some inability to satisfy everyone and every demand made upon us. For many centuries Christianity has been there to help multiply our guilt. This has been true, at least partially, because we have been given an ideal that, while possibly practicable for a saint, was not immediately possible for the rest of us. We can only honestly solve our problems in terms of the kind and degree of generosity and foresight we now possess, not simply in terms of some ideal that demands here-and-now solutions beyond our strength or development.

After trying to know well what is possible for us now—with God's help, prayer, and a reasonable amount of time—we must make decisions. Then we must face the fact that we are not going to make everyone in our environment equally happy. We cannot fault ourselves for a variety of reactions to ourselves over which we do not have complete control. If all is done out of love, what more can be asked?

August 28

We've probably all been turned off at times by encountering individuals whose conversation is so formal, so programmed that we feel we're speaking to a wall, at most to a company man or woman, someone who does not allow himself or herself to think, to feel, outside of what is prescribed by some external structure or group. Or it may be a specialist in some field, from theology to Scripture, where the terms and language seem all to have been given in advance and just loaned and repeated. I feel that way hearing a Scripture-filled evangelist speak, addressing every situation and person with a quotation, usually with chapter and verse, rather than betraying any personal assimilation of the meaning and depth of those phrases.

In a situation where we know no one very well, at a cocktail party or reception, we easily meet a whole set of stock phrases that leave us longing for even a good spat with a friend or family member as a relief. The same thing can happen in religion or our relation to God. We often use a language that is certainly not our natural usage. The prayers of the liturgy, of public worship, rightly have a certain kind of general appeal, at times they may amount to a sort of blandness or neutrality. They must be broad enough to include the basic desires and prayers of a nintey-year-old widow and those of a twenty-two-year-old man in love. A prayer that would suit perfectly and exclusively one or the other of these two would certainly not be very appropriate for the other or for any of the rest of us.

But there must be in personal prayer, the prayer of daily life, a real effort to use some language that is meaningful to me, that enables me to express my desires worries, hopes, faith. Without these, we are in a sense keeping God at arm's distance, using language that never opens up our feelings and self, that inhibits a personal relationship from developing. It's like ordinary human relations. With friends we must get beyond "How do you do" and "Pleased to meet you" to words that open us to the other. Only in this way can real intimacy develop. So with God and prayer. There has to be some time in prayer that is independent of printed text, time for prayer that only I can utter.

August 29

"What we need are more kindly friends and fewer professionals" (Peggy Ann Way). Whether it's true or not that Christians need to recover much of the task of comforting or helping the burdened and troubled, from professionals (counselors, psychologists, psychotherapists, social workers, etc.), it is probably unarguable that there is no way to follow Christ without being concerned to help the troubled. To carry out the imperatives of Matthew 25: "As often as you did it to one of the least of my brethren, you did it to me." I don't think such a recognition devalues the work or necessity of professionals in such matters as alcoholism, depression, abuse.

The reviewer quoted at the beginning is writing of a book very critical of therapists of various types. She is saying that the Christian heritage, the demands of the following of Christ, requires that we "be present to hurting folk." She says that caring for others, helping those who are in any need, is a simply human duty flowing from baptism, not simply attendant on ordination or professional training. She suggests, too, that Christians, because of their union with Christ and his work and love, have an insight into human suffering. They are warned against self-seeking, encouraged to be truthful, and taught to see that both healer and healed share a common condition before God.

Who is to say that we need "fewer professionals"? Possibly, but the more important point to make is that we need more caring people, that there should be more willingness, more competition, to do something about disaster, suffering, pain, need, poverty, injustice when it comes to our notice. There should be more of us willing to help by doing what our circumstances and life allow. The problem should be for those in charge to know where and how to use all the offered help rather than having to plead for it or look in vain. Christianity does not despise human science, expertise, know-how, training, but it does encourage *all of us* to be anxious to do something about the suffering, pain, anxiety, and need around us.

August 30

"It is more important to be aware of the ground for your own behavior than to understand the motives of another" (Dag Hammarskjöld). Another good reason not to worry about analyzing, knowing, worse yet, judging, the motivation and actions of others. Many of us need reminders about withholding or restraining our wish to understand the motives of others or, more often, to judge them. We do it easily in our harsh or biting language and comments, our lack of trust.

One of the best ways to inhibit or lessen this tendency, which can easily become habitual, is to do what Hammarskjöld suggests: Each time the temptation arises to judge Joe's or Karen's behavior or words, we could profitably turn that penetrating searchlight on ourselves and ask, What makes me tick? Why am I doing this? Why do I do anything?

Christians have in one sense a basically easy answer to the question, easy to formulate, that is. The followers of Christ should be motivated as he was by concern to do what honors God and to love those we live with and with whom we work and associate. As I said, easily said. Not so easy to do.

The effort, though it seems to be primarily in the mind, to understand and purify our motives is important, one we should return to often. We can help it along by trying each day in our own words and manner to formulate the basic intention behind our actions and words.

Besides our prayers for others, for ourselves, our thanks for life and gifts, our requests for help and strength, the prayer that sends us off in the morning should include an attempt to focus our life, our talents, our energies, on the service of God and the good of others. But once again, it will be more honest and efficacious if we do the wording ourselves, make it fit our heart and intentions.

Lord, help me today to live truly for you, and help me to do all I do that those around me may benefit.

August 31

At the risk of being considered an airhead or flippant, I still think (this far into the year) that in general our world is too grim. Especially we who have it relatively easy, so comfortable. Why such headlong and unremitting seriousness, such unwillingness to laugh off the details, the inessentials, our own self-importance?

Very seriously, I think humor is sadly underrated. I think that part of the development of the human race, of the change in our way of thinking and acting is just this, the ability to take ourselves and the incongruities, the absurdity of human life, with some lightness. The New Testament writers seem to show little evidence of anything we would call a sense of humor. I suspect that is related to custom or their time, place and way of thinking, not necessarily an example of how the finished or developed human being must necessarily act.

Typical of our undervaluation of humor is this judgment of a Los Angeles psychiatrist on comedians, "They use humor as a defense against depression and never develop anything deeper." Granted, comedians are not identical with just any ordinary human being possessed of a willingness to use a sense of humor. But I think the criticism still shows this inability to appreciate humor. To say that humor is a defense against depression hardly condemns it in my eyes: Isn't much of life, our activity, everything from work to art, psychiatry, similarly constructed? A sense of humor can attest very well to the seriousness with which one takes human existence and its real terrors and absurdity. We must look at life occasionally with some distance, some proportion, some detachment, or we could easily be continually depressed.

"They never develop anything deeper." How do we know? Why can't humor go along with other approaches to human existence? While I trust in the Savior for final help and deliverance, what is wrong with laughing off some of the smaller pains and difficulties in my own life? Why let them cloud over my confidence and joy in living?

September 1

Christians who lived through the last few decades and know the thrill much of the world felt at the expansiveness and warmth of Pope John XXIII and the surprising open-mindedness of the Vatican Council of the early sixties may feel there has been a withdrawal, a retreat. A restrictive and cautious spirit seems to replace all that. Many Churches today are pessimistic about the prospects for more unity between Catholics and Protestants, Orthodox and Anglicans. There are those who seem intent on bringing back a Church of rules and regulations, of narrowness and even some paranoia. Not only does the Catholic Church seem more fearful and less open to other Churches, but within the Church, too, there are moves toward rigidity and a cramped spirit. There is a chill in the air.

The man considered the greatest Catholic theologian of this century, Karl Rahner, back in 1965 wrote of the possibility of such a reverse. Threats to the more open spirit would come, he wrote, from a "wave of caution," "fear of one's own courage" and "terror of false conclusions that people may like to draw." But he was confident that the seeds of a "new outlook and strength to understand and endure the imminent future" had been sown and that God would provide the climate in which the crop could grow. Remarkable changes recently in so many parts of the world should encourage us about the Church itself.

In saying all this, Rahner was certainly not suggesting that we sit back and wait. It is up to all Christians to counter caution with boldness and new ways of cooperating. It is up to us to counter fear of our own courage with trust that generosity of spirit and the accompanying daring are part of the following of Christ. To us it belongs to demonstrate that the teachings and spirit of the earlier decade can produce a more catholic (the word means broad, comprehensive) Christianity. Much more can and will be done for the reunion of Christians over coffee or at a barbecue or by our daily working together than by official decisions and meetings. "Hope in him, hold firm and take heart. Hope in the Lord!" (Ps (26) 27:14).

September 2

The important among us (that really doesn't leave any of us out, does it?) often gravitate to the VIPs in the world. We feel that our talents and abilities are better used "cultivating" influential people or being sure they know we exist. The spirit and practice of our society encourage this. But, as so often happens, a look at Jesus' attitude and practice puts a question mark after ours.

The little ones, he tells us, have angels who are before God all the time (Matt 18:10). In other words, the humble, the unimportant, are the objects of God's special love. In a number of parables Jesus speaks of God's concern for the least, the lost, the uncared for or forgotten. In his practice and especially at meals (according to Luke), to the horror of his contemporaries, the Lord associates with outcasts, the wretched, the crippled, beggars, tax collectors, those ostracized by the customs and religion of the time.

What kind of people do we avoid or consider to be just outside our consideration? Are the determining factors income, style of dress or speech, type of work? Possibly much of this is unconscious. Who are the nerds, the "unwashed" in our eyes?

To give consideration, respect, even love, more generously and broadly is to model ourselves on the life and behavior of him who told us to imitate the Father's all-embracing love: "Be merciful as your heavenly father is merciful" (Luke 6:36). God lets the rain fall and the sun shine equally; God's love makes no distinctions. The love and consideration Jesus gave to outcasts and despised should console those of us who have to admit that we just aren't very important, may not even be "in" this season or any season.

Finally, Jesus' teaching is that everyone, each of us, is important to the Father: "You are worth more than the birds." Trust in God for your worth, your value, for full appreciation. And if all are so important, so valuable to God, who are we to undervalue or, worse, degrade or despise any of this creation, ourselves included?

September 3

Before the prince or princess of our dreams comes, there needs to be some experience of what is being offered these days in the way of princes and princesses. It would be surprising if the first Millie or Mort we ever fell in love with turned out to be the only one for us. Similarly, the first job we get may very likely not be the only and ideal one for us. Time spent looking further afield in both cases is no waste. We don't have to live all our life in one day. Time allows grace and reflection to strengthen us and lead us to a choice that is not too quick or arbitrary but responsible.

In one sense, Adam had it easier. After ruling out panthers, pythons, and pelicans as adequate companionship for a human being, God made the woman, the only woman, Eve, not a whole crowd of them, Becky, Cindy, Carol, etc. Our situation, unlike Adam's, offers a lot more diversity and, in a sense, requires more responsibility. Adam didn't have all the options in regard to a mate nor the need to decide between something in computing or chemistry.

Choices and commitments are vital elements in every human life. They require time and reflection, may even necessitate some risk, some error, danger. At life's smorgasbord we need to saunter a bit and not be pushed into precipitous decisions by the thought of all those delicious desserts down the way. Further, we need time also because it isn't simply a matter of finding the right or perfect person or position, but of making ourselves worth finding also. Too much concern about the perfect person or position can be a way of avoiding any commitment ever. If we're ever going to make a hit, somewhere along the line we'll have to stop aiming and shoot. Eventually happiness depends upon making some decisions, giving ourselves to some commitments, choosing this kind of life, this action, or this person. Even our daily happiness and satisfaction depend on giving ourselves fully to what we have at some time promised or proposed.

September 4

To those familiar with the old Latin celebration of Mass and sacraments in the Catholic Church or even those familiar with sacred music, the Latin opening (also the title) of Psalm 130 is famous for it use in the Mass for the dead: *De profundis,* "From out of the depths." The opening two verses pleading for God's help well suit many a grieving person: "Out of the depths I cry to you, O Lord, Lord hear my voice!" And the great trust in God's forgiveness well suits any of us.

In the psalm itself "out of the depths" likely refers to some great desolation or agony and, in view of the references to forgiveness, possibly to serious moral failure, sin. We might say—I'm at my nadir, the pits; I can't get any lower, the bottom of the well. Though it is a moving and beautiful prayer, it is one that in many ways we all hope will not have to be too frequent a refrain in our prayer life. Implicit in the prayer is the recognition that we all sin and have need of forgiveness. Verse 3 says that if God were to make, as we would say, a "big deal" out of every sin, no one would go unscathed.

While the psalmist is evidently crushed by whatever has happened, we too often are crushed by our sins or failures because *we* have let *ourselves* down so badly. The psalms by their very tone teach us a sorrow for sin based on our having let *God* down.

Verses 5, 6, and 7 speak of waiting for and counting on the Lord, on God's word, and longing for the Lord. The psalmist seems to be saying that he trusts the Lord for forgiveness and hopes to see evidence of that in a change in his life, in happier days. Even apart from the context of sin, waiting for and counting on the Lord should mark the Christian anytime.

Finally the psalmist, no matter how real the agony, does not leave us in the depths, but expresses hope and trust that the Lord who is merciful will free us from all our faults. "My soul trusts in God's word. My soul waits for the Lord. . . . For with the Lord is kindness and with him is generous redemption."

September 5

"The kindness of strangers" is, unfortunately, not the whole story. There is also the ill will of strangers. I have used elsewhere that line of Tennessee Williams about how we all depend on the services of people we often do not know; how we are blessed through strangers. Apart from the occasional grouch or uncooperative personality, there are—at least for most big-city dwellers—real fears that the stranger is a threat, someone likely to harm us. Caution, if not a very real distrust and suspicion, marks many urban people as a consequence. This makes it very difficult. What can you say? What policy can you suggest? What Christian approach can there be to the real danger that many of us sense is as close as a car breakdown on a city street or in the deceptively friendly person who is out to swindle or worse?

I don't know if our Lord's words about being as simple as doves and as crafty as serpents are meant to apply here, but they seem to describe the necessary attitude. Christian trust, love, hope, willingness to see and to help bring out the best in others cannot be innocent of common sense and its judgments. This meshes with a truth that seems intrinsic to God's whole approach toward us. God's care and concern for us and for our world do not in any sense replace our own intellect and our ability to think and plan, both given by our Creator. Ordinarily our house, for instance, is going to be secured by locks and warning devices, neighborly help, not simply the trust that God loves us. We're going to be safe on the streets because of prudence and good government, not because we've been baptized. Christian trust in a loving God is never an excuse to let the city, our world, our neighborhood, go down the drain by neglecting what reason, cooperation, and prudence can provide.

September 6

While this is not by any means a book of suggestions for reform of the Church's services, I think the service can bear a little scrutiny and criticism at times. A Lutheran preacher writes of coming to a church one Sunday to preach. The opening words of the service were; "Oh Lord, we enter into thy holy place this morning conscious of all those things of which we are ashamed." He thought: "Oh Lord, is this the only way to enter the house of God? Why should we not equally well say, 'Oh Lord, we enter into thy holy place this morning astounded by all those things in which we are delighted' "? The same idea has often struck me when I've heard college students voice a complaint about how the Mass always opens with a "downer," a confession of sins and that plea for mercy. Elsewhere I read of a young lady complaining about the prayer before Communion: "Lord, I am not worthy to receive you. Say but the word and I shall be healed."

We can point out, of course, that opening the Mass with a recognition of sin is a way of asking to be cleansed by God to be fit for God's presence, the proper approach of the creature to the Creator. The prayer before Communion, too, is basically not simply an avowal of our shamefulness but a word of trust and confidence. Like the man in the Gospel who said, "Lord, I am not worthy to receive you under my roof. . . . Say but the word and my servant shall be healed" (Luke 7:6-7). Like him we express our great trust that in the Lord's coming to us we will be changed, healed.

Granted all that, there's nothing to forbid and a lot to commend our coming to worship, to church, to prayer, with a heart full of wonder and thanksgiving for all the things that delight us in our life and world. Maybe a change in attitude and mood is due even in our liturgy. Whether that's true or not, we certainly do well to begin the day, begin our prayer, our worship, with joy and delight, astonishment even, at the wonders that surround us. "This day was made by the Lord: we rejoice and are glad" ([Ps 117] 118:24).

September 7

When we speak of the hazards of wealth we mean the way we can be hindered, dragged down by our attachment to it, our search for it. And, paradoxically, it happens so often that what we possess really possesses us. Just having a lot of things ties us down, makes us less free, makes us worry and spend time trying to insure that no one walks off with them. Our freedom is limited by things; we must stay alert to keep them or, better, to make them more productive.

But it isn't just wealth or objects that possess us; it's also what we do or achieve or think we do that can chain us. We end up measuring ourselves in terms of what we accomplish.

But Jesus came to free us also from our achievements, our works, from the temptation to think that our value, if not in what we have, is in what we do. Neither what we have nor what we do is the sole measure of what it means to be a good human being. We are much more than what we have or do. Our value lies in what we are and that is, first of all, a gift. A gift we need to use and develop, certainly, but still a gift.

This was all brought home to me when college graduates were having a tough time getting jobs. By way of conversation on running into a former student, I was easily tempted to say, What are you doing these days? I soon gathered that this was really embarrassing to many and switched my question to Where are you these days? I found that this could be answered either in terms of geography (Dallas or Ottawa) or in more abstract terms ("I'm hanging loose" or "between jobs") with no embarrassment for not being the VP or a VIP. The graduate didn't have to feel he was being evaluated as a success or not in terms of what he or she had done.

All this is not to oppose our work, our achievements as part of life, an important part. Basically, the problem comes in when we no longer see them as a part of our life but as equivalent to our life, our meaning. When wealth or accomplishment are identified with the meaning of a human life we are close to a form of idolatry, putting our hope and trust in something less than God.

Our personality and our worth both exist before we work, when we are not working, and after we have finished working, have retired. We are first of all persons, created out of love by God to share and transmit God's love even apart from what we are able to acquire or accomplish. That forms the basis for our dignity as human beings, a basis for self-respect and mutual respect.

September 8

Living in the present is often perceived as the preserve of Zen Buddhists or as something foreign to the following of

Christ. Christ, it is believed, tells us to live for the future, in hope and expectation.

However, even while talking about the end of things, Jesus puts a strong emphasis on the present. He says, for instance, in the middle of one such discourse on the end: "Happy that servant whom his master discovers at work on his return" (Matt 24:46). He is blessed or happy for being discovered at work, not necessarily even at prayer or in church.

Preparing for the end, for the future, is not, in the teaching of Jesus, some specialized activity. It occurs in the faithful and generous discharge of our commitments here and now. We prepare for the future by repairing that car now, by preparing dinner or doing the laundry, studying for the test today, rehearsing for tomorrow's talk.

For us academic types, teachers and students, early September is always a new beginning. For many others it is, too, because their lives are affected by children or spouse resuming school or beginning courses. For all of us, this time of the year is as good as any time to encourage ourselves by seeing our daily work, some of it a grind, some of it exciting, as the most wonderful thing we could be doing now. The Lord asks nothing better than to find us devoted, awake, attentive, to our immediate commitments. All that should be additional motivation for us to face them, undertake them, with joy and wholeheartedness.

September 9

So often we think that we could do something better, something great even, if we were in different circumstances, living elsewhere, had a different job. And there's some truth here: There is the possibility that in a new situation (beginning college away from home, a new job and new neighborhood, etc.) we could make a radically new start and change more easily some bad old habits. But despite the relative ease of movement and change in our world, there is a real necessity that we see our responsibility and our happiness as attached to what is right before us and around us. In the Hebrew Scripture we hear the Lord telling the people: "This command which I give you is not too mysterious and far away—not up in the sky or across the sea; no, it is something very near to you" (Deut 30:11).

What God asks of us is usually not something requiring an airline reservation for Sumatra or Buenos Aires, a particular education, or some special kind of intelligence. It is something right here, close at hand. Above all, it means loving and serving those with whom we live and who surround us.

The same point is made in what seems at first glance a very unusual, strange practice: the celebration of the Lord's Supper or Mass. Looked at from the outside or in terms of the externals, it is indeed an odd rite. Someone in clothes one never sees on the street goes through some fairly odd gestures with token amounts of bread and wine, and those present receive equally small portions of the same, all the while singing and responding a bit like a chorus in a play.

But what is going on at the altar is making the same point: God's demands on us are very much in the world immediately around us. The bread and wine of the Mass signify the most ordinary food of human life (an equivalent in our day might be a hamburger and a cold drink or coffee). If Jesus himself is present to us in the celebration surrounding this very ordinary food, one of the conclusions we are to draw is that God, too, is as close as that to us. God is met and served in the circumstances, the people, the responsibilities, of daily routine.

September 10

Elsewhere in these pages you will come across suggestions to let go, to allow God to work, to be more relaxed, to trust more, to not think that everything, every movement, every task, is solely up to your strength and know-how. Well, that has to be balanced by the opposite emphasis. Somehow all of us have to learn to balance the two approaches in our life, learn to know when to use one, when to stop, when to use the other. Nothing but our own experience can actually teach us that.

In the parable about the manager who is going to be fired (Luke 16:1-12), Jesus commends the crooked manager for preparing before his dismissal for his future by getting in good with the boss' creditors. As in all parables, the story is told to make one point, not many points or to commend anything immoral. It's a bit like a detective commenting on how ingenious and clever a thief was in the way he broke into some establishment. He is not commending the thievery but marveling at the expertise. Similarly, here Jesus commends the initiative, planning, thinking of the dishonest manager, not the dishonesty. And there is plenty of space in our daily lives as Christians for more initiative, more effort, more ingenuity in following him, in cooperating with him in overcoming injustice, suffering, and oppression. If we are willing and able to put so much time, foresight, effort into our golf or tennis game or into our investment portfolio, why not into our efforts to forward the kingdom of God?

Our Lord remarks how astute the worldly are in their management of affairs and how lagging and sloppy by comparison often are the "children of light," his followers. A good thought to get us going more efficiently and energetically today at our tasks, our life as his followers. Is it time perhaps for a decision about our schedule? About when we pray? About reading and reflection on Scripture? About some further religious education? About a retreat, about some specific, neglected, long-delayed service to others? Initiative and energy generate more of the same. Let's move!

September 11

Our world is full of service. Just open the yellow pages sometime: weed control service, beauty service, leasing service, data-processing service. We're nearly drowning in service and services. But, of course, a bit of reflection shows us that while these do represent cases where someone can do something for someone else, it is usually at a price. We need to rescue the word for "religion" and think of service as something one does for another out of love and concern. Jesus said he came among us as one who serves. But granted that, there is still a need to purify the term. We all in a certain sense like the idea of service; doesn't it easily mean that we expect the world to provide help and comfort for us? Don't we often presume that mother or wife or roommate is there to pick up the dirty socks or the empty cartons as we drop them when and where convenient? We often expect others to wait, to serve; if they don't, they're just not laid back. How often do we men still presume that women are there as our natural servants? We act much of the time like dethroned royalty used to butlers and maids.

But service can be the right word for the way in which we should carry out the command to love our neighbor. All of our lives we need reminders that following Christ means not conquering others but surrendering to their service. St. Benedict in his guidebook for monasteries says that the monastery is a school of the Lord's service. Being a follower of Jesus means learning to serve God, to serve God primarily and most often by learning to help those around us. It's a school from which there is no early or easy graduation. It means working to reverse the usual egotism of our existence, imitating the teacher who demonstrated in all of his life how we can serve our neighbor.

Among Christians it shouldn't be a matter of some people learning to serve and others accepting service; there should be a lot of competition to serve. For we claim to follow, after all, one who said: "Anyone among you who aspires to greatness must serve the rest; whoever wants to rank first among you must serve the needs of all. The Son of Man himself has not come to be served but to serve" (Mark 10:35-45).

September 12

The best hours of our day and our week are spent in work. For some, retirement can't come too quickly, and real life has to wait till 5:00 P.M. or for the weekend. For others, life away from the job may be a letdown. The thought of quitting it leaves them desolate. In between there are, one hopes, those of us for whom work is perceived as having some useful purpose and also as satisfying us personally. And yet, we're ready to have a life apart from it, to appreciate vacations and time with people other than our fellow employees.

Beyond being necessary for survival, our work may be fulfilling, contribute to the world's development, help continue in some ways God's creation; it may provide necessary and good services to many others, maintain and improve the world around us. But this is one of the areas where all the best theories are most frequently inapplicable. The way our economies run, many of us must work at activities that show us so little in the way of any of these ennobling motives or purposes. If it isn't drudgery, work is often at least something that seems to have so little meaning for the individual, for me, beyond the immediate task. It requires effort, often great effort, and involves pain or weariness, at best boredom.

All the talk in Christianity about self-denial or sharing the cross may find its most obvious application in our work. If we have no choice but to go to a job that is unsatisfying, something we have to put up with, something full of annoying and difficult moments and people, something that relates little if at all to our own interests—if this is so, we have a kind of unavoidable cross like that of which Jesus speaks. He says that all who would come after him must take up their cross (Luke 9:23).

Certainly, a great part of human effort should be spent in making jobs and people match, making work more human, more satisfying. But in the meantime, rather than looking for special penances or crosses—foods to abstain from, simple pleasures to deny ourselves—we have our work to endure, to "offer up," to bear with Christ. What more selfless cross is there than the kind we cannot really avoid and which seems necessary for the good of those who depend upon us? As Christ took up *his* cross, so we often find ours in our work.

September 13

Though we are often tempted to think that our times or our decade has invented greed, already several hundred years before Christ the Hebrew prophets took after those who resented the time lost to acquiring when they observed a day of rest, the Sabbath. The prophets blasted their fellow Hebrews, who panted for a return to the meaningful (i.e., profitable) activity of the business week and pawed the ground impatiently during the quiet of the Sabbath, our Sunday. The Sabbath, after all, signified time and energy for God and for what makes us more human and adds nothing to the GNP. Even if we don't gouge and exploit others, our legitimate concern for a livelihood, can make it difficult to focus on who we are apart from our getting and spending.

Sundays ask us to put the accent on being rather than on doing or on working or even on the social whirl. Even if we don't have to work at our jobs on Sundays, our recreational activities may still be pursued with the same dogged energy. Possibly they, too, are a threat to the Sunday. But at least with these there is more probability that we can give time to the specifically human: to our choices, relationships, values, integrity, self-worth, compassion, the happiness of others.

But beyond these human but financially nonproductive activities, we should aim for time for something like reading and thinking about Scripture, for prayer. "Slow down; you move too fast." The daily lives of all of us show that these priorities (prayer, the needs of others) cannot be taken for granted. Time for the Gospel, time to see why we work and acquire, time to slow the hot pursuit of things and time to turn from, say, the latest NFL star on the tube to the needs of a suffering or lonely friend or family member.

As a beginning, let's not let Sunday pass without getting away for a few minutes from even our most decent human activities. And in that time, let's look beyond the present, beyond our needs, to being what we hope and know we should be and can be with the help of the Lord.

September 14

Some Churches, some preachers, St. Paul, too, in places, emphasize or preach a "theology of the cross." It's a heavy term for most of us who don't have much of an idea of what theology is, let alone when linked to another word. And it can sound pretty stark and forbidding. The cross itself is clear enough: For Christians it refers to the awful instrument of the death of Jesus, a crossing of two huge beams on which a man is nailed as punishment. Someone from a more psychological point of view has said that the cross in its construction symbolizes well the pains and difficulties of life. Make the vertical beam our life and its direction, our hopes, our aims, our wishes; the other beam signifies all that opposes that, goes against it, crosses it, as we say. The cross is a sign of how life and hopes are contradicted by misfortune, unhappiness, ill health, suffering. And all these are very real; we need reminders that the cross is part of any ordinary life, so much a part that I doubt we need to make a special search for it. Yet it is not right for Christians to rest in the thought of the cross as a sign of the wretchedness and misery that infect every human life. The "theology of the cross" that St. Paul preaches and, one hopes, others who claim to preach it, is full of hope and even joy. Paul sees in it the extreme extent of God's love for us; his love will stop at nothing in an effort to be made clear to us. It "shows God's commitment to humankind; he is indeed a God bent on the salvation of humankind" (*Dictionary of Theology*, pp. 92–93).

Too often in Christian practice, emphasis on the cross has meant—as in some of those interminable and dreary Good Fridays—that we must feel wretched and miserable. No, the cross is not the end in the teaching and work of Jesus. It is meant to point to God's love for us, the extremes he will go to in order to save us, to deliver us. Like the early Christians we should see the cross as filled with hope and promise; they even went so far as to make crosses studded with precious gems as signs of glory, victory, happiness, joy. Why shouldn't we also?

September 15

Judging from my own experience, I would guess that most of us are susceptible to the mood-changing influence of music.

We may use it that way with happy results. In the middle of Psalm 27 is a positive and musical phrase that sets the jubilant, confident tone of the whole psalm: "I will sing and make music to the Lord" (v. 6). Facing enemies, false witnesses, an army, the author expresses the strongest confidence: "Though an army encamp against me, my heart will not fear; Though war be waged upon me, even then will I trust" (v. 3). The Lord, he says, "will hide me in his abode in the day of trouble" (v. 5).

In words taken from human relationships and applied to God (what else can we do?) the psalmist prays: "O Lord, . . . Hide not your face from me; forsake me not" (v. 9). We may feel the same way; feel surrounded by hostile forces, impossible tasks, depressing duties, heavy burdens. We may cry out: Don't abandon me now! Throughout the psalm, despite the author's insistence that God remain faithful, is the strong confidence that God is absolutely dependable. "Though my father and mother forsake me, yet will the Lord receive me" (v. 10). As if to say: Impossible as it may be that father or mother should ever forsake me, still, you Lord, are even more faithful, more sure, always there.

But surrounding this are clear, forceful statements of trust: "The Lord is my light and my salvation; whom should I fear? The Lord is my life's refuge; of whom should I be afraid?" And the final verse: "I believe that I shall see the bounty of the Lord in the land of the living. Wait for the Lord with courage; be stouthearted, and wait for the Lord" (vv. 13–14). If the psalmist says in the middle "I will sing and chant praise to the Lord," we have here the text of that song and one that we could easily make ours.

"The Lord is my light and my salvation; whom should I fear? . . . I believe I shall see the bounty of the Lord in the land of the living. Wait for the Lord with courage; be stouthearted, and wait for the Lord."

September 16

In Psalm 8 the writer, seeing the grandeur of the heavens, the moon and the stars, remarks on how extraordinary it is that

God still has thought for such frail creatures as ourselves. "Who are we that you should be mindful of us . . . that you should care for us." For some, of course, it is primarily a philosophical problem. They ask themselves, Is it really possible that the God who has set in order this vast creation should have any concern about what you or I do, bits of sand on a planet on the edge of a galaxy being whirled through this vast universe? From the purely human standpoint it does pose a problem.

Yet for the believer there is the assurance from God in Scripture that God is concerned with the least of creation, that, in exaggerated terms, God has numbered each hair of our heads. There is no real Christian belief without the conviction that God is concerned about me, about us, and does care. The history of believers from Abraham through Jesus and his followers is very much a recounting of how they felt or experienced the hand of God in everything, from deliverance from slavery to resurrection from death. The believer does believe that it is remarkable, wonderful, incredible but true, that God does see my tears and hear my cries, knows my pain and intuits my unspoken and almost unspeakable longings as no one else can.

We probably have our best evidence of God's love in the undeserved and unimaginable love all of us have experienced from parents, families, friends, a love that we generally in no way have caused but that is freely given. Our thought often should be, Why do they keep me in mind (send me letters, call me, check on my feelings), visit me when I'm sick, cheer me when I'm down? Who am I to deserve such a gift? What can I do in thanksgiving?

September 17

"If everybody contemplates the infinite instead of fixing the drains, many of us will die of cholera" (John Rich). There may be little danger of too many of us "contemplating the infinite," that is, devoting all our time to meditating on or thinking about God. More often, we regard ourselves as useful and productive only insofar as we *do* fix the drains, master the computer, or attend meetings.

Yet the temptation does cross the mind of serious followers of Christ that they should give more of their life and time simply to prayer. Hardly anyone would dispute this. And in the story of Martha and Mary in Luke (10:38-42), Jesus seems to commend Mary for sitting at his feet and listening to him rather than preparing the salad and meat in the kitchen. As if to emphasize this difficult and critical balance between active and prayerful life, Christ in the same chapter defines the neighbor as the one who does something for the man beaten by robbers.

Today, let us think for a moment about just one side of this issue: that we should not let prayer and meditation take the place of or hinder our genuine responsibilities to others and to our world. For most of us—and it is for these I write—life must be a mixture of prayer and action with the action necessarily taking more of our time since our livelihood and that of a family depend on it. Prayer and reflection should fortify and strengthen that activity, provide its foundation and inspiration, without reducing our commitment to it.

The drains, the garbage, the streets, the meals of the children, exercise, taxes, keeping up our friendships—all these must be given attention. Or cholera, chaos, and confusion do lurk around the corner. Put another way, "A man gazing at the stars is proverbially at the mercy of the puddles in the road" (Alexander Smith).

September 18

In these pages you will come across some warnings against nostalgia or the view that everything good has already happened in our lives, in our world. "Those were the days, my friends . . ." But as with almost any truth, Christian or otherwise, there are always several aspects. The past has much to say to us.

Recalling the past need not just hobble the present or put us in a dream world that makes no demands. On the contrary, recalling with appreciation the wonderful people in our lives, the grace-filled events or happenings, can give us renewed hope and courage for the present and the future.

Stuck in a movie theatre once, much too early for the film (and being in a rather mellow mood), I spent my time in a sort of silent prayer of thankfulness, thinking of all the lovely people and happy circumstances that I had encountered in my life and career. Any of us could take a bit of time and try the same: Thanks, Lord, for letting me know Jake, always so positive and generous: what an inspiration and encouragement. Thanks for Tom, such a wonderful combination of tenderness and strength, so justly proud and snappy and at the same time so sensitive and willing even to shed a tear, to show genuine love to his friends. Thanks for Kate, so thoughtful of anniversaries, birthdays, moods; so ready to think of surprises and events for others. Thanks for work where I can be both satisfied regarding my abilities and able to do something useful for others. Thanks for a mother so faithful and loving of the Catholic tradition and so happy to see the Church move toward other Christians; thanks for a father so critical of religion. Thanks for life among college students for so many years, always surprised by their mischievous inventiveness, their bouncy sense of humor, their fresh attitude toward life, their infinite hopefulness.

You can do your own list. Recalling the blessings of the past, of friends and situations, can drive us to use the present better, to sense a need to return to the world and those around us some of the good we have received.

September 19

"The tidal wave of grief that followed the murder of John Lennon on Dec. 8, 1980, flowed from several sources. Perhaps the most gaping of these was the shocking obliteration of a decade's worth of hope. Millions woke one morning bleak with the promise of winter to learn that now the Beatles could never get back together, that the expansive spirit of the '60s had definitively expired ten years past its prime" (*TIME*, book review by Paul Gray, September 12, 1988).

Human beings, extraordinary and famous like John Lennon, John F. Kennedy, Dag Hammarsköld, give us hope or, better, serve as signs, vehicles of the hope that comes from the one unfailing source and ground of hope, God. A Christian may be a bit defensive about hope being so centered on one human being or even a human movement, yet ordinarily and for the most part, our hope is going to be made flesh, situated, made real and present, for us in human beings and their works and words. That's the way God works, remember? To get across the message of hope most completely, God chose to have Jesus become one of us and shine on this earth in human form for some thirty years.

Seeing our hope made present in others, in human movements is partly a matter of walking the line between idolatry and simply seeing them as means used by God for our encouragement.

Hope comes to us first, probably, from encouraging and trustworthy parents, then loved and admired teachers, friends who pat us on the back, bolster us on bad days, revive our drooping spirits, encourage our talents. We shouldn't fear to accept the hope given or offered by human movements and persons. But at the same time we must recognize their frailty and that the final support, the reason for our hope, cannot be some soon-to-disappear human being or movement or "a decade's worth of hope," but the author and source of all their gifts and inspiration, God in Jesus Christ.

September 20

The kingdom of God is like a wedding banquet, not a wake! Jesus used many images for the kingdom: treasure, pearl, city on a hill, salt, lamp, leaven, field. But he never compares it to a prison, an army, a crusade, a concentration camp, an exclusive club, or even a dormitory. It's a feast we're called to, not a funeral; a party, not a purgatory. A supper we're offered, not a subpoena; a banquet, not a burden. In Scripture it's apparent that God can think of nothing more descriptive of the joy that should flow from God's limitless love and hospitality than a great dinner, a glorious celebration open to all. We're supposed to think of the sounds and sights that meet us as we come off the street to a wedding reception: music, laughter, lighthearted talk, a lot of people looking their radiant best with smiles enough to make power plants obsolete. Jesus himself, in St. John's Gospel, begins his public career by adding to the effervescence of just such a wedding, that at Cana. The same John pictures Jesus after the resurrection having brunch alfresco with Peter and the disciples on the shores of a lake.

But let's face it. So often Christians give the impression of being sentenced to Christian life and faith rather than blessed with it. Where's the joy and generosity, the freedom and expansiveness? Too often it looks like a grim duty, painful obligation, an irksome millstone, a dogged battle. If it's a banquet, why do we so often take our place at the table as if in an electric chair? Instead of a festive supper, we seem to view Christian life so often as life in a dismal barracks, hemmed in by a thousand regulations. Karl Rahner says that one often gets the impression that Christian life exists when a person respects certain laws or norms, moral, cultural, or ecclesiastical. What a cramped view! Jesus calls us to a banquet, an Oktoberfest, a homecoming, and we treat it like a briefing by the warden or an appearance in traffic court.

But the kingdom of God, the banquet we're called to, asks a personal decision, a response that is not identical with a set of rules but is rather a call to a more sensitive conscience. The implications of my following the Lord are never satisfied, whereas I can know very well when I have fulfilled some law. Unnecessary rules give us a false sense of security and a grim-faced religion!

Let's not fall into that trap. When someone asks what it means to be a Christian, the answer is not, A Christian must . . . a Christian has to . . . a Christian is obligated to. On the contrary, a Christian is one who has accepted an invitation to a life and faith, an invitation to appreciate the goodness and beauty of creation, of the world and God. Murder, hatred, exploitation, deception, jealousy, injustice, insincerity, war, racism, prejudice are all sin because they prevent that celebration, prevent us from being hospitable and friendly to the person sitting next to us.

"The Christian is one who believes that life is essentially a call to celebration, a banquet, not a wake. . . . Confidence and joy should flood everything. . . . Christians should be marked by enthusiasm, interest, faithfulness, even a bit of craziness and humor," not by grimness.

September 21

Seriousness is more dignified than just being congenial or, worse, a bit light or humorous. As someone has said: You never see a picture of Abraham Lincoln grinning. Our national heroes must *look* like weighty men. It's unfortunately all too true that along with a suit and tie for us men, a tense, headlong look guarantees that others will know we're important and that if our jaw were not set so firmly, the world might stop revolving. Our chances of getting that loan from the bank are immeasurably helped by businesslike dress, in fact, by looking as if we didn't need the loan. Otherwise we are presumed to be irresponsible. In many ways, seriousness and conventionality are cheap ways to respect. It seems that we have to play this game. But let's not take the game too seriously; let's keep in mind that it is a game and that in a more ideal world it wouldn't be necessary.

As a step toward that better world, the realization of the kingdom of God here and now, we need to forget ourselves a bit, to take ourselves more lightly. In this way we allow some room for God to act in us. If we aim at the illusion of absolute control and self-determination, we pretty well exclude God's action.

Taking ourselves lightly is really much better than taking ourselves so seriously. This is no invitation to flippancy or an easy cop-out. For it's tough for us even to laugh off petty things. We all have our lists of concerns and matters that cannot be joked about: our politics, our schedule, our taste in food, our favorite team, and so forth. Just being awakened at two in the morning by noisy neighbors can require more patience and perspective than most of us have. What is being recommended here is very demanding even though it may not gain us much publicity. We're noticed more when we file a lawsuit, throw a tantrum or our weight around than when we ignore an insult or a slight.

Being willing to pass over imagined and real injuries, to think more of others' problems and pains, to really forget ourselves, is like taking ourselves with some humor—lightly.

September 22

Some days, even some hours, we do rightly feel that to have survived is an accomplishment. Today will be such for a young businessman I talked with last night. He has to evaluate others' work and give reports; one of them today will have to be unfavorable. He will be the target of heat and resentment. May the day pass quickly. Basically to survive our days in general without becoming bitter, resentful, continuously angry, is an achievement. Most of us do not need to look for more exotic challenges. To face the life before us with its warts and pimples, its pains and pettiness, and to do that with some grace and gentleness is a high accomplishment. (If I'm not saying enough for you, drop this book and go out and buy one of those drugstore paperbacks that tells you How To Set the World on Fire in Five Easy Lessons.) You sense the accomplishment in these small things when you run across in the indifferent haste of a big city the pleasant, helpful, friendly, maybe even respectful salesperson or bureaucrat. We're all—unfortunately—surprised at meeting these individuals.

And to answer queries all day long and still maintain some civility and patience is an accomplishment. At a big railway station in a large European city I recently witnessed a woman asking the man in the information booth for information on something the railway just did not provide or do; he explained that very pleasantly. She was disappointed. To my surprise, a few minutes later, she stopped by to compliment him on his civility and pleasantness. And rightly so.

We may not need to compliment ourselves or pat ourselves on our back—that's best left to others—but deep down we should realize that doing what we must day by day with fidelity and the best spirit we can muster is an accomplishment. As the infamous Jim Jones said, with more truth than he knew, encouraging his nine hundred followers to drink the poisoned potion: "It's hard only at first. *Living is much, much more difficult.*"

September 23

The list we call the Beatitudes (Matt 5:3-12)—Blessed are they who mourn, who hunger, who are merciful—represents such high ideals that most of us specialize in one or the other. If we think we're pretty great at being clean of heart, we may not be terribly meek about it. Since we are so selective in this I propose to be selective, too, and limit myself to one facet of "Blessed are they who mourn, for they will be comforted."

Think of how half-hearted and dull we can be at worship and how grumpy we can be in the corridor or the workplace. Sometimes you'd think this beatitude was more of an eleventh commandment: Thou *shalt mourn*. Or an extra beatitude: "Blessed are the grouchy, the grumpy, the gloomy and glum." Wouldn't it be a great step on life's path if we could show more joy, enthusiasm, unforced generosity in our service of God and others?

If we believe even half the teachings about Jesus, we have sufficient reasons to lighten up a bit, to present the following of Christ as something downright attractive. We know that God loves us; God is not some sore-head waiting to pounce on us. We know that the Lord, brought down to the sorrow of a dreadful death, was raised again with the promise that we, too, can rise not only from sin and death, but *here and now* from self-pity and pettiness, from laziness and boredom, from indifference and envy. We have every reason for hope, joy, confidence, trust, even a smile, some laughter.

"Blessed are they who mourn, for they will be comforted." Surely; definitely. And the occasion for mourning, for sorrow, *will come;* none of us needs to go looking for it or practice a sad face and grim behavior. We will, sometime or other, be driven to real sorrow, to tears: a parent will die, a friend will be maimed in an accident, someone we have loved and trusted will prove disappointing . . . Mourning and sorrow will come.

In the meantime, why spoil our youth, the present, the lives of family and friends, our great opportunities by moaning about everything, pitying our generally comfortable, middle-class selves when our present sorrows are often no more serious than cold vegetables, a cloudy day, having our sacred routine interrupted, or being unable to afford designer jeans. At times we tend to think too easily that we are among the blessed who are insulted and persecuted when really we're just touchy and self-pitying. Why not counteract gloomy days and hypersensitive people with more easy smiles, joy built on faith, and offset the seriousness of our work and duties with laughter and humor? Blessed are they who rejoice and are glad for they bring joy, comfort, hope and strength to all the rest of us.

September 24

A beautiful, sunny, mild day in the fall after a week or more of gray, dismal days. (If this doesn't fit the day on which you're reading this, jump to another and keep this for an appropriate day.) Certainly a reason for being happy, contented, thankful. Being thankful for the good is surely no refusal of the bad or painful that will inevitably come. But we do not have to put them on the same level, nor do we have to claim that we are indifferent, despite what may have appeared in some religious writing. Jesus came to do away with evil, suffering, death, probably even depressing days or weather. He spent much of his time giving suffering and illness a knockout blow. The idea that Christians should love, pursue, or especially value what is painful and difficult is inconsistent with biblical teaching, the teaching of Jesus.

Christians have to learn more to rejoice unabashedly in what is good. It's what God intended to begin with, as Genesis tells us. To cry out in revolt or pain against suffering and evil is the decent response to something so contrary to God's design.

Rejoice in the beautiful days, the lovely things, the radiant, kind, handsome people that surround us. They reflect clearly the God who loves us, and they are among the many reasons we have for loving God. Why should we picture God as someone who has it in for us or who rejoices in giving us a hard time? This is one of a number of inconsistencies in many views of God. For some reason, we often bend over backward trying to see even the bad and unpleasant as coming from God.

It's a refreshing, sunny day; why not simply be very happy about it and hoard some of that brightness in our heart for the days that follow? Christians are meant, like the Savior himself, to counter evil and pain—even miserable gray days—with some joy and generosity.

September 25

Despite the awful exceptions that appear in the media, most human beings seem enraptured, awed, lifted by the beauty, softness (that velvety skin!), and mystery of babies. As the young father who called last night from across the Atlantic to tell me of the birth of his first child said, reaching for words: "It's hard to believe." We think: What are they thinking? Are they? Those big, beautiful eyes, spontaneous and random movements; do they mean anything? What's going on? Bring a little toddler, just able to walk, or even a slightly older mischief-making bundle of energy into a dormitory of nineteen-year-old boys/men (all very conscious of how macho they must be), and they are transformed, one would almost say liquified, into worshipers. Entranced, intrigued, fascinated by this form of life, everything else is dropped, forgotten, at least momentarily.

There are at least two kinds of awe present: (1) our awe at them, our sense of the mystery at the human being growing from this beautiful beginning, messy as it may be at times, and (2) their apparent awe or wonder at all around them, their sense of discovery, sometimes of fear, at all the new things, people.

Our awe and wonder, their awe and wonder—that should somehow be kept. How it livens and brightens our lives when we have it; how deadened things are when everything provokes a yawn of déjà vu in us. We need more appreciation. Abraham Heschel points out that really what we need—not what we are being given—is not more information (who can use all we have?) but more appreciation, more reverence, wonder, even excitement, before what is.

Heschel speaks of the need to contemplate, appreciate the uniqueness, the irreplaceability of this moment, of this person, every person. I'm sure we can move toward that by thinking more often of it. As he says, maybe a mantra, a motto for the day, for many days, might be, "What was shall not be again." What we see, experience, the people we meet, the event before us, this will never happen, they will never be again in the same way. How wonderful, how rich!

September 26

For many of our contemporaries the primary feeling in facing the universe is one of isolation, lostness, even loneliness. We seem to be in a universe that is basically indifferent to us, to our aspirations and hopes (catastrophes and horror seem to be distributed impartially). It seems cold and silent in the face of our questioning and our fears, unmoved by any hope we may have. We are left, at most, to put arbitrarily some meaning into it. We seem, in the scientific view of many, to be an accident thrown up by ages of cosmic turmoil and change. One conclusion may be that it is everyone for himself or herself; hence, possibly, some of the rawness of the struggle around us.

What Christians call God's revelation is the belief that in various ways over the centuries but above all in Jesus Christ, God has broken that silence to give us a Word, a Word of promise and encouragement, a light shining in the darkness. What God has given us is not a blueprint making science, technology, philosophy, and human thought irrelevant but a promise that we are not alone and that the universe and all of us in it are on the way to fulfillment.

In the Son of God, his life, words, death, and rising, we have given to us for our hope and our spirit, a model of the promise of God for us, a promise of final overcoming of pain, separation, disappointment, injustice, and death.

This is all meant to sustain us as we live our lives, do our work, and love our friends. But for most us it can do little of that without more reflection on and thought of the risen Christ and his promise. Further, it can do nothing for others around us lost in the darkness of an indifferent universe unless we are more often inspired by it. The Lord is our strength, our song, our Savior, but this only becomes apparent and effective when he is a stronger part of our consciousness.

September 27

"Loss is a part of life—of being alive—of being human." Loss of family members, friends, associates. Not loss as the opposite of gain or success. That's another topic. And I write as a professional loser: a professor at a small college where one gets to know many students, some of them quite well, and then must see them leave after four years at the most, some earlier. Some, I will see again and again, possibly for many, many years. Others, never. Others maybe twenty-five years later for a brief moment at a homecoming or by chance in a city street. "Born to lose."

Parents often "lose" their children, too; just their leaving home and going on their own must be a wrenching experience after eighteen or twenty years of loving care and watching them grow. Or we lose, worst of all probably, friends and family members at what we call an "unexpected" age, at a time when we hoped to have them with us for years to come, through death, accident, suffering, mental illness, or simply through the demands of employment that takes them to Saudi Arabia while we remain in Newport. When it concerns our family members or close friends, any age is an inappropriate age to lose them. As we grow older, the tendency to read the obituaries grows—rightly, in many ways; after all, the names we read there are the people we grew up with or knew for many years. We're surrounded by loss.

The Christian needs to have the faith and trust that those whom we cannot follow, for whom we can do nothing, with whom we cannot even talk, are also in the care of the great Lover, of God, of the Lord. It is certainly a good form of remembrance, something much better than just nostalgia or sentimental grieving, to keep them in prayer to God daily, to lovingly remember them, their graces and goodness to us, even their quirks and traits, to keep their memory fresh along with our hope. We could be overwhelmed with gratitude sometimes if we sat down and thought of all the great people who have helped us over the years.

September 28

I think music is one of the most powerful creations of human beings, one of the inventions, if that's the term, that can do so much for so many of us, our happiness, for human life, for raising it above a simple struggle for food and shelter. Even those for whom this struggle is so bitter and all-consuming are often remarkable for the vitality and strength of their music.

Religion, the Church, has made great use of music, and even apart from strictly sacred or religious music, music serves a great function for the human spirit. It can soothe our spirits, excite them, help recall great moments, inspire us, energize us, lift us from a bad mood. And why not? If God does most of God's activity in this world only with and through our help, our work, our smiles, our good words, why not through our music and dance? Music and dance are "luxuries" that do a lot for many of us. Without them, we would be much worse ogres than we are.

The very last of the psalms is a hymn to the importance of music. The psalms themselves are meant to be songs, most likely accompanied by some instrument. Appropriately, therefore, they sing the joy and the use of music to praise God. The author sees music and the sounds of instruments used to praise God as part of all the praise that creation itself gives God by growing and being:

> Praise the Lord in his sanctuary, . . .
> Praise him with the blast of trumpet,
> > praise him with lyre and harp,
> Praise him with timbrel and dance,
> > praise him with strings and pipe.
> Praise him with sounding cymbals,
> > praise him with clanging cymbals.
> Let everything that has breath
> > praise the Lord! Alleluia.

September 29

In a novel I read years ago, a character dying in sordid and easily misunderstood circumstances says, "What does it matter? Grace is everywhere." The words have application not only in extreme circumstances but in the very ordinary, too. We shouldn't be too snooty about where our inspiration or encouragement comes from. God, who chose to bring victory and grace out of a kind of death considered disgraceful, can use all of human life to come to us. If something seemingly as unimportant as a song, a refrain, even merely a melody, helps us keep alive in ourselves and in our daily behavior a kind of hope or joy or peace, why not use it? The only mantras, phrases for meditation, aren't lines from Scripture.

Humming or carrying in my head the whole day a melody that comes from almost anywhere, bluegrass to rock to Mozart, may give me a lift, help me rebuff some of the more unpleasant possibilities of the day. Why not? Not everything that inspires me to a more generous or joyful life has to be a doctrine of the

Christian Church or a verse of the Bible. As I write this I find myself on a schedule where, after a brisk hike, I catch a radio program playing as its sign-off a fetching song by Louis Armstrong, "I see skies of blue, clouds of white, the bright blessed day . . . and I think to myself, what a wonderful world." Even when the skies aren't blue or the day is heavy with disappointment or confrontation, I'm reminded of the other side of things.

Over the centuries the Church with more or less success has tried to put to music the words and phrases of the Bible that sum up God's love for us and our gratitude and hope. Why not accept the same wherever it comes from and use it to make our life and the lives of those around us more joyous, generous, satisfying?

"Grace is everywhere" if only we let ourselves look everywhere and not just to the Church or the prayer book or the Bible.

September 30

Reforms in religion often mean simply stripping away useless complications in our relation to God, elaborate ceremonies, excessive regulations. Our prayer to God hasn't been spared this kind of complication. It often is treated as if it were some very specialized activity. We hear that we should practice a certain mode of meditation, follow different steps in the ladder of prayer, possibly even follow prescribed physical exercises. Much of this represents an option available in both Eastern and Western religion, but hardly a demand of the Lord. As so often our vision is cleared up and the world of religion touches human life more directly when we look at the Gospels. One can't help but wonder whether the insistence on these so-called higher forms of prayer hasn't actually destroyed prayer for many or made it seem as accessible as a second BMW or January on the Riviera.

Most of us would benefit immeasurably and give our life in Christ more realism if we would follow the directives of the New Testament, few as they are. There we are told nothing about methods, stages, or levels of prayer. Rather, we are told to speak to God: to express our faith or doubt, hope or discouragement, love or repentance, our thanksgiving and hurt, praise and petition. The Our Father models much of this for us, and elsewhere in Christ's teaching we are encouraged to be persevering, trusting, and accepting of God's will in our prayer. Not only the words of Jesus in the Our Father and various parables but his praying before important decisions and moments teach us.

Every day should have a moment—probably before sleeping or on rising—when we do these things: ask, forgive, praise, repent, express all that is important to us and our lives. The words of the Our Father were probably given us more as a model of priorities in prayer than as a formula to be memorized. We need to avoid letting our prayer be a matter of memorization. We can avoid that by putting before God, simply and directly, concrete requests or aspirations: Help Anne in her worries; be with Harry in this time after his marriage has broken up; strengthen Helen and me to be more patient with Jim; I thank you for all that Mike has meant to me. This provides for the genuine communication that any living relationship needs.

Before concerning ourselves with more fashionable and "advanced" forms of prayer, we should get habituated to this daily addressing God about our own lives, worries, relationships, work, hope, joys, and disappointments.

October 1

"Alleluia! I love the Lord for he has heard my voice" Psalm (116). The psalm that begins this way has the double beauty of being applicable anytime for the Christian and of being appropriate to more particular moments. We can all use it as a hymn of thanksgiving for what we have in Christ, for the hope we have, for all the signs of it in our personal lives and the world around us. The author starts out in a high mood and stays on that level:

> Alleluia!
> I love the Lord because he has heard my voice. . . .
> Because he inclined his ear to me the day I called.

The third verse summarizes in more detail what Christians believe the Lord has done for them. He has delivered us from "the cords of death," "the snare of the nether world," distress and sorrow. "Gracious is the Lord and just; yes, our God is merciful. . . . I was brought low, and he saved me" (vv. 5-6).

Even apart from this more complete and final picture of what the Lord has done and for which we are grateful, the psalm can be a help to expressing our gratitude in particular instances: recovery from serious illness, deliverance from a dangerous situation, from a loss of faith and hope, from misunderstanding, despair, hard times. We can name our own.

Especially, the psalm expresses gratitude for God's response to our prayers: "Because he has inclined his ear to me the day I called." The Lord has been gracious. Simple thoughts and words that should express increasingly our own attitude, as we reflect with faith on our life.

"For he has freed my soul from death, my eyes from tears, my feet from stumbling. I shall walk before the Lord in the land of the living" (vv. 8-9). I will try to remember this God who has been so good to me. Alleluia!

October 2

We only see what we expect to see. And there certainly is no assurance that what we expect to see is identical with all that is actually out there. Apart from whatever else faith is—and like any decent bit of reality it has more than one meaning—faith is a way of seeing. It leads us to expect to see more. The Letter to the Hebrews (11:1) says that faith makes us certain of realities we do not see—at least not with the standard brown, blue, green, or gray orbs.

Realities we do not see: God's presence, God's gifts in the world and in people around us—often their goodness, simplicity, freshness and depth, strength and gentleness; their sufferings, fears, and worries. The beings we call angels are reminders, representations of the richness around us, and of all God's gifts we so often miss.

Faith enables us to see more than what can be measured or weighed, or conceived by reason or imagination. But besides that, faith is also a conscious choice on our part, a decision to look for the signs and hints of God in our world and life. It is correct, faith tells us, to see the divine reflected in our world, to interpret experience from that vantage point—gullible and quaint as it may seem to nonbelievers.

So often, either in word or attitude, we accuse reality of being stale, dull, dreary, empty. Isn't this partly due, at least, to the nonexercise of faith as much as to anything else? These thoughts always remind me of words of Francis Thompson in "The Kingdom of God." One verse is especially fitting:

> The angels keep their ancient places—
> Turn but a stone, and start a wing!
> 'Tis you, 'tis your estranged faces,
> That miss the many-splendoured thing.

October 3

A line that has remained in my mind ever since reading it years ago is Alexander Pope's "Hope springs eternal in the human breast." In periods of pessimism or discouragement it has been like a prayer or a reminder that these days are not the definitive ones; that there will be again or there are, even now in the midst of this discouragement, reasons to hope. In fact, just continuing with life and work and relationships is itself a kind of hope. Otherwise, why bother? But it also strikes me as true that worries, too, spring eternal in the human breast. When one worry gives way to resolution or something better, or proves groundless or misplaced, there are always new ones queuing up, waiting their turn to take over, to furrow the brow. One worry goes, and the place of worry apparently abhors a vacuum; new ones come. We stop worrying about our health because it has proved to be okay and we start worrying about son Tom or daughter Cathy, or the review coming up, or taxes and bills, or plans for a visit. We get the car fixed and then know we can always worry about that new garbage disposal we have installed. The worry over son Jim's progress in math goes away to be replaced by a worry about the people he's with tonight.

We try all the remedies, sometimes with little result; we go out and play a game of tennis or handball, cut the grass, listen to music, ask someone else how their life is going, visit a sick friend. Sometimes these things help, at least the effort is worth it.

We certainly should not shortchange all the interim remedies we may try and find helpful for banishing worry, but fundamentally we need to reflect and pray more that our hope and trust grow more real, more profound. Ultimately, they have to be deeper and more firmly rooted than our worries to outlast and even help dissipate the latter.

"God is my refuge and strength, my helper close at hand. In time of distress I shall not fear even though the earth rocks and the waters rage and foam. . . . The Lord is with me" (paraphrase of Ps 46:2-4).

October 4

Grandmothers and many a host at a meal are famous for such lines as "You're hardly eating" (to someone who has already had about twice what he or she usually eats) or, "Is that all? Have some more." This insistence, so hard on the waistline and at times intimidating, comes ordinarily, one can safely guess, as a sign of love and care. The same people will offer a "little something" for your trip, a little something that is many times more than what an inactive person sitting in an auto really needs. But love has its own logic.

The Eucharist is rooted in a similar idea, that eating a meal together signifies friendship, love, community, good will.

Though somewhat lessened by instant fast food, and the difficulty of getting a family together for a meal, the idea is still strong. We celebrate great occasions of love and friendship with anything from an intimate dinner for two or more to a huge banquet for the whole Democratic party. In the Middle East where our Lord lived and taught and ate the Last Supper with his friends, a shared meal was the essence of hospitality and brought with it solemn obligations to ensure that no harm came to one's guests. Much of this has a vague or taken-for-granted character in many of our meals, too, but it would help our celebration of the Body and Blood of the Lord if we recalled more often that we are there as a sign of our unity in Christ, to strengthen and reaffirm it.

The peace greeting, an ancient custom, is a great opportunity to make this real. *But* we need to extend that greeting, that peace and love, to someone besides those with whom we came. We can greet and kiss them anytime. It's meant to extend our love to strangers, to other neighbors not so well known. We don't need a church service to kiss husband, wife, or boyfriend, but we do need such encouragement to greet and show good will to the others who form with us one body in Christ.

We need to bring more of this attitude to our celebration of the Lord's Supper and take more *away* from it. The effectiveness of our shared meal in church appears in our determination to extend our good will to those we meet outside the church.

October 5

A young friend, nearing thirty, writes that "my wisdom is still too rough around the edges for publication." The same caution about what he has learned at college, in travel around the world with the Marines, and in a position with a large corporation appears toward the end of the letter. He says, "When my college friends and I get together once a year we play a lot of sports, have serious discussions, tell stories, and, in general, realize that we are still as dumb as we used to be but better dressed." I like that. It's a pleasant contrast to our tendency to be "too sure too soon about too many things." In reality, we may be able to spend more on our wardrobe, but the mysteries remain; we're as "dumb," as mystified, as ever.

Living with some uncertainty about life is more realistic and healthy than claiming too soon to understand and comprehend—worse yet, "see through"—everything. Life is a bit like the tormented young Hamlet in Shakespeare's play who objects to anyone supposing to know his problems any better than he does, to know "his stops," and to be able to play him like a musical instrument. Most of us feel the same way when faced with the manipulator or counselor who claims to know us so well, the salesperson who tells us what kind of jacket we need by reason of a few prying questions. Both we and life are more complicated, more complex; neither easily gives up all its secrets.

Everyday we face a world and life that may look an awful lot like yesterday's, but let's recall how much mystery there still is in it, how different today is, how many things we do not completely understand, how many questions life still poses, how much we and others should be allowed some inscrutability. Facing that uncertainty and lack of clarity, even some confusion, is good ground for more trust and confidence where it should be, in the Lord who is "the way, the truth, the life." Following the Lord does not mean *knowing* all the answers but trusting him to bring us to peace and contentment, no matter how little we see or understand.

October 6

In some of the current debates over how God should be spoken of, as he or she, father or mother, there is sometimes voiced the idea that we could solve all that by calling God "it" and avoid giving offense to either gender. Scripture itself speaks often, of course, of God as Father or he or in masculine characterization, king, shepherd, Lord, even warrior. It also speaks of

God caring for the people like a mother or looking for the lost individual like the woman looking for her missing coin. Probably in the society of Jesus' time, it would have been unlikely to call God by anything but masculine terms. Jesus tells us to call God our Father in the prayer of the same name. In fact, strictly speaking, according to specialists, the word Jesus used for God is not "father" but more like "daddy." In attempting to speak of God, a reality beyond our language or comprehension, Scripture reaches for expressions of all kinds. Impersonal terms are used for God, too: He is called rock, fortress, and shield, for instance. These terms have the advantage of expressing well the notion of enduring strength or dependability, protection.

But before we are tempted by the idea of "it" for God (as in it saved me; it loves me) as a solution to the often sharp disputes about sexism in regard to God, we should at least see what insight is contained in calling God Father. It means we think of God as a person, think of God as having in some way the qualities we revere and honor in persons: knowledge, the ability to respond to others, accountability, ability to care and love, to feel with, to sympathize. An "it" can do none of these, it just is. It is unresponsive, impersonal, removed, unmoved, incapable of being moved except by a tractor or an earthmover. We should be happy in the revelation given us that God does have—no matter how much more magnified—the qualities we prize in human relationships, the qualities of a person. Further, "father" itself is not at all to distinguish God from a mother but to denote the ideal qualities of that parent—strength, security, loving care.

Whether we think of God as male or female is a quibble compared to the difference between thinking of God as personal or impersonal. We should be happy to call God him or her, he or she, father or mother. It means we believe God hears, loves, answers, cares.

October 7

A college graduate of some five or six years ago writes, "I quit my job with _____ after four years. They treated me well but the work was just no longer interesting to me. Perhaps I ask too much of a job. I'd like to have it provide the means for living, of course, but also provide me with some inspiration, some zest for living. I'd like to be able to contribute something to others in the course of my job. A lot of what I did at _____ was convincing people to do what was best for us and not for them."

Even in an era when so many seem only interested in what can bring them immediate wealth, it is surprising how many people one meets like the man quoted above. They recognize that paying for a house and supporting a family are unavoidable realities, but they would like their work to contribute something to others, to the wider world around them. While they're making a living, they'd like to be serving some real human need or adding something of light and sparkle to human life.

In talking to "hard-headed," "no-nonsense" types who nevertheless want to be Christians, one realizes that this concern, to be of help or comfort or joy to others, is one way in which the following of Christ must restrain the tendencies of the marketplace. As the Gospels make clear, the Christian can never be driven simply by the desire to accumulate this world's goods; that must be subordinated to other, more simply human goals, goals demanded of one who takes the following of Christ seriously.

As we go about our work with all its here-and-now emphasis, it might comfort us to know that there are others around us who also would like to soften the rigor of competitive business life with a more basic concern for other persons. And we need to remind ourselves, too, that people, the good of those we live with and work with are goals worth keeping foremost in our intentions.

October 8

Tony was a walking, rather bouncing, picture of the American ideal of a college-age man when I knew him as a student. Of course, he played football and rugby. He was of medium height and very husky. I ran into him frequently in the student dining room or going across campus. There was always a very hearty, confident greeting and a smile. Just meeting so much friendly energy was always a tonic. It could lift the lowest-hanging chin and make you wonder why you thought things were so bad. I suppose you could attribute this to (what seemed to be) very robust health, maybe a comfortable family and standard of living. And these undoubtedly help.

But why not value such buoyancy and such a manner of brightening up dreary days without worrying too much about the genetics and environmental factors that may go into it? Like the rest of this world's beauty and surprises, it seems best taken for cash, for what it is. It seems to me that maintaining such a spirit must require some effort, at least at times. Tony must at times have done more poorly than he expected on a test or paper, had a spat with someone, maybe even had a cold or the flu, run into some annoying bureaucracy.

So at least once, maybe more often, I complimented him on this spirit. (I've learned more and more not to save all the compliments for the wake. Why save it for a eulogy that only comforts the survivors?) I remember saying something like: "Tony, I appreciate that great smile and friendly greeting. It always makes me feel great. How do you keep it up?" He flashed another smile (a bonus) and said something like: "Why not? The other approach doesn't do any good, helps no one." I thought that it was a real achievement for a twenty-year-old, especially when I looked back at my turbulent and unpredictable college years. What a great way to approach life!

This fall while away from the college and writing this book, I had a letter, delayed by a postal strike, from a classmate of Tony's, saying, "I assume you heard of the tragedy with Tony. For someone that athletic and positive to be hit with a physical ailment is startling." I hadn't heard but the next information I had was in another letter. Tony had died at twenty-three years of age of a heart attack. I doubt whether he knew his robust and fresh years would be so few. Or did he? I don't know. But in any case, in terms of what I witnessed, he lived them in a way that was a genuine blessing, gift, joy to those who knew him, as I did, in these casual contacts.

October 9

"Look at the birds of the air: they do not sow and reap and store in barns, yet your heavenly Father feeds them. . . . Consider how the lilies grow in the fields . . . ." (Matt 6:26, 28). Or, in Luke: "Think of the lilies; they neither spin nor weave: yet I tell you, even Solomon in all his splendor was not attired like one of these" (12:27). In a way, we Christians have been fairly selective about which "commands" of Jesus we take seriously. A great deal has been made about certain commands and much theology built up over the centuries on fairly slim foundations. But there is great power and comfort for us in some of the more neglected "commands," like the ones that begin this page.

So often it's the poets and artists who catch the point. American poet Emily Dickinson said that the only command she never broke was, "consider the lilies." Our world would probably be a good deal better off if more of us took these commands to observe, to contemplate the birds of the air and the flowers more to heart. To do that suggests at least two points to me. I hope you think of others.

To observe them means, for one thing, to appreciate, take time, for the simply beautiful and, to our often limited viewpoint, nonuseful elements in creation. "To smell the roses," as the cliche goes. Cliche or not, such directives in the Gospels are worth taking as seriously as the more materialistic cliches that apparently motivate so much of our lives: make money, produce, get results, advance our careers.

Basically, we fail to value what God has made and done when we limit our "obedience" to these other commands given, not by God, but by our society and world.

The other very important point in these famous lines is the appeal to confidence. If God can do so much for these idle-appearing flowers and carefree-appearing birds (we, of course, know they work hard), why not trust more of our future and our lives, our hope and desires, to God's loving hands and care? What freedom and joy that could bring into our lives!

October 10

One reads continually of beautiful evidence of how various Christian groups work to help the suffering, the diseased, without judging that this illness or suffering is some sentence from God. We shouldn't be surprised at this, yet we sometimes are because we've heard enough of Christians who do make the business of judging theirs instead of God's. The Los Angeles Diocese has a counseling program to help women deal with postabortion stress. One can safely presume that such a program is not a matter of berating suffering women for having failed to live up to Catholic ideals. Individuals, hospitals, and hospices all over are rallying to the service of victims of AIDS. One hears of Catholic institutions that seek to be helpful to married priests and their families.

Every bit of suffering that crosses our path is a call to sympathy and help, not to an inquisition into some real or imagined cause. The desire to link suffering and sin has been given a number of blows in the Bible, despite an earlier attitude there that sought to link the two. The Book of Job is all about a man who suffers way beyond anything that he knows to be wrong in his life. And Christianity is built around the suffering person of Jesus, also known to Christians as the Sinless One, the Innocent.

The first sentence of the previous paragraph, I realize, is open to difficulties: "*every* bit of suffering." Obviously, none of us can handle every bit that we may encounter unless, possibly, we live in a fairly remote and isolated spot. What some have called "compassion fatigue" sets in for individuals as well as for nations. In the case of the latter, wave after wave of refugees have often numbed our sense of compassion or made it seem impossible to do more. Christians probably should be the last to speak of fatigue in this area.

But within the limits of our strength and faith and hope we must try to have an open ear and heart and hand to suffering.

October 11

According to one of the most important authorities on the New Testament, St. Paul pictures Christian life as standing "in the light of Easter morning, in a new life" (J. Jeremias). Despite the fact that Valentine's Day, Christmas, New Year's, Halloween, and Thanksgiving get much attention from the advertising world and our society in general, there is no getting around the certainty that Easter, the resurrection of Jesus, is the central, foundational element in our faith. Because of it we celebrate Sunday each week.

Even apart from trying to recover some of this appreciation each Sunday, we would help our spirit much if we could, as part of our morning prayer, think of ourselves as standing in the light of Easter, by our faith and baptism able to walk in and live a new life. Even though we have the same colds, the same bills, the same fears and worries about pollution and nuclear accidents, the same concerns about our old age or an aging parent—even though all this remains true for us as for any unbelieving neighbor—the reality is that our life has been bathed in the light of the resurrection, that we do have a new kind of life in Christ, a life of hope and even joy.

If we are fortunate enough to be able to look out and see the eastern sky early in the morning, we may see the sun breaking through; in many places certainly one of the most beautiful sights. If there are only clouds, rain, and darkness, we know that, somewhere behind all that, the sun does shine. Too, beyond the sometimes depressing cast of our life, we can remind ourselves that the sun and vitality of God's life in us do still exist. Until the dawn breaks forever we need by faith to realize that even now the light is there, in our lives and hearts, no matter how hidden or unable to be felt. If we aim with God's help to fill our actions with love, to have them flow from love, the light is there and will shine, probably more visible to others than to ourselves.

October 12

Despite what may seem to be very minimal results, I did spend a good year working on these pages. But they remain words. Words, words, words. The word has a significant place in Christianity, but we need at times to remind ourselves that it can be overemphasized. A great many people on our planet rely hardly at all on the written word. The word is both powerful and poor. Maybe I could use a few words today to urge on you and myself that we realize the limited place of words, that we understand there are other, often much more important ways in which the Gospel, the life and message of Jesus, is made present.

Most Christians recognize, though to varying degrees, that the Gospel is made present in the actions and rites of the Church, in the service, above all in recalling the life, death, and resurrection of Jesus in our gathering around the altar and sharing the meal he left us.

For no matter how much we say or write about it, the only satisfying way to comprehend (if that is the word) what is going on in the Lord's Supper is to participate in it over a long period and preferably in an honest and careful celebration. The same could be said of baptism where water, the being plunged into it, and light, oil, all have probably more to say than the words alone. The building, too, and its arrangement help or hinder our understanding of what is going on. The art and music are all part of the fuller expression of the Gospel.

But possibly there is nothing to equal encountering the Gospel made flesh in another person, in someone's gestures, life, actions, smile, sensitivity, just plain goodness. We, faced with the power and impressiveness of the written and oral word, are at times inclined to think of ourselves as second-class citizens. But none of that, eloquent, moving, or effective as it may be, really equals the value of seeing the Gospel in the good qualities and life of those around us. Let's try to read the Gospel daily in them and also illustrate it for them.

October 13

In many churches we are used to seeing the cross with a representation of Christ on it, a crucifix, as we call it. This has gone through a number of changes historically. Not so many centuries ago the figure was often depicted as realistically and gruesomely as possible. Sympathy and feeling for the crucified Savior seems to have been the theme. But the earliest Christians put no body at all on the cross. In fact, the cross was often studded with gems and made of precious metal.

In St. John's Abbey Church in Collegeville, Minnesota, at a side chapel there is a crucifix by contemporary artist Joe O'Connell that has the body of Christ on the cross but as if rising, and with the bands of his burial dropping from his body. On the side of the crucifix an angel swings a censer smoking with incense, honoring the glorious resurrection of the Lord.

The point is one that should never be absent from our gaze at the cross. The cross is the means by which weakness, suffering, humiliation, poverty, were victorious. Through it came finally the vindication of the all-good one who hung there. The victory of the cross, the death *and* rising of Jesus, tells us over and over again that the elements most likely to be worshiped in our world even as they grind the poor and the no-account—power, prestige and might—are overcome by God for the one who lives for God.

In Christian thought and in our prayer life the cross and resurrection of Jesus should not be separated. Together, his suffering, death, and resurrection form one great action by which we are saved. Sunday was set aside by the early Christians to commemorate Jesus' rising on that day. Every look at a crucifix should also fill us with the hope that the unavoidable cross in our life is only one part of the mystery. "It is Christ who died, and, more than that, was raised from the dead—who is at God's right hand, and indeed pleads our cause. . . . For I am convinced that there is nothing in death or life . . . nothing in all creation that can separate us from the love of God in Christ Jesus our Lord" (Rom 8:34; 38-39).

October 14

"I'll stay in Minnesota if I never see a mosquito or the temperature below 65," or probably more often we say, "I'll be there," and left unspoken is, "unless something better turns up." In some way or other, we're frequently tempted to limit our commitments. After all, to some degree they are demanding, even frightening. In fact, hearing them expressed at a wedding often leaves people in tears. We are more used to and ready for the kinds of promises expressed in that first sentence, or "Sure, I'll help you move," and to ourselves, "if I'm not duck hunting."

But if we never commit ourselves to anything beyond the next ten minutes, it may be very difficult for us ever to be ready for lasting faithfulness. Till we have some real expertise in carrying out these lighter commitments, we're obviously not ready for the heavier ones. Why enter a marriage or accept any other major responsibility if we can't be sure we'll be back to take Mrs. Green to the hospital? Each day asks for short-term faithfulness, living up to a determination to limit our drinking, being dependable in the discharge of a job, sticking to our diet or the universal gym, to regular prayer. We need practice in such short-term commitments. At times, too, we are better off focusing on smaller and more immediate commitments while resisting the lure of grander ones, especially if we think of them as cures for immediate problems. A student can be lured into a premature decision on a college major because of worries about financial security, certainly, a shortsighted view. Or the pressure to make new friends at college or in our new life with the company in Atlanta can fool us into a hasty sexual relationship or a too-exclusive commitment. Tough as loneliness is for the single or the separated, living with some of it for a while seems preferable to an instant but treacherous solution by way of an unprepared-for involvement.

There is a place and time for short-term commitments. Exercising faithfulness now in smaller matters can help prepare us for the more lasting decisions. The person who specializes in the no show, who never meets a deadline, is he or she going to be there for another in marriage? Let's be there for that appointment this morning, attend that meeting now, and carry out both our promises and the garbage—today.

October 15

Our inner life is often like a professional wrestling ring complete with Killer Bees and Midnight Rockers locked in combat. Teams of intentions pull us in opposite directions. With St. Paul we can agree: "I can intend what is right, but I cannot do it. For I do not do the good I want, but the evil I do not want is what I do" (Rom 7:19). Like the two sons in the Gospel story (Matt 21:28-32), one side of us says yes to what should be done and leaves it undone. The other says no and, if we're fortunate, finally does jump to it.

We pledge obedience to our best ideals but find that today is too soon to carry them out. We make a promise while sick to visit someone who's bedridden and forget about it when we're back on our feet. We start a new phase of our job or a new school year determined to avoid last year's procrastination and failure and find ourselves following the NFL more closely than the program or the syllabus. We say amen to Jesus' ideal of selflessness and find ourselves ready shortly afterward to demolish a competitor whether it's in the dining room or the office.

What we need to do, of course, is put our blood, sweat, and Gatorade behind a unifying ideal and move with it. And for Christians there is no question about the ideal. We describe it in various ways: love, self-giving, or concern for others. In any case, it's tough. One good way to begin our day—no matter what yesterday's failures—is to aim and pray to unify our life and actions around this ideal. St. Paul puts that ideal in one demanding phrase after telling us that our attitude must be that of Christ, who gave up his status as God's Son to accept even death on a cross for us. "Let all look to others' interests rather than to their own" (Phil 2:4). What an inexhaustible ideal! It doesn't leave much of our daily activity untouched. What an incentive to pray for help.

October 16

The first book of the Bible, Genesis, in speaking of the origin of all that is in God, lists item after item, the stars and planets, the plants and trees, the animals, the human beings, and says repeatedly. "And God saw all that he had made and it was very good" (1:31). The need to emphasize that all that God had made was good existed at a time when neighboring peoples were saying that material things, including the body, were evil. We still need reminders of how basically good all of creation is when we see so much that is bad, so much suffering and evil. And we can focus on either the good or the evil. "Two men looked out their prison bars; one saw mud, the other stars" (Oscar Wilde). Genesis has long coexisted in Catholic tradition with prayers that speak of our world as "a vale of tears."

Every one of us must have moments when we think that true, when we think it even worse than a vale of tears, when we think it's a sewer or a prison. And what happens to us or what we witness can easily drive people to such an attitude. We certainly are out of order telling someone in grief or the victim of serious disaster to simply cheer up and pull out of it. All of us have to be allowed periods when it's hard to even see through the tears.

But we can help ourselves revive or sustain a more positive vision of our world with a habit of praying exultant hymns of praise like Psalm 148. The author starts and ends it with an alleluia. In between he calls on segments of creation to join in his praise of God, the Lord. Praise God, he says: heavens, heights, angels, sun and moon, shining stars, waters, sea creatures, fire and hail, snow and mist, mountains and hills, beasts, birds, young men and maidens, the old together with children.

Again, as so often, we do not simply lighten our spirits by making the effort from within to think that way but also by opening our mouths to words and sentiments that easily enter into our hearts and minds once we get rolling with them. Psalm 148, a good psalm, hymn, to use to balance our darker moods, to recall us to hope and joy. "Alleluia! Praise the Lord from the heavens,. . . . Praise him, sun and moon,. . . . Praise the Lord from the earth,. . . . . young men and maidens, the old together with children."

October 17

More morality; the Ten Commandments; return to standards; attention to ethics. In an age and time like ours when government officials at all levels are indicted for dishonesty and misuses of power and position, when stockbrokers and cabinet ministers alike resign, are thrown out, are jailed—or, worse yet, continue in their office—when marriage seems to be an old-fashioned custom to many, when children don't obey parents—in such an age, the frequent cry from preachers, parents, columnists, is for more morality. Teach the commandments once again, drill them in and this won't happen.

It's like the tendency in education to offer a new course whenever something seems to be wrong. Ethics will be big in the nineties, one columnist prophesies. Too bad. We've really had enough ethics and simple moralism over the years. Do this, don't do that. Nothing is less inspiring and less helpful in the long run. It salves the consciences of those who feel they must do something: sure, why not just go and tell everyone what is right and what is wrong.

Catholic theology, probably more than most, over a number of centuries became very sophisticated in analyzing sins and degrees of sin, of providing lists to be used before confession, where you could just check off the sins you had committed. It's all starting at the wrong end. Politicians who are honest, government and stock exchange officials who obey the rules, public individuals who are what we call moral, will be such, not because they've learned for the first time what is right and what is wrong from lists of sins and virtues but because they've been impelled by (1) visions and ideals and (2) a sense of responsibility, a need to respond to those values, ideals, better yet, to that person, Jesus Christ, to God.

It's not a matter of know-how (we think everything is on that level, hence the multiplication of how-to books) but of know-why or, better, of believe-why. For ourselves and those we teach or influence, our children, a good life is one lived in loving response to the God who first loved us, who has revealed that in Christ and through the many whose lives and words have blessed us. To live up to that love, to respond to it, that is the basic morality.

"He who loves his neighbor has satisfied every claim of the law" (Rom 13:8).

October 18

Why do we postpone happiness? Are we afraid of it? Don't we consider ourselves worthy? Is too much happiness always the herald of something bad? Will we have to pay for it later? Some of these ideas may sound outlandish, but I suspect that some of them are operative in us or at least cross our minds at times. But Christianity does not consider that there is anything wrong with being happy. And we can do a great deal about being happier ourselves and even promoting happiness as a more generalized practice! Part of the approach lies in our attitude toward whatever is before us: work, obligations, opportunities, friends, problems.

We follow Christ in the life that is before and around us, in this neighborhood, this job, with these people, this family, even this climate. True, we can make—and sometimes must—real changes in job, friends, neighborhood, many other matters. I'm not trying to rule them out but only pointing out that somewhere along the line finances, health, other considerations may determine that we must "settle down" here. Our happiness depends a great deal on finding and loving the good that is here, not simply elsewhere or at some other time. A delicate balance has to be struck between our desire to always improve matters and the need to appreciate what is. The point for today is that all too often we fall under one of these categories: "The unhappy waiters and killers of time, . . . students who can't be happy until they've graduated, servicemen who can't be happy until they're discharged, single folk who can't be happy until they're married, workers who can't be happy until they're retired, adolescents who can't be happy until they're grown, ill people who can't be happy until they're well, failures who can't be happy until they succeed, restless people who can't be happy until they get out of town; and, in most cases, vice versa, people waiting, waiting for the world to begin'' (Tom Robbins).

So often we don't expect to be happy till the weekend comes, till school is over, till Christmas comes, till the vacation comes. We act as if we are only in an orientation period; we dance around the ring and never make a hit; we're always rehearsing rather than putting on our show; we devour the days and hours by living only for the next one. Why? For some reason we think that only a change of time and space will help. But happiness more profoundly seems to be within us, within our power under God's grace—here and now. To love and live the present is to make ourselves and others happy.

October 19

What is our deepest desire? Many believe it is for meaning, significance, for a sense of our value, to be loved. Each of us may have a way of putting it. Personally, I suspect that whatever we call it, the desire centers around how we think we are valued. Much of our behavior seems to stem from this, everything from our first tantrums to our adolescent efforts to stand out, to be noted. Why limit it to adolescence? It continues. Clothes, behavior, appearance in general, the way we push ourselves or demand space and attention, even fame, to be seen with the "right" people—all of those may be expressions, even if a bit twisted, of this same desire to be valued.

With more honesty and time we may come to admit that it is most profoundly a desire to be loved, to be befriended at a level that shows most of our relationships as lacking. Our desire seems limitless. Someone has written that no amount of attention is ever enough for the egomaniac. Does anyone of us ever receive enough attention, enough love?

We spend much of our time and effort in trying to earn that love, that respect, that position, prestige—to use some of the synonyms that we let pass for the real thing. But there is always a distance between what we deeply desire and what we can earn. We can never earn or buy enough of it.

At the heart of the Christian message is the belief that God gives us—does not present it to us as reward or in return for what we have done—simply gives us the love we ask for in our final fulfillment. The Protestant Reformers made the point by emphasizing that God accepts us apart from what we can do or merit. Such an awareness can free us from our need or desire to be acceptable, can free us to trust and confide in the Lord, who already loves us. "God has first loved us" (1 John 4:19). Jesus discloses to us the friendship of God given to all by his special treatment of the despised and the lowly, the poor, the apparently lawless among his contemporaries. Accepting this love often seems more difficult to us than it would be to earn it.

October 20

"I will be glad in the Lord" (Ps 104:34). Christians for various reasons have at times accented that line variously. "*I* will be glad in the Lord," or "I will be glad in the *Lord*." In the case of our more puritanical colleagues it has meant that any other joy or gladness (in friends, good food, entertainment, beauty) was in competition with or incompatible with this other joy. One would suggest that, unlike others, I find my joy in the Lord; another would argue that if I am glad, it is somehow in the Lord, not much related to mere earthly considerations.

But, darn it, I think our joy in the Lord most often comes in and through other people, their accomplishments, or events and elements in nature. And whatever they offer of joy and gladness comes, of course, ultimately from the Lord. But we shouldn't make it an either/or affair or even act as if human joy ordinarily came directly and only from the Lord. Our joy in the beauty, softness, and innocence of little children, the buoyancy and freshness of adolescents and young people, the gentleness and serenity of an older person, the thoughtfulness of another—aren't all these originating in the power and creativity of God, of the Lord?

We need more unashamedly to rejoice in the beauty and lovely things and persons around us without feeling guilty because he, she, it, is not simply the Lord himself. There is a current in Christianity that seems to teach that all of these are only of worth if we love them because or for the sake of the Lord. But why devalue my wife or husband or friend by suggesting that he or she is not lovable for what he or she is? Where else does that lovability, those charms, come from except the Lord? Does the Lord require constant acknowledgment of his presence in order for him to be properly honored? Why not praise the Lord by appreciating what God has made?

In prayer and at the Lord's Supper we do acknowledge that all good comes from the Lord. Cannot that attitude persist in human life without our having to make a big deal about how "I love you," but, of course, "because of the Lord"? Why even suggest that anything worthy of love, appreciation, our joy and excitement, could come from anywhere but the Lord?

October 21

I once spent a month replacing a chaplain at a nursing home, and I must confess, after over thirty years with college students, I found it very hard. The sight of failing bodies and minds was crushing. Not that what I see in the mirror is all that encouraging. Yet even in the environment I am more used to, one is hit often enough by evidence of the fragility of human life. In the small college I am used to, a few thousand students, one averages, I would guess, almost a death a year among people between the ages of seventeen and twenty-two. Car, train, and bike accidents, even cancer and heart attacks, not to mention the mercifully more rare suicide. Which situation strikes one the most? I have no settled opinion.

In either situation, ever-present ill health or the shock of death among the young, we are given the opportunity of becoming more acutely aware of both the importance and brevity of the present moment. If we do not allow ourselves to become hardened, this experience tells us over and over again to value the present, to use it well, to live now, not just in the future, to do now what we know we should do and not simply wait for a better time. There is no better time.

In the famous now-almost-classic American play *Our Town*, the young heroine after dying in childbirth asks to come back to her family for just one day, and she is granted her wish to visit them on her twelfth birthday, to relive that day. A most poignant moment comes when she tugs at her mother, begging her to take a bit of time from household tasks to really see her and live and love the moment.

We too easily have let Christianity at times seem to be entirely oriented to the future. We live in hope for a better life. That is true, but it isn't the whole story. We prepare and bring about that future partly by entering more wholeheartedly into the present, by being where we are. It is a mistake to leave the present to the "eat, drink, and be merry, for tomorrow you die" crowd. We, *too*, have every reason to love and appreciate it as God's good creation given to us as the scene of our activity, our loving, our suffering.

Let the memory of that dear friend cut off in youth or those falling around us like autumn leaves remind us to say now the complimentary things we would have wanted to say, to commend another's work, to thank those who may have all unwittingly done so much for us, to enjoy the goodness of the simple things before us, the beautiful day, the radiant faces, the bumptious spontaneity of the young. The wonderful and miraculous things are right here if we only open our eyes. The insight is expressed well in a Zen verse "How marvelous, how miraculous; I draw water, I gather fuel." Or, how wonderful, how unbelievably beautiful, I meet Lucie for coffee, I pick up the kids after school, I run into Jeff on the street, I see the Nelson's new baby.

October 22

We all say foolish things. I would suspect that among the 365 reflections in this book you could find some foolish things. St. Augustine went through his many volumes in his latter years and wrote a volume of corrections. And a much-revered philosopher of our century, revered also as a human being, Albert Camus, wrote some words that age might have made him question. Unfortunately, Camus died young in an accident.

He wrote: "At 30 a man should know himself like the palm of his hand, know the exact number of his defects and qualities, know how far he can go, foretell his failures—be what he is. And above all accept these things." That underestimates the complexity of the human being and how much time and experience contribute to our self-knowledge. (Interestingly, another philosopher, Thomas Aquinas, argues that a person could only become a philosopher at about forty.) All our experiences conspire to aid our understanding of our selves, to correct our idea of what we think we are or must be. Why foreclose the whole subject so early? It puts the other thirty, forty, or fifty years in a straitjacket. While the quotation on the face of it seems so confident, it is basically hopeless.

As each year goes by, we are capable of learning much more about ourselves. Gradually it will become evident that some aspects of ourselves are pretty strongly ingrained and not likely to change significantly. And these we must learn to accept. But there is much more to ourselves than we ever know at thirty or probably even at the end of our lives. All that is reason for hope: hope in our ability to change, to improve with the help of God, to be able to alter our behavior, attitudes. To be able to junk worn-out and useless conceptions and rigidities.

And finally, the Christian must have hope that God can do much more in him or her and that what will seem unfinished can be entrusted to God. Christian belief carries in itself the conviction that our fulfillment may be beyond our imagining and, too, beyond this life. At some point our hope must include joyful surrender to a mind more profound than our own and a heart more concerned than our own, a trust in the mind and heart of God.

October 23

To say, as some famous thinkers have said, that God is dead is open to different meanings. With one or the other, the believer can possibly agree. For Friedrich Nietzsche in the last century, the "death of God" was necessary so that human beings could really live, or more specifically, that his kind of human being could live. He felt that the idea of God only served to enslave human beings and to deprive them of the energy, the will to change, that they otherwise would have. As long as they believed in an all-powerful God, they could rely on God to do everything. Why should they knock themselves out changing the world, which God could change with the flick of the wrist?

But without having to subscribe to some lofty philosophical or theological idea about the death of God, we can recognize how easily God can die in human lives. If there is no strong influence in human life holding back our self-seeking, our aggressiveness, our willingness to trample on other's rights, if nothing limits the ways in which we think it legitimate to make money or gain position, or more mildly, if life can go on without any thought of God, no prayer or little prayer or perfunctory prayer, then in practice God is dead in our lives. God has died for us. Our God is dead.

Another, less dramatic way of looking at the same issue is to think along with Jewish philosopher Martin Buber of God as being eclipsed. Instead of positively excluding God from our thoughts, activities, life, we let God's existence, power, and influence be covered over, blotted out, as the sun itself could be by an eclipse. Our obsessions, egotistic concerns, forgetfulness, concentration on the here and now, absorption in making money or gaining power and position, can leave God out.

All this may strike us as extreme, but it is a reminder that for God to be alive in my life means more than lip-service. It means setting aside time for God, for worship and prayer, probably for some specific personal practice of my faith, some activity that clearly has its origin in my desire to respond to God's love, to follow Christ. God may not be dead for us or dead in our lives but there is always the great danger that the reality may be, at least, not in good health.

October 24

One of the most common names for the Body and Blood of Christ is Holy Communion, though other terms are more and more used: Eucharist, Lord's Supper. Holy Communion has fallen into some disfavor for suggesting that receiving the Body and Blood of the Lord is a purely private meeting between me and God, me and the Lord. If that's how it is viewed, it does stand in need of an injection of reality and vitality. Communion is not meant to signify the moment during which you or I individually go to the altar and are joined with Christ in personal union, which is helped by closing my eyes, shutting out completely everyone else who is present, and speaking to the Lord.

Communion comes from words meaning to unite with, to be united with, in association with, and not simply with "my" God but with "our" God and with all others who share at the table of the Lord with me. The communion, the sharing, is not only up and down—from God to me and me to God—but sideways, from me to others and others to me, reflecting the essential Christian belief that God comes to us and that we serve the Lord primarily in what we do for others.

From this flows the importance of all our efforts at the Lord's Supper to be aware of others, to be of good will toward them, to even express it in a greeting, a sign of good will, given, preferably, to people to whom we are not already committed to giving good will. Holy Communion signifies a large network of people all joined to each other and to Christ by the sacrament. St. Paul is strong on this (1 Cor 10:16-17). Offering the sign of peace before Communion is the ancient custom, attested in the earliest Christian writings, of underlining that our union with Christ is, in fact, unrealistic, even false, if it does not include a willingness to be concerned about all those who also are in this "communion."

Rather than allowing our Communion at Mass to reinforce any simple me-and-God version of our faith, we need to let it expand our willingness to serve the one next to us, the neighbor.

October 25

There's evidence in the letters of St. Paul that some of his early followers understood—or misunderstood—his message to be that the Lord's return or the end of the world was about to happen. As a consequence, why bother going to the office, getting a haircut, or raking the leaves? Evidently a good number of early Christians, even if they did not go that far, did feel that God would bring down the final curtain and they would see Christ return in their lifetime.

As the years rolled on and with the help of some correction from St. Paul himself, they recognized that life had to be lived, work done, friends cared for, and promises kept. They could not just idle the engine but had to get in gear. They realized that one could no more simply live in the future than in the past.

We still live, as Christians, with the belief that there is to be a final wrapping up of our world and human existence, but we have no certainty about *when* any more than we do about the end of our own lives. Like the early Christians the lesson we are to draw to is to live now.

Real life is here, not in some imagined, fabulous future on the Riviera with a professional athlete's bank account. Living in readiness tells us how urgent and important is the work of becoming that self we know we should be. It tells us what a waste it can be to live only for the blatant and coarse satisfactions of life, to live only to fit someone else's expectation, to be hemmed in by silly customs or what others think. Those things have their—limited—place but all too often we let them limit true living.

The end of things tells us to live fully now, not back in high school or in some imaginary future when we will be some combination of Walter Payton and Lee Iacocca or Margaret Thatcher and Jodi Foster. It tells us to live today, whether on vacation or at work, at a game, with friends or alone, to do what we do. It tells us to live Monday through Friday with all our strength and vigor and not to fool ourselves into thinking that the only life is on the weekend or on vacation or, worse yet, at work. The end tells us to live now from the depth and richness of our nature, not on the surface, not putting off generosity and love, contact with friends, or help to the sick and lonely. Not to let bed, booze, and barbiturates shield us from real life. By being awake and alive now we are always ready for what is and for what will be.

October 26

Recently I read an interview with a singer of sad country western songs and blues. Seeing a jovial and prosperous person before him, the reporter asked if the singer really suffered as much and lived so constantly in pain as his songs suggested. While granting he had his share of bad times and days, the singer admitted: "I don't live as sad as I sell."

It works in the other direction too: We don't live as "good" as we preach or profess. Lutheran theologian and historian Martin Marty tells of being heartened to discover something similar in Martin Luther. One of Luther's friends had been building St. Paul up as a great hero of faith. Luther burst in: "I don't think Paul believed as firmly as he talks. I cannot believe as firmly, either, as I can talk and write about it."

St. John in one of his letters writes that if we say we know Christ while disobeying his commands, we are liars. But I'd add, in some way all of us do disobey the commands or fail the ideal. While it is not desirable to be a liar, part of the human condition is that we are all, in some sense, liars. There is, in other words, always a gap between what we say we believe, what we want to be, what we have vowed to be, what we preach or teach, and what we are. In ideals, words, and profession we are always beyond what we are, ahead of what we actually do.

Part of that is simply idealism. We all needs ideals, and they only remain ideals insofar as we do fall short of them. Trying to bridge that gap sums up in many ways the work of Christian life. And it serves two good purposes: We always have something to strive for, reasons for not being satisfied, and secondly, it is good reason for a continuing sense of dependence on God and trust in God for what has not yet come to pass.

October 27

Jesus was able to die at what most of us regard as a very young age with the words "It is finished" on his lips. We may feel justified in using the same words for some phase or situation in our lives, but many of our experiences seem unfinished. They are and our lives often are unfinished symphonies or at least serenades. Possibly, our loves seem to have an unfinished character about them.

Dear friends and family members die before the promise in our relationship has been realized. Or they move away to be seen rarely again. Or a serious change in attitude or values on our part or theirs leaves a great awkwardness in the relationship. It's never the same again, no matter how much good will may remain.

Even our best friendships and loves include serious difficulties, disturbing disagreements, lack of understanding, an uncertainty about how the other feels or thinks, a failure to be near on some issue close to our heart but apparently not to the other person's. Children leave our lives—at least in terms of distance and preoccupations or even decisions—when we have just begun to understand one another or have an easier relationship than that turbulent one of the teens. Worse, a misunderstanding cools a warm and longstanding relationship in a way that no simple gesture or a few words can easily change. Our love for and attraction to another is limited by their disappearance from our life and milieu. Another relationship, at least in their minds, means they must lessen the one with me.

Even in more perfect relationships there remains a part of the self that is incommunicable to others, incapable of being shared. We are such genuine mysteries to ourselves and to others. Maybe there always remains a part of us that cannot be shared with another.

This persistent imperfection in our relationships points to the Lord and God in whom all is fulfilled. The impossibility that our capacity for love will be totally fulfilled here and now points most strongly to another world, life, and lover, God, in whom love will come to fulfillment. The imperfection of love here is meant to help us hope. The recognition that there is something so great to hope for as the perfection of love is reason for us to take every love so seriously—even to tears at times.

October 28

From conversations I've had with successful business people, mostly former students, it's pretty safe to say that academics have a certain air of unreality about them. Business people tend to think that professors are not in contact enough with the realities of the marketplace to speak about economics and politics.

More and more, I think the world has to move along by a balancing of the forces of realism (their chosen word) and those of idealism or otherworldliness, though that flatters me when I think of how I love Brie, good wine, movies, and the like. Nevertheless, there is a sense in which my type does represent another viewpoint, one that is always pointing beyond what is to something more ideal, more just, more gentle. There is little danger that the forces of realism and market know-how will fade away for lack of interest or because the world in general has turned to contemplation, to Plato, Chinese sages, Old Testament prophets, or to Jesus. Granted all that, I think the world can tolerate some idealists, visionaries, dreamers, too, if you want, and not be fearful that self-interest is going to disappear from the face of the earth.

A former president of Princeton (you know the type, now) is reported to have said to graduating students, "If you feel that you have both feet planted on level ground, then the university has failed you." If we feel we have tendencies toward this idealism, this otherworldly vision, we should not fear it. In fact, we need to nurture it and keep it alive and accept being among those who are continually, as they hope, in imitation of Jesus, pointing to ways in which the world could go more justly and kindly for all. If we have shelved our ideals in the interests of hard reality maybe it's good to dust them off and take a look at them. They could just inspire us and affect reality.

October 29

Those Jews who several centuries before Christ were uprooted brutally from their homes and taken into exile in Babylon experienced more acutely than most of us the confusion and incomprehensibility of human life. Exile or Babylonian exile has come to mean in our language a sense of being out of place, lost, alienated. Overcoming that and finding happiness, peace, and satisfaction likewise has come to be described often in terms of return from exile, homecoming.

For the Christian, the believer, human life has aspects of an exile, a less-than-perfect time where all is not what it should be, where we are not in ideal closeness to God and each other. And, while age and a kind of wisdom can bring us more peace and understanding, we are just as likely to sense more intensely the incomprehensibility of life.

We find ourselves sitting in the late evening with our eyes closed wondering about how strange it all is, how utterly beyond us. What does it mean? Why do things happen the way they do? How or why have such wonderful things happened to me or in my life? Why have such tragedies occurred? The more we think about it the more dense and impenetrable it often seems to be. We may find this simply baffling or realize that like so many elements that go to make up human life (suffering, love, death, children), it just has depths and mysteries always beyond us.

For the believer, the only way to handle all this is to allow it to shore up our confidence in God who alone has the whole picture. The obscurity of our understanding of life should be accompanied by a greater realization that our only sure footing is in Jesus Christ, in faith, love and trust in him. Like us, with fear and trembling (remember his prayer in the garden before his death) Jesus faced suffering, death, and the future. His resurrection is our assurance that in his loving company, fortified by his body and blood and his word, we can daily walk the same path. All is not and will not be clear, but we have one in whom to put total trust and confidence.

October 30

A woman who took part in the prayerful chanting of the psalms at a monastery came away impressed by a whole new experience and particularly with one line of Psalm 46 lingering in her mind. "Be still and know that I am God" (v. 11). I think the silence that was observed between the psalms was, to her, very striking, probably a new thing for that mother of six. Be still, quiet down, and you will be able to know that I am God, that I am here, that I am in this busy world.

Even though not every line or verse of the psalms may make immediate sense to us (some have reference to long-forgotten events), still, there are often such lines that make our attempts to pray them worthwhile. This same psalm, though, has a more general and powerful theme, which inspired Martin Luther very much. His famous hymn, now fortunately no longer considered simply a Lutheran treasure, begins with the first lines of this psalm in an older translation: "A mighty fortress is our God." The idea is the same, though my translation reads: "God is our refuge and our strength, an ever-present help in distress. Therefore we fear not, though the earth be shaken and mountains plunge into the depths of the sea. . . . The Lord of hosts is with us, our stronghold is the God of Jacob." (We don't have to have a historically accurate conception of "Lord of hosts" to realize that it means to speak of God as mighty, nor of Jacob to realize that the writer speaks of one of his great ancestors who trusted in the same God.)

Granted all that, we can use this psalm as a powerful prayer of confidence. The writer and we, too, can express our conviction, ever in need of renewal, that God is our refuge, our strength, someone powerful and close at hand in every difficulty who should calm our fears no matter what turmoil seems to engulf our world and life. God is for us a refuge and strength, a helper close at hand. We shall not fear. The Lord is with us. God is our stronghold. "A mighty fortress is our God."

October 31

The horrors on Elm Street or among the Living Dead are clearly but, maybe oddly, entertainment. Many of us can accept an artificial chill or thrill or scare. In fact, many can and do, as evidenced by the popularity of films where incredible creatures ooze through the cracks in the wall to fasten themselves on someone's body, or human beings are transmogrified into wolves or vampires while in the crib. People not only take that, they enjoy it, love it, are basically "entertained" by the bloodletting and terror of such films and similar novels. Manufactured horror becomes entertainment, an escape from reality. Judging from popularity, we'd rather face an invasion of incredible beings from outer space than more immediate horrors like starvation, cruelty to children, cruelty of adults to each other in war and fighting, torture of dissidents.

Someone has said that we cannot face very much reality; we need to retreat from it, hide from it, be shielded, gloss it over, make it acceptable by some distance or by making it fantastic and unreal. All of this is understandable; however, we do need to face real suffering and pain around us and in our world to keep our hearts open and sensitive, to do what we can in our situation to relieve or assist the misery of others. There may be a place for escapism and a real need for it in our lives, but it cannot replace our obligation to face reality, to face unromantic and painful events around us and in our world. As Christians, we face them like any human being—with tears and often a sense of helplessness but also with a determination to help whom we can and to hope and believe in the power and presence of God in our world.

November 1

There's a story about a Christian hermit coming back to his hut and finding some robbers taking all he had. He joins them, finding stuff they missed, puts it into their bags, and waves goodbye. Sort of like you or me coming on someone walking away with the TV set; we throw in the CD player and a few good suits and wish him a nice day.

In reality we find those words of Jesus in the Gospels (Matthew, chapters five, six, and seven) about turning the other cheek, giving your coat to the thief who has taken your shirt all unreal, impossible. Rather than blessing those who curse us, we're more likely to fuss, cuss, and demand justice. Competition, standing on our rights, are all part of everyday life. None of us can avoid aggression and rivalry.

But the words of Jesus still have a place. None of us wants a world where the only principles operating are: Get yours; tit for tat; an eye for an eye. Do we want to live in a world where we can never let someone get ahead of us in line or take that parking spot, where we'd never forget the two dollars Jill borrowed, where we can't take another's weakness into account? But then, a moment later, we're back to thinking: we don't want to be someone else's doormat, everyone's sucker, the last boy scout in the world.

Part of the problem is thinking that Jesus is simply teaching us to be victims. On the contrary, his words tell us to take the initiative in showing love, forgiveness. In the teaching of the Lord, we are in charge, not someone else's ill will, anger, smallness, insensitivity. Jesus teaches us not to return evil for evil. But further, he tells us not even to return love but to be the first to give love, like God.

November 2

Echoing what many, many people feel, P. N. Furbank writes: "Why am I so frightened of an atomic war wiping out the bulk of mankind? After all, whereas an atomic war would leave some humans alive, my death, so far as I am concerned, would leave none whatever." I don't know how many of us think much of death, or how we think of it. I'm not privy to others' minds, and the topic is not one that people use to fill in the spaces at a cocktail hour or a wedding reception. But I think Furbank makes a strong point: My death is really what counts, from my unavoidably self-centered perspective. When death and/or catastrophe strikes near me, I think of how fragile, fugitive, my life is. The death of young people, such as I've had to experience nearly every year of my teaching career, especially brings home the fact of death. If someone so young can die, what about someone who has lived many more years? Woody Allen says, "It is impossible to experience one's own death objectively and still carry a happy tune." Deaths around us, illness, often the progression of some illness of our own that medicine can only allay for a while, all force us to think of death, no matter how little it pleases us.

And the thought brings a whole train of others after it: How little I've done of what I wanted to do; this project is so incomplete, my work unfinished; how much my self is unfinished, still plagued by the same bad habits and tendencies of decades ago; what failures in human relations, within myself, I have to face. I think the lines one reads occasionally about how great everything has been, how happy I will be to go, are inflated dramatizations meant as public relations releases or even whistling in the dark. More typically, it seems to me that the Christian looking back, at whatever age, needs to practice putting all in the hands of the Lord. He came not just to fulfill, as we say, various Old Testament prophecies, but to fulfill us, too, to make up for what is lacking, to forgive, and by his grace to fit us for life with God. In that we trust; for that we hope. It isn't just *our* life, *our* project.

November 3

Throughout much of this century there has been a movement among Christian Churches called "ecumenical." Protestant missionaries in what we now call the Third World became increasingly aware of how confusing their conflicting claims were to the people to whom they were trying to bring Christ. Hence, an effort to reunite or bring closer together the various Christian Churches. Only toward the middle of this century did Catholics start to show much interest in this, and only with the great Pope John XXIII and the Second Vatican Council in the early sixties did Catholics really become more serious about joining this effort, which is called "ecumenical" from a Greek word meaning world-wide.

One of the great results of all this has been a softening of formerly rigid positions among Catholics and Protestants and a realization that both lost when they broke with each other in the 1500s. One significant gain from this movement for all of us today is, on the one hand, a renewed appreciation of and devotion to the Bible in Catholic life and worship and, on the other hand, a greater appreciation for the sacraments, especially baptism and the Eucharist, on the part of Protestant Churches. While Catholics realize more and more that an important part of the nourishment and strength the Lord left us is in Scripture and particularly in *his* words, Protestants see more and more that God acts on us also through the actions of the sacraments. Protestant Churches emphasize more the celebration on Sundays of the Lord's Supper. With this in mind all of us perceive much more of the strength and life present in the words of chapter six of St. John's Gospel. We can summarize them with a verse or two: "Jesus said to them, 'I am the bread of life, whoever comes to me shall never be hungry, and whoever believes in me shall never be thirsty' " (John 6:35). We live not by bread alone, even high-fiber, preservative-free bread, but by every word that comes from God. The word here is that Jesus remains present to sustain and strengthen us both in his words (Scripture) and in the sacraments, in his body and blood received in Communion. In the same chapter: "I am the living bread that has come down from heaven; if anyone eats this bread he shall live for ever" (v. 51).

November 4

"Go with it" usually suggests to us moving with either a football, soccer ball, or some proposal we have or charge we've been given. In the teaching of Jesus there is a frequent alternation of "Come" and "Go." He asks us to follow him, to come. And once we've received the invitation and heard what he has to say, he tells us to go, to preach, to heal, to help (Mark 6:7-13).

Not everyone is called to "go" in the same way or same direction. No matter how well we recognize the problems of the Sahara, Bangladesh, or the lower Bronx, we may not personally be called to go there. Going might involve abandoning our immediate and also very serious responsibilities. It could be a bit like fighting racism in England while still practicing it in our own neighborhood. The more romantic, ego-satisfying work may not be where we are called to put our energy and drive.

But each of us does have some way of "going." If we have a gift for being a good listener to others, then we should go and do that willingly; if my gift is for consoling or inspiring others, then I should go use it. If a gift for saying positive things about others and about life, circumstances, work, is mine, then I should not be afraid to speak, go to it, now. Each of us can think of a particular gift in his or her own case. And then, as we offer ourselves and our lives with Christ to God in prayer or at Mass, let's ask that we may more generously give of what we have received or perceived. If we have ever looked carefully into ourselves at some time or other, we have heard a call in some sense. Now let's be willing to be sent, to exercise the healing power present in our own gift. "Go with it."

November 5

The electricity, the enthusiasm, the energy of the young: infants, two-year-olds, children in general, teenagers, even those in their twenties. It's a kind of, or an aspect of beauty; something that lights up the world and tells us of its possibilities and the possibilities of eternal life. That glow, that gleam, that human sunshine.

At a certain age, of course, we may not really appreciate it. College students *must* disdain the enthusiasm and energy of high school students; at that time it's an embarrassing reminder of where they came from. They can, however, appreciate and melt in the presence of a preschooler. And the enthusiasm and charm of teenagers may easily be lost on their harried parents at times; that enthusiasm and excitement is often reserved for conversations with their peers. With parents and elders many a teenager wishes to give the impression of boredom. Viewed from outside, they are often pictures of enthusiasm and vitality.

But I think this bubbling energy should be something we contemplate, rejoice in, and find encouraging. Think of the joy and light they bring to the elderly; how a visit from a child can light up the faces and hearts of those whose own bodies do not permit them to express or experience the exuberance and joy their hearts and minds may feel or treasure.

Psalm 8, which celebrates the glory and beauty of creation, seems in many ways to express well the joy that comes from just seeing (and hearing!) the exuberance of happy and excited young people.

> How great is your name, O Lord our God,
> through all the earth!
> Your majesty is praised above the heaven:
> on the lips of children and of babes. . . .
>
> Yet you have made us little less than gods:
> and crowned us with glory and honor,
> gave us power over the works of your hands,
> put all things under our feet. . . .
>
> How great is your name, O Lord our God
> through all the earth!

November 6

It's perfectly proper and even productive to argue with some of the lines of Scripture. After all, our belief in its inspiration and preservation from error regards its overall teaching on human life, not a whole set of opinions on everything under the sun. I read some time ago of an English writer disagreeing quite vigorously with a line or two from Psalm 39. The line (in NEB) reads, "Lord, let me know my end and the number of my days: tell me how short my life must be." The writer, Samuel Butler, says, "Of all prayers this is the insanest." He says it must indicate an emotional state of the author, certainly not his considered thought about the issue. And he adds, "It would have served the maker of it right to have had it granted. 'Cancer, in about three months after great suffering' or 'Ninety, a burden to yourself and every one else.'" Put that way, we see his point. Would any of us want to know in advance the full truth of our decline, especially when there is so little to be done about it?

Finally, Butler says that the writer and all of us could probably better pray: "I thank thee, Lord, that you have hidden my end from me." And that's the way it is ordinarily, fortunately. We do not know the end; we do not even know the next thing, really. We plan and work for some sort of security. And in doing so we exercise our freedom, make our choices, make our decisions, and to some degree help form our futures. But many elements of that future are hidden, unavailable to us, beyond our control.

We're not just "left with" the need to trust and have confidence but *allowed* to have a trust and confidence that is one of the glories of our existence. Our life is more in the hands of God, of someone wise and more caring about it than we could ever be. We can trust God. "I bid you put away anxious thoughts about food to keep you alive and clothes to cover your body. Life is more than food, the body more than clothes. Think of the ravens: they neither sow nor reap; they have no storehouse or barn; yet God feeds them. You are worth far more than the birds! . . . Think of the lilies: they neither spin nor weave; . . . you are not to set your mind on food and drink; you are not to worry. . . . No, set your mind upon God's kingdom, and all the rest will come to you as well" (Luke 12:22-31).

November 7

"Alleluia" begins the shortest of the 150 psalms in the Bible, Psalm 117. In its essential content it rebukes all those who take so many words to repeat the important message we have from God: God is concerned for us and deserves the praise of all.

> Alleluia!
> Praise the Lord, all you nations,
> glorify him, all you peoples!
> For steadfast is his kindness toward us,
> and the fidelity of the Lord endures forever.

The two verses offer examples of the Hebrew practice of rhyming ideas rather than words. Praise the Lord, all nations; glorify him, all peoples, illustrates this perfectly. The second verse does the same but with a slight addition: God's love for us is steadfast, reads the first part; the second part stresses that it is unfailing, everlasting. That's how strong it is. Whether we're products of a more skeptical age or whether we feel a bit sorry for ourselves, we're tempted to say: Why praise the Lord? The answer, of course, is given in the second verse: because God's love for us is so strong and everlasting. Pushing it further, we probably wonder at times how we know of that love. Why should we, why should I, praise the Lord? One way to answer that is to ask, Why not? That suggests we do some comparing with others, immediately around us or further afield. Are we all that much worse off than these? More positively, aren't there many signs, above all in the kindness and love of others, of God's love for us?

The message of this psalm, which I said was so plainly at the heart of our belief, comes from the time before Christ. Yet what Christ said and did does not alter it. Jesus is the most definite, perfect, in-the-flesh statement of how much God loves us. In Jesus we see how enduring is God's love. The evil of our world, to which Christ was no stranger (more than that, he entered into it completely) and which we all share in some way, is overcome by the love of God. "For I reckon that the sufferings we now endure bear no comparison with the splendor, as yet unrevealed, which is in store for us" (Rom 8:18). "God did not spare his own Son, but gave him up for us all; and with this gift how can God fail to lavish upon us all there is to give?" (Rom 8:32).

November 8

Related to the idea that actions are often better witnesses to faith than words is the notion that prayer is the real test, the real evidence of faith. If we really believe that God is personally concerned with our calls for help, that God responds, strengthens, consoles us, then we show it by turning to God in prayer. Without prayer, our claim to believe that God cares for our world and can act through us is simply theory.

What do we do in prayer that makes our belief clear, makes it have consequences? In the most basic prayer we simply acknowledge that our world and our life is lived in God's presence, that we are dependent on that presence for every minute, every day, of that life, every bit of good that may be accomplished in it. In prayer we ask for help, for strength, for courage, for perseverance, for hope, joy, trust. Or we ask to know what we should be doing, how we should be living. Or we praise and thank God for all that is and has been and all that we have received. Or we express our trust and confidence, that amid tragedies and disappointments, God is still there, able to bring good out of it somewhere, sometime. In all of this, we express an awareness of God's presence, our dependence on our Creator.

Prayer is the test and the evidence for belief, trust, faith. But conversely, too, it builds up and strengthens that faith, just as conversation and other forms of communication with a loved friend build and develop the relationship, keep it alive, give it more substance. Out of sight is often out of mind. Similarly our faith cannot long survive being without expression, without prayer.

November 9

Weakness has nothing to do with it. It's all about strength. So often we excuse our tears and mourning for a dead husband, wife, or friend by saying something about how sorry we are that we are so weak. We're used to that language, but it really comes from a non-Christian idea that showing feeling is wrong and a sign of weakness. In reality tears of mourning and grief come from a strength, the strength of our love for someone. Love and attachment in Christianity are not wrong but signs of a correct appreciation of the good God has created. An important relationship has been broken or seemingly destroyed by death, and we rightly and profoundly regret that he or she is gone from our life.

The only proper reaction to the loss of a loved one is grief and enough of it to allow us to express our appreciation, our thanksgiving for the time we had with the person and all he or she meant to us. There is no healthy way to just ignore grief or loss, to hide it or make believe it doesn't exist. We need time to absorb, think about, feel deeply, the loss of someone who may have been in a very intensive way part of the good things of our life. Why should we want to erase something so important, so vital in our survival? To attempt to forget it, though odd currents in our society urge it on us (Cheer up; enough is enough; etc.), is really to cut off the thanksgiving we rightfully feel for another sign of God's grace that has been taken from us.

In very beautiful words François Mauriac says: "We are, all of us, molded and remolded by those who have loved us, and though that love may pass, we remain none the less their work. No love, no friendship ever crosses the path of our destiny without leaving some mark upon it forever." All of what remains of our life, in some ways, will be partially spent in absorbing the good they've done us. There is no reason why we should aim to forget that or act as if they never were. Obviously, all normal activity cannot cease indefinitely so that we can mourn and grieve; that would hardly honor the memory and inspiration of the dead one. But we rightly resist the impatience of our society with our human need to cherish, remember, and be thankful for the good the dead have given us.

November 10

Much of our life, especially, say, the first eighty years, are spent taking ourselves, our development, our future, very seriously, teasing our hair into the right style, choosing a vocation, making our résumé look impressive, firming up those thighs, wondering how Joe or Cathy really feels, learning self-defense, making the case for our promotion, and so on. We take ourselves and our future even grimly at times. I suspect that some of this is unavoidable. But there should be more periods when we take ourselves lightly, when we forget the self, prick our self-importance, experiment with the paradox that we find ourselves by losing ourselves. Taking ourselves lightly is really another term for having a sense of humor. When we are dreadfully serious about becoming vice president of IBM or having our first million by age thirty, it is, of course, hard to lighten up, to let go for a moment. If our goal is such a heavy one we may be pretty solemn about it. I'm not denying that some, maybe a great deal, of that is necessary. But there is also a very great value in *not* taking ourselves so ponderously all the time, in being able to see ourselves as slightly comic, to see that every event of our life, everything we are doing, is not something to be measured on the Richter scale.

Could we learn to step back at times, maybe daily, and have a bit of a laugh at ourselves? At our earnestness about winning every racquet ball game we play or about our dignity or how macho we are or how sensitive we are? We easily live and act as if every project, sentiment, or notion of ours is the most momentous thing to hit the planet since Velcro or the compact disk. Is it?

November 11

In centering the faith of his followers in a meal that was to be "in remembrance" of him, one might say Jesus capitalized on a strong but underrated human tendency. I mean our tendency to remember. One realizes, of course, once that's been said, how dangerous it is to give the past this kind of position. (The good old days include some bad old times of putting to death those who disagreed with you, of anti-Semitism, of putting men and women through ordeals by fire or water because they "looked like" witches.) But to keep this page manageable, let's simply think of memory here, in terms of your life and mine.

Each of us has—at least it is to be hoped that it isn't just the experience of a privileged few of us—moments in the past when something great happened to us: when someone showed us exceptional and lasting love, care, concern, came to us in difficult times. While it may be pleasant to look at the photos and the movies of these days, people and places, our recalling them can also be an occasion for thanksgiving and an inspiration to act now.

If we have been so blessed by others, by events and time, we have every reason to try to share the same with others, to make sure they have similar memories, but, first of all, that they have similar care and love shown them. For example, the sick and housebound, the lonely and elderly, the neglected, those finding life very difficult and painful. Our judicious intervention and help can thank God for the good we have received and make it productive of more of the same, a chain of blessing. What a way to live: to see ourselves and our actions as enlivened and energized by the good done to us in the past as that was energized by the good to others before . . . and before that . . .

The great good God has done for us in Jesus and the many reflections of that in our own experience can move us to something similar today.

November 12

The great minds of our time, whether scientific or philosophical or theological, often seem to be convinced that prayer is self-hypnosis. Or if more sympathetically inclined, they believe that given some more thought, we're going to figure out how our prayer and God's governance of the world actually work to produce particular results. They find the views and practices of much of humankind quite naive or simpleminded. Maybe so, but I doubt that human wisdom and research are going to come up with a good formula for the problem.

It seems to me there is more wisdom and more of a solution to the problem in the often naive-sounding lines of simple believers. For instance, in the words of a Negro spiritual: "He may not come when you want him . . . but he's right on time. You can't hurry God."

These delightful lines sung to a very lively tune don't replace human speculation and thinking about the problem. Certainly, if we have the time and the ability, we must face it and see what human reason can say about it. My point is not to deny that or forbid it but to suggest to those of us who have often read such treatments and thought about the problem ourselves that after a particular point we may want to get on with our life of faith and trust. And remind ourselves that God may not come when we want, may not snap to it in response to every prayer and wish of ours; that's obvious. "My hour is not yet come," Jesus tells his mother in John 2:4 in answer to a request of hers. But eventually, in whatever way God chooses to answer our prayers, it's in the right way, the right place, the right time. Along with our petitions must always go, "Thy will be done." God does what is ultimately best for us, no matter how hard it may be for us to understand the answer God gives. God may not come at our command, but God comes and we can trust that the coming is timely and appropriate. God will help bring about what is best.

In that sense, you can't hurry God. To learn not to hurry ourselves may be a great part of learning to know and accept God's will in the complexities of daily life. "God's right on time."

November 13

It's amazing how many ways there are of defining what it is that makes us human, what sets us apart from other animals with many of the same capacities and needs. One will say it's the ability to reason or think; another the ability to feel; another a sense of humor; another our capacity for making and keeping promises. Another definition is contained in this quotation: "If we were to live here always, with no other care than how to feed, clothe, and house ourselves, life would be a very sorry business. It is immeasurably heightened by the solemnity of death. The brutes die even as we; but it is our knowledge that we have to die which makes us human. . . . Knowing it to be inevitable, that to every one of us it will come one day or another, is a wonderful spur to action" (Alexander Smith).

Here, to be human is to know that we will die, to have a kind of consciousness that gives us a sense of the value of this moment, this day. In fact, more immediate deadlines also give us a push. We have only a few more days of vacation left; we want to finish a piece of work during the break or during this period between jobs. And everyone knows how the end of the semester or a final test can galvanize an otherwise carefree student. Or how the impending wedding day gets us into action.

If the thought of our eventual death gets us to give our work, our friends, our families, our world more generous and unstinting service and care, it is a "wonderful spur to action." If it helps us keep the emphasis on living each day as well as possible (not in tense straining), then the thought of death really does give a great dignity to our lives.

We might go one step further and add that the ability to hope for more beyond death, beyond the grave, to trust that we go to a loving God, that, too, is a distinctively human quality. Help us, Lord, to live and do our best now and, for the rest, to hope and trust completely in you.

November 14

There have been times, places, and people for whom prayer for the unity of Christians meant either that all of us become a kind of Baptist or that all come "home to Rome." In our prayers sometimes we tend to specify such items for God in a way that shows little trust. Looking at the four centuries since the Protestant Reformation and all that has happened in the Churches, above all at the changes in position and practice, it becomes more and more chancy to try to predict how Christians will become more united. There seems to be little question that we should be more united in the sense of recognizing and accepting each other's witness to Christ. But *how* remains a challenge.

This is all part of a larger question regarding our prayer. How much do we need to specify for God what we want or need for ourselves or others: that Tom be promoted to full manager? that Mary find a good Irish-American husband? that Dan, sick for years and in his late nineties, be restored to full health?

A couple of points may be helpful. First, strictly speaking, God does not even need our information about the state of Tom, Mary, or Dan. That doesn't mean we can't or shouldn't mention it, but it does tell us that our prayer is partially at least an exercise of loving care on our part in which we ask one who loves our dear ones more than we do to protect and care for them.

Further, we can show by our prayer for others more trust in that loving care of God by including some willingness to have God's will be done. Maybe Tom would be better off with an entirely different company; maybe Mary will do better as a single person; maybe Dan is about ready to leave this life. We don't know what is best in each case—and we should be on guard against thinking that we do.

Part of our prayer, for Church unity or for the health, welfare, and comfort of others, should always be some surrender to God's loving will, some willingness to allow for solutions that are beyond our limited minds and hearts to conceive. Lord, keep in your love Tom, Mary, Dan, the Church; be with them.

November 15

"We don't know how many future generations we can count on before the Lord returns." That line came from an American Secretary of the Interior not too long ago who seemed hesitant about serious management of our natural resources. When it's on that level and tends to resignation about the destruction of our forests and waterways, this attitude undoubtedly scares most of us. Carried a little further, it might suggest more: Why bother with the garbage or the potholes or cutting down on alcohol-related deaths or even cancer? Implicit in this attitude is the belief that since the Lord is coming to clear up and clean up everything, why should we preempt him?

Even St. Paul in his time had trouble with people drawing similar conclusions about the possible and always-near coming of the Lord, his advent. Paul had to deal firmly with disciples who thought that they should just sit on the back porch and wait or put the engine in neutral. But throughout Jesus' teaching there is a strong and clear emphasis on using the talents and gifts given us here and now, on the fact that we will be judged by how we have served him in the hungry, the imprisoned, the sorrowing. The unknown time of the end of our world as we know it is not an excuse for sitting idly, for letting evil and suffering go unchallenged, for letting the laundry pile up, the weeds grow, or the trumpeter swans be destroyed.

Instead, the always-near coming of the Lord should drive us to lessen the misery of our fellow pilgrims in the present. Instead of unproductive carping, ineffectual and self-serving criticism, we need to spend our precious minutes, our youth and/or health, full time—in forgiving, inspiring hope, inducing some laughter and happiness, letting the light of Christ brighten the gloom. Instead of making us hesitant about buying green bananas, the thought of the end of life or the world should urge us to visit that sick friend today, make that phone call now, write that letter, give that bit of praise or thanks before we forget, call on that neglected parent, or surprise that depressed friend.

November 16

While we may need anything from a glass of milk to a little walk to a glass of brandy or even a prescription to at times get to sleep, as we grow in our following of Christ we can hope that our faith and trust in him will help. Psalm 4 goes: "As soon as I lie down, I fall peacefully asleep, for you alone, O Lord, bring security to my dwelling" (v. 9).

That may sound too simple and absolute to be true, but it may be a good prayer in any case, as is the rest of that psalm called a "night prayer" in my translation. It's one of those psalms that reinforces our trust by helping us put it into words: "Know that the Lord does wonders for his faithful one; the Lord will hear me when I call upon him" (v. 4).

A bit further we read: "Many say, 'Oh, that we might see better times!' " The second part of the verse suggests an answer to this prayer: "O Lord, let the light of your countenance shine upon us!"

We shouldn't be misled by the simplicity of these statements about how God, the Lord, blesses us, hears us, brings us happiness, makes us go to sleep peacefully and without struggle. As the history of God's dealings with the people and the experience of all of us shows, God's goodness to us comes more often then not through some kindness, some love, some joy given by another. A woman (in a novel) speaking of a man who rescues her from loneliness and a hard life says, "He was a glance from God." God's glances, touches, encouraging words, peace, come most often through people around us. When we become more willing to see that and less expectant of command appearances by God, we gain more reason for trusting that our prayers are heard, that God will light up our life, that we can lie down to sleep with utter confidence.

November 17

To expect or, worse, to demand that we have a blueprint for the future, that we know when the end or our end is going to be, to know what is going to happen—ignoring Jesus' reminders that we do not and cannot know the hour or the day—this amounts to a rejection of our freedom and responsibility. If it's all up to the stars or to some plan of God's that does not involve our efforts, then what we do is of no consequence and we are simply robots.

But the future comes through God's grace *and* our work and life. To insist on a complete itinerary for what is to happen and when it's to happen is to reject the great dignity we have in our ability to cooperate with God. It is to refuse faith and demand, instead, God's knowledge. Part of the human condition is to learn to accept uncertainty, or put more positively, to put genuine trust in the God we believe in who brought Jesus through awful suffering and death to resurrection.

Even our faith that we, too, will rise does not take away our worry, though it certainly should give us trust. It does not give us knowledge; it gives us assurance that "he has the whole world in his hands."

We need some of the faith and trust expressed so beautifully in the words of Cardinal Newman's famous hymn: "Lead, kindly light, amid the encircling doom, / Lead thou me on, the night is dark, and I am far from home. / . . . . / I do not ask to see the distant scene; one step enough for me. . . . / His power has blessed me for so long, / Surely it will still lead me on . . . . / till the night is gone."

Doesn't, as he says, the past, our experience of the Lord's love—he has blessed me for so long—argue that we can trust him for the future too?

November 18

"The Word, Christ, became flesh and dwelt among us" (John 1) summarizes the tone of the New Testament accounts of Jesus. And the other three Gospels in their own way insist on how the Son of God lived human life and died human death. In between, Jesus' involvement was so total that he was blamed for hanging around with vagrants and gluttons, people in sordid professions, and those nonobservant of the religion of the place. Yet despite all this, in the Christian tradition there has been a good slice of emphasis on avoiding human contact, on withdrawal from the world in order to find God somehow apart from and despite the created world and our fellow human beings. A very famous and oft-reprinted book, *The Imitation of Christ,* is especially strong in arguing that mingling with the masses is always bad for the "soul."

Fortunately, there are other approaches in our tradition that recognize that if God has chosen to be with us through and in a human life and in this world, then we might reasonably expect to find God there, too! Above all, the great and justly prized St. Francis of Assisi exemplifies this positive appreciation of God's creation. His famous *Canticle of the Creatures* is full of it:

> Be praised, my Lord, with all your creatures, especially Brother Sun, who brings us the day, and through whom you give light; he is beautiful and radiant with great splendor. He shows you to us, God Most High.
>
> Be praised, my Lord, for Sister Moon and the stars; you have formed them bright, precious and fair in the sky.
>
> Be praised, my Lord, for Brother Wind, and for air and clouds, calms and all weather you give us.
>
> Be praised, my Lord, for Sister Water, who is humble and dear and pure.
>
> Be praised, my Lord, for Brother Fire, through whom you light up the night; he is beautiful, strong and joyous.
>
> Be praised, my Lord, for our Sister Mother Earth, who sustains us and holds us to her breast, who produces abundant fruit, flowers and trees.

And we can go on, can't we? Be praised, my Lord, for good food and meals together; be praised for the sight of great gymnasts and dancers; be praised for Tom, who is so fresh and light-hearted; be praised for Susan, who is always there to help; be praised for John, for cooking a great dinner; . . . be praised for . . . .

November 19

A few years ago Bruce Springsteen sang: "When I look at myself I don't see the man I wanted to be. . . . I'm caught movin' one step up and two steps back." Even our best efforts so often leave us feeling the same way. And it's discouraging. The temptation, the immediate reaction, is to grit the teeth, harden the jaw, and determine that I am going to do differently. And undoubtedly there is a time and place for all that, at least for some of it.

There's also a more radically Christian approach, one that leaves less space for self-satisfaction but allows real peace. Possibly, after years of battling the same old bad habit or personal stupidity, it's time to say: Lord, you know and see how little I live up to my ideal, how I keep falling back from my best efforts. Maybe this is what you came to save us from: not just these faults but our excessive dependence on ourselves, our trust in ourselves, our pride in what we can do.

Why does every Christian worship service begin with a prayer for forgiveness, a recognition of sin and the need for mercy? Isn't it because no matter what we do, we always have a need for forgiveness, for the voice of God saying: I know you bumble; trust me and start again. Trust me, even when the starting seems to get you nowhere.

A great part of the Christian message is that it isn't simply a matter of me looking at myself and not seeing all that should be, but of recognizing that my becoming what I should be is gift, a work of God, a matter of grace. On our part what's needed is trust, humility, confidence, letting go.

November 20

"I thank God in all my remembrance of you . . . from the first day until now" (Phil 1:3-5). Our thankfulness is largely fed by remembrance of something past, some happening or event or, more likely, someone from our past—our parents back in Madelia, friends at another school, old chums separated by a continent or two from us. We remember Jill's great laugh, Lou's improvisations at the piano. We remember Miss Snodgrass who spent all that time helping us get the math, or the great times we had hiking with Bill, and a crowd of similar matters. It's a truly odd person who never thinks of good things that have happened or lovely people from the past. Our faith, too, like the Jewish faith, is built around remembrance of something past. We assemble around the altar for the Lord's Supper because he told us to do it "in remembrance of me." Each celebration of the Eucharist is a recalling with thanksgiving of what Jesus has done by his dying and rising; it brings before us the suffering, death, and resurrection. Eucharist is an English version of the Greek word for thanksgiving.

But we thank God, give praise to God, not only by recalling with gratitude what *has been* but also by our life and words here and now. We thank God by our manner of life, our spirit, our enthusiasm, our joy, the attention and care we give to who and what is before us. Possibly we need to give more attention to the present, to being thankful for what it holds, for what is before us, what we have of opportunity, friends, possibilities. Too much or exclusive thinking of the past can easily only leave us dissatisfied with the present; we hanker only for the "good old days." The same for the future: If it has too strong a hold on us we never really live in the present, now; the "good old days" in that case are yet to come. To be alive now means to be present to what is before us, not to let the present pass while we dream of the future or regret the past. Every day should begin with an effort to open our eyes, ears, and minds to all the goodness, beauty, wonderful things and people around us, so that all our thanksgiving isn't only after the fact but accompanies what we do and enjoy right now. Today.

November 21

Learning to take ourselves more lightly is partly a matter of seeing life and its details as part of a larger picture. Obviously there are some matters that cannot, no matter how we look at them, be dismissed lightly: our responsibilities, other people's troubles and feelings, cancer, famine, war, death, sin. But we shouldn't too readily put everything on that same level. After all, besides Beethoven and Tchaikovsky, there's also Weird Al Yankovic and Bobby McFerrin. The point here is that we handle little injuries better by laughing them off than by some big show of macho might or pouting. To be taken advantage of is not the end of the world. "It's those who won't be taken who cannot seem to give."

By putting things in a larger perspective we mean primarily (1) situating the issue in a longer period of time, (2) seeing it in terms of more than our own backyard, and (3) seeing it relative to the problems of others. (1) A Japanese writer says: "An event becomes humorous, loses some of its apparent heaviness when it is taken out of its limited frame and placed in a larger one." Time and distance easily turn today's sorrow into tomorrow's smile. With enough time and distance we can even take some of those heartbreaks more lightly, like the fellows in the country western ditties who turn heartbreaks into corny lines like my favorite: "She stepped on my heart and stomped that sucker flat." (2) We easily get so close to our work or concerns that our world—academia, politics, business or finance, competition of some kind—becomes grim, something not to be joked about. "The grave world," someone has written, "is indeed the world of the grave."

(3) Finally, our worries, projects, lose some of their world-shaking importance and tragic dimensions when put alongside those of others. A little listening to them and some imagination can make us realize what others are going through. Our worries about a promotion or getting to South Padre Island for our vacation becomes pretty forgettable and petty when compared to those of the sick and bedridden, those struck by famine and drought, the unemployed, the high school friend who has lost an arm or a leg. The things we rage, worry, and fume about can seem pretty lightweight.

Someone expressed it well in a letter: "When I remember that the sun sets this week in Alaska, and will not come up again until the end of February, the gray skies here in Minnesota start to look pretty good."

November 22

Speaking of the end of things, Jesus says in Luke (12:35ff.): "let your belts be fastened around your waists and your lamps be burning ready." A reminder about readiness for the return of Jesus or even for the end of life. And he adds: "The Son of Man will come when you least expect him."

All this is a very good reason to ignore the dozens of paperbacks that will be coming out between now and the turn of the century telling us that the year 2000, that nice round number, will be the end. And a lot of these will be written by people who pride themselves on taking the word of Christ and the Bible very seriously. But what are they doing with Christ's words about the *unexpectedness* of the time of his arrival, the fact that we will not know the time, the day, the year? They seem to have decided to ignore that teaching. I sometimes think that these people aim to be a sort of churchy equivalent of popular horror movies.

Earlier in this same section our Lord says: Do not live in fear. His message, in other words, is not an invitation to a sort of religious terror, to anxious fear and worry, but to generous, confident living today. We should always suspect that religious messages purporting to be Christian yet aiming to terrify, have more to do with Stephen King or Frankenstein than they do with Jesus. What possible excuse is there for thinking of the Lord as some kind of terrorist? Unavoidable as fear and worry are for all of us at times, still, our ideal should be to have that kind of confidence in the love and concern of Jesus that drives out all fear and permits us to live in joy, trust, and courage.

November 23

We may get to Lourdes or Rome or the Holy Land, but even then our pilgrimage is not over. To be a pilgrim fits any Christian, booked on Holy Land tours or not. We're always pilgrims, never totally at rest in our following of Christ. Till the end of our time we are always on the move. At any point along the way, we are, to varying degrees, a mixture: both converted and sinful, trusting and yet doubtful, loving but petty. By our baptism and faith, the New Testament tells us, we have become new creatures, new persons in Christ, given the strength to live in him, risen from the dead and victorious over sin and death. Yet we know there are always elements in our life that look in another direction or pull us elsewhere. There are situations where we are governed more by self-seeking than by self-giving.

We trust and believe that we are on the way to a final resolution of life's conflicts, disappointments, pains. We trust, even though we walk in the shadow of death, that God is with us and active in us. Yet we do at times feel lost, hopeless, despairing: "My God, my God, why have you abandoned me?" At least emotionally, it seems very uncertain that any happy and satisfying solution will come about.

When all this makes us even doubt the reality of our new life in Christ, we should be encouraged to realize that conversion, begun in baptism and in our first decision for Christ, is a gradual affair. It is not ordinarily (is it ever?) a matter of a single, decisive moment. Rather, there is always some need to be open to God, more willingness to trust in God's power and love.

Further, the whole trip is never in isolation. The following of Christ, despite the distinctive individual differences we all have, is made in a caravan, a convoy. There is a crowd going along with us, people seeking the same final likeness to Christ, the same life in God, not always recognizable as such by membership in a Church. Thankful for their encouragement and, more often, for their example, we move toward a lasting meeting with the Lord. And, despite our own weakness and sense of incompleteness, we can always offer others some encouragement and hope.

November 24

This is supposed to be my book in some sense, but very often I realize someone else has said it all so wonderfully. For instance, a great mathematician, physicist, and thinker on religious matters of the seventeenth century, Blaise Pascal said: "We think of the future as too slow in coming; we recall the past only to stop its too rapid flight. . . . We do not think of the only time which is really ours, the present; and if we do think of it, we only use it to arrange the future. And so we never really live, since we are only hoping to live, and, since we are always preparing to be happy, it is inevitable that we never really are happy."

Certainly the future worries us: Will the bomb go off? Will the ozone layer fail? Will our food be contaminated? Will population outrun food supplies? Will Bill get the promotion? Will we be able to pay the bills? Will the biopsy be positive or negative? No one denies there is enough to keep us awake nights. But, really, what better can we do for the future than to work, live, love, act well now, put all our heart into improving this day, this life? Why shouldn't our uncertainty about the future be a strong reminder of how important this place, this November, this responsibility, these people, this job, is? We spoil our time now by looking ahead, only to worry and by neglecting the good before us. As someone else has said: "There is nothing rarer in human life than a moment when we want to be where we are, doing what we are doing." But we need to multiply those moments.

In one of those famous stories, St. Francis de Sales is supposed to have been asked while he was playing pool what he would do if told the world or his life would be over in half an hour. He said he would keep on playing pool. Readiness for the future consists in doing well *now* what we should be doing, whether it's cooking, raking the leaves, going to committee meetings, playing pool, cleaning a room, comforting someone, enjoying a meal or a party. The present is undeniably ours; why not use it with no holds barred, giving it everything? The Lord whom we await is already here now, if we'd only open our eyes to what is now before us.

November 25

The Gospels, St. Paul, Luther, all of Christian tradition, warn us against trust in our works, against thinking that somehow we run up a credit balance with God. It's probably because our society and our world seem so often to value people for what they achieve that we carry such a thought over even into our relations with God. We more or less think, whether we say it or not: Well, look what I've done; aren't you proud? The problem isn't with our working unflaggingly for God and for others. It's with our temptation to think that this is some great good we're conferring on God. In the Gospel (Luke 17:7-10) Jesus tells us that all this should be a little more matter-of-fact. When we have carried out all that we've been asked to do we should say, "We are servants and deserve no credit; we have only done our duty."

For most of us it might be immediately helpful to look at these words as offering a cure for self-pity. After all, it is a dull somber day, the leaves have all fallen, the sky is leaden, it's the middle of the semester, of a trying project, the weather for the past weeks could not have been drearier, and who of us isn't overworked?

Most of us, I would suspect, are tempted to think in very low moments that we are being singled out for harsh treatment, that we're one of those "rare victim souls who are meant to live out their days in shadow and not in sun, sitting among the ruins." After all, who else has such noisy neighbors, such health problems, such scheming colleagues, a malfunctioning radiator, or so many buttons falling off clothes?

Though the words "we have only done our duty" sound so matter-of-fact, the ideal is very steep. It tells us not to pity ourselves, not to dramatize our suffering, not to subtly advertise for pity or gratitude. The ideal is so high and difficult because, in yet another way, it asks us to cease living and thinking as if everything were owed to us. It asks us to recognize that all we have and are are gifts.

We pray to be taught that what we do or have done is but what should be expected of those who have been given so much.

November 26

Frankly, some of the psalms that form part of the everyday religious life of many priests and religious women are in some of their detail plain boring. Recounting in detail long-forgotten battles with the Amalakites or the Perezites often doesn't inspire a twentieth-century American very much. To be fair, they are not simply recounted by the writers for the sake of the history but to thank God for delivering them from this or that enemy. In this way, too, the modern reader or, better yet, the one who prays, can find lines that apply to his or her life. In Psalm 78, for instance, the psalmist says that all this should be recounted to one's children in order that "they too may rise and declare to their sons / that they should put their hope in God, / And never forget the deeds of God."

Those of us who have lived long enough in the Christian faith and in trust in God have our own reasons for being thankful and hopeful for the future. We may not have overcome the Amalakites in battle with God's help, but we do know how we were delivered from this illness, this misery, this danger, so many times and given the life we still have. Our reasons for living life generously now are often that God has done so much for us in the past; we have experienced in the love of others for us the assurance of God's loving care. We should tell our children that they, too, should hope in God and never forget what God can do.

But we'd do better in not taking that injunction too literally. What do teenagers revolt against more than being "told" again and again how grateful they should be? We should concentrate more on simply living a life—minus a lot of direct preaching—where we trust in God, put our hope in God, are basically happy and thankful without constant carping, preaching to others, to our family. Won't our trust in God come through by the values we exhibit, the things we consider important, where we put our trust? Even when children do not seem to see or appreciate what we believe and feel, we can trust that faith and gratitude will "out," that they will have an impact.

November 27

Peace and love, harmony and tranquillity; yes, of course, but not prematurely or at the expense of justice and respect for others. The rush to declare that all is peace and harmony can be at times a covering up of real problems, wishful thinking. The word "peace" can be used as a sort of tranquilizer, a way to hush up difficulties and suffering. Peace, like love, truth, hope, has to be won, earned, learned, be the result of justice and truth. Peace without that foundation is a bit like the false smile that hides enmity and differences, a mask of serenity put over a grimace.

Fairly often in Christian history peace and harmony have been sought with too little regard for those who have every reason to regard the present situation as intolerable. Rather than face injustice, degrading poverty, aggravation, insults to human dignity, peace has been used as a sort of club to beat down agitators, troublemakers, subversives, prophets. The justly valued idea of harmony and unity signified in the Eucharist has been used too easily as an excuse for harsh uniformity, conformity, surrender of rights, or abdication of needs.

In our pursuit of peace we need to face the difficult task of balancing the legitimate needs and rights of others against what may seem to be a disturbance of someone's peace. The Lord, the one we follow, was not at all reluctant to disturb the peace, to provoke the guardians of what was and of vested interests. With it all, Jesus still maintained and has come down to us as a picture of peace and harmony. Somehow the two can be reconciled. If we regularly seek peace and reconciliation as goals in our lives, let us ask ourselves whether we accept the legitimacy of disturbing that peace in the interests of truth and justice, even of honest peace.

November 28

Laypeople are at times justifiably confused (to put it most mildly) or, worse yet, irritated by the jargon of contemporary theology, which sometimes comes across in sermons untranslated. Some of the terms that seem to be jargon are forgivable attempts to recover something, for example, eucharist, meaning thanksgiving. Some of them just seem trendy. The words "minister," "to minister," and "ministry" may have been common among Protestants but are relatively new in their common use among Catholics. I suspect they are here to stay, and basically they are not of the same objectionable quality as "eschatology," "preferential option for the poor," and "praxis." In fact, "minister" and "to minister" enshrine a very down-to-earth and important part of our following of Christ.

They come from the Greek word for serving, for waiting on someone. Christ defined himself as one who came to serve, not to be served. With insight reflecting this, the popes have been called, not always with corresponding behavior, "servants of the servants of God," ministers. But service, ministering, is by no means limited to the Lord, the Savior, and to popes or to mother, father, or nurses. It is a consequence of becoming members of the body of Christ by our baptism. We are plunged into the life of Jesus dying and rising in baptism in order ourselves to learn to die and rise, much of it through our willingness to minister to the good of others.

The term "minister," even in its present use in the Church, can be given very specified and even official meanings, but the reality of service, of actually doing something that helps make the kingdom of God real by using any talent or goods for others is something that doesn't wait on official recognition by the Church or anyone else. It is our following of Christ. Like him we should rejoice that we are able to, this day, minister to those around us: the sick, the young or elderly, the poor, the lonely, the wearied, the confused, the groping and discontented, the unhappy.

November 29

Good shepherd, king, light, rock, fortress, the way, the truth—we're familiar with these titles or comparisons for the Lord our God. But thief? I Thessalonians (5:2) makes the comparison: "The day of the Lord comes like a thief in the night." And in Matthew's Gospel (24:42-43) the Lord himself says: "Keep awake, then; for you do not know on what day your Lord is to come. Remember, if the householder had known at what time of night the burglar was coming, he would have kept awake." Bible scholars think this is a sure sign that this is an exact recounting of something Jesus himself said. No early follower would have dared compare the King, the Lord, the Light of the World, to a thief.

Yet despite this and similar ideas expressed elsewhere in the New Testament, "It is not for you to know about dates and times" (Acts 1:6-7), there are regularly people who insist that they can tell us when the Lord is returning or when our present world will end. One of the most memorable was an American named William Miller who announced that March 21, 1844, was the day. His followers let their fields go unplanted, gave away their money, and settled their debts. When nothing happened, it was rescheduled for October 21 of the same year, again with equally disappointing results.

Dates have been set in every age: 1260; 1533; 1752; February 28, 1763; June 12, 1933; and January 1972. Undoubtedly that nice round number, the year 2000, will attract another set of predictions. The paperbacks should be arriving at the drugstores right now. One well-known TV evangelist, while not specifying the date, has already given us a detail: He will return with Jesus. The last days, too, it seems will include reruns.

But this defiance of Scripture about how unexpected and unknown the end will be is simply dangerous and misleading. The point of the scriptural teaching of Jesus is to stress just the *unpredictability* of his coming. We're supposed to learn from all this to be always awake, watchful. We're to live *now* in vigilance and wholeheartedness, not in terror and fear. For while the Lord's coming may be like a thief in the night, the one who comes is our light, our rock, our fortress, our shepherd.

November 30

We are often baffled at the behavior or response of others, and if we're honest, we're also baffled at our own behavior, dreams, thoughts, and desires. What is going on? we often think. We are mysteries to ourselves and all the more to others. How much more likely it is that others are mysteries to us. Why should they be any easier to understand than we are? Love of others, of course, tries to bridge the gap, to make up with sympathy and patience what is bound to be lacking to our understanding. But still others are to a degree forever incomprehensible, forever cause for amazement.

Because we are such mysteries to ourselves and others, however, it is still valuable for us to give some attention to what others have to say or think about us. No matter how off the course their judgments may be, they usually contain a kernel of truth worth using for self-examination. At the same time, knowing how imperfect their judgments of us are, we should be wary of our judgment of them. The extreme of our judging others is what we call prejudice, literally, to judge others beforehand, before we really know what they are like. How we cut off our understanding and love of others by terms that are meant to definitively categorize them: farmer, city boy, executive, housewife, black or white, lawyer, nerd, spic, wop, redneck. J. P. Sartre has said, "We only become what we are by the radical and deepseated refusal of that which others have made of us." That may be a bit overstated. But it might encourage us to respect more our own mystery and that of others.

To respect mystery and incomprehensibility in ourselves and in others is a way of recognizing the depth of God's gifts to all of us, a way of keeping wonder and appreciation alive in ourselves. What better way to greet each day and each person than with expectation, wonder, a willingness to be surprised, to have our guesses, judgments, and prejudices overturned.

December 1

Waiting, as I've argued in other places, can be a waste of time. It is a waste when it means we give short shrift to the present, fail to take it seriously, to give it our all. But waiting is an undeniably important part of our life, of the spirit that keeps us going and moves us. We wait for a baby to come, maybe especially the couple who wait their first. They know it will be something great, entirely new to them; they probably have little idea or possibility of even imagining how much it will change their lives.

We wait for the visit of a dear friend from whom we have been separated for a long time. Or for a son or daughter away for the first time to come home—even with a bag of laundry, an earring, or spiked orange hair. Or those who are elderly wait for any little sign that they are still remembered or count: a phone call, a card or letter, a visit. Life may depend on such moments.

We wait expectantly and anxiously for a vacation, a chance to ski or golf, for the relief of a weekend after a hard time at the office. Waiting and expecting implicitly show that we recognize things as they are—not perfect, they could be better. We need hope, things to hope for, to live for, friends to want to see and hear from, unexpected happenings and events. They are like bursts of energy in our life, pushing us on, helping us to face the present with more verve and vitality.

Because they mean so much to us, we can and should realize how much they must mean to others. How much *we* can help provide that lift for others by our kindness, thoughtfulness, by remembering them, introducing occasionally the unexpected and joyous into their lives, a visit, a phone call, a letter, a greeting.

December 2

What do the drug culture, some of our evangelists, and sponsors of seminars on how to turn your life around all have in common? I'd say a denial of a basic condition of human life: that we grow and that we grow most often gradually. The attraction of those movements and preachers is the promise of immediate change or transformation, immediate relation to God or experience of God. It appeals to our impatience with the grind that is the ordinary path of human development. We somehow think or at least wish that a perfect relation to God and to others should be attainable in the same way that a hot cup of coffee is. Possibly we need to have tried to be another Greg Louganis or Bonnie Blair or Wynton Marsalis in order to realize that perfection comes about only through blood, sweat, and tears or, at least a lot of perspiration and patience. Even when it's a matter of allowing the all-powerful Lord to act in us.

Interesting experiments have been made with people taking LSD or some chemical equivalent, some drug that gives the recipient at least a facsimile of the presence of God or something extraordinary. During such sessions the clients have often felt an ocean of love washing over them and all of creation: "I love everyone," they murmur. Coming back to reality after the drug has worn out has not only brought a letdown to ordinary earth and human life but also painful realization (at least to others) that the egoism and selfishness present before the drug are still there. There is no instant way to selflessness or genuine love for others. As someone has written: "When you see the psychedelic leaders of the world, after a gorgeously mystical brotherhood love session, as they are coming down, having a bitter argument about who should wash the dishes, a sense passes through one that somehow sainthood has been missed" (Leech). We're better off imitating the selflessness and perseverance of the saints among us than expecting to be instantly transformed by some ecstatic experience in drugs or prayer.

December 3

Coming on the expansiveness, confidence, and downright exultation of St. Paul's faith in the Lord, we realize how reluctant, how cautious and timid ours seems to be. In Ephesians we have this, for example: "In him [Christ Jesus our Lord] we have access to God with freedom, in the confidence born of trust in him" (Eph 3:12). Or, in another translation, we hear of the "boldness and confidence" with which we may approach God through Christ. This spirit of freedom, boldness, confidence, is not simply Paul's gift for us to admire from the outside. It is open to us in the same way that it was to Paul; not by some overserious striving on our part but by surrendering ourselves to the loving care of God. To face the business world, our competition, and daily challenges, we are told to "put on" the right kind of clothing, a confident air and step, a positive attitude. In the following of Christ, this boldness and confidence are not our production but something we open ourselves to by more childlike surrender to the power of God. Lord, replace our weakness and timidity with trust and joy rooted in our certainty that you support and lead us.

All the stress in this book on confidence, trust, and even joy in the Lord is not meant to be an invitation to some private, cozy comfort, to suggest that we can sit in the corner or by the fire (or in air-conditioned comfort) and let the rest of the world go by. My hope and belief—for you as well as for myself—is that the strength coming from such trust and even elated confidence will provide us with the foundation for facing an often discouraging, even hopeless-appearing world, a frightening world, or at very least, a simply dull and tiring world. Just as Scripture tells us the Word of God is not given just as an ornament in this world but to bring about change (Isa 55:11), so God's power in us and our resolution and boldness are meant to help us bring to this very broken world the help, courage, and joy we have received. We should approach our world with the freedom, boldness, confidence, that is God's gift.

December 4

The Book of Sirach says, "If a man is to be wise he must be relieved of other tasks. How can a man become wise who guides the plow, whose pride is in wielding his goad, who is absorbed in the tasks of driving oxen . . .?" (38:24-25). The suggestion is one we're familiar with, that one needs time or withdrawal from ordinary occupations to know ourselves, our relation to God, to better our following of Christ, to be "wise." The passage seems to accept the idea that wisdom and ordinary occupations (we would probably say business, politics, professional work, any work) are incompatible, an idea I would hope most of us would reject.

To say that following the plow, riding the tractor, facing the computer, guiding a case through court, or any other occupation must prevent us from gaining wisdom seems to show some lack of appreciation for learning that may be found in our daily occupations. Don't we—or can't we?—learn something of significance to our following of Christ in facing the problems of our daily work: the difficult people, the knotty dilemmas, the delicate balancing of sensitivities, the boredom of a particular activity, the tiring hours, the unrequited generosity and good humor we must show?

From all this a kind of wisdom can be learned that we need to value more, not less. Doesn't daily work teach us about patience, forgiveness, respect for others, for the world, the needs of others, loyalty and honesty, perseverance? Toward the end of this passage Sirach comes to a more positive evaluation of daily work: "But they [these workers] maintain the fabric of this world, and their prayers are about their daily work." It recognizes that our daily work is a necessary contribution to human existence; and that correctly we include its concerns in our prayer.

Without abandoning or ignoring the value in the withdrawal afforded by retreats, time for reading (a book like this), time for prayer and reflection, can we not also see that we gain some insight in fulfilling the responsibilities and needs of daily work? Possibly the Church would gain from being more willing to learn from baptized Christians who spend a great part of their lives in what we so easily call "secular" occupations.

December 5

"It is in giving that we receive, in pardoning that we are pardoned" (words from a famous prayer attributed to St. Francis of Assisi). Giving has a much more basic place in the following of Christ than we customarily realize. Our widespread misunderstanding of the word "sacrifice" lessens our appreciation of giving. So often, "to sacrifice" (or "a sacrifice") in our understanding means to give *up* something. I sacrificed my time for such and such (I gave it up to do this other thing); people make sacrifices during Lent; they give up pleasures, satisfactions. "Christ gave up his life on the cross" fits the same understanding.

But "sacrifice" or "to sacrifice" means simply to give something, to give a present. It follows that an essential part of sacrifice is that the person to whom the gift is given accepts it. In ancient times the burning of the animal sacrificed, given to God, was taken as a sign of acceptance. Jesus gave his life, offered it to God; God accepts it by giving Jesus a new life, the resurrection and ascension.

It would give our life as Christians a more positive note and show that it is not motivated by some hatred of our world or its goods if we would think of sacrifice as giving. We give good things to God or to others *because they are good,* not because they are evil or dangerous. Please take into your love and care so-and-so, whom we love so much but whom we cannot care for at this distance. We give him or her to you. Our offering of ourselves, in prayer or at the Eucharist, with Christ, is a giving of our lives, our work, our talent, and achievements to God, from whom all these good things come in the first place. We give them to others, too, insofar as we serve their needs or help them to live.

December 6

In the time of Jesus there were names traditionally used in certain families. One didn't casually decide to call one's son Perry when all the firstborn sons in the Swenson family had been called James for generations. In the account of the expectation of the birth of John the Baptist, we are told that to the surprise of the neighbors and family, John's father Zechariah said that the boy was to be named John instead of one of the names traditional in the family (Luke 1:57-64). The change in tradition was not because the parents or father had been so impressed with a movie idol or a popular rock star named Iggy or Nigel or John. No, the name change would signify some hope or faith of the parents. In this case, giving the child the name John, which means God is gracious or God's gracious gift, was thanksgiving for the child to be born to an elderly couple.

Further, the name given to this boy who was to announce the coming of Jesus also signified that he was to proclaim in Jesus God's great gift to all or Jesus as the sign of God's gracious love. The prayer that Zechariah uttered was one of praise and thanksgiving to God for the son who was born and the Savior who was to come. Mary's famous prayer in the same chapter of Luke (2) is similarly filled with gratitude and praise. In putting these before us Scripture is not simply recounting something historical but illustrating the response and spirit with which we, too, should serve God (modeled for us in people like Zechariah and Mary), a spirit of thanksgiving and faith.

We can do two things with this: 1) We can let praise and gratitude liberate us from our smallness and self-centeredness and keep before us that all of life is a gift, a truly liberating and heart-expanding attitude; and 2) we should move this attitude out from our prayer life into ordinary life and conversation. Before asking ourselves or God why some disappointment or pain happens, we should at least aim at more appropriately asking why we've been so blessed, so gifted with friends, love, and even with more mundane things such as comfort, leisure, health.

December 7

Someone has defined the bureaucrat as a person who knows he or she will eventually give you what you need but who always says no the first time you ask. Whether it's a genuine bureaucrat or a supervisor we must deal with, an official we cannot avoid, someone who has charge of something we have need of, there are in all of our lives inevitably some difficult individuals. Possibly everyone is someone else's difficult person. These people keep us awake the night before as we worry about our reception and what they or we are going to say. We put off seeing them if possible. We do without whatever we need rather than face that stomach-churning encounter. Perhaps more of us serve the same function in the lives of others than we realize. The possibility that we may be such a terror to others could help keep us a bit more humble and make us more sensitive.

But what do we do about the ogres in our lives, our apartments or neighborhoods, our offices or places of business, at the checkout counter or at the government office? I'm still not sure. Following are some suggestions, rooted, I think, in an effort to look on our world with love.

We could regard such encounters with more of a sense of humor, thinking how funny it is that another human being can make me tremble so or frighten me. Maybe it's their only way of realizing some sense of importance in a dull job or one filled with exasperating encounters like the one with you or me. Maybe the person who seems to terrorize us is having a bad day, has a lot of them (is chronically sick or beset by financial problems or worries about a sick child), or would rather be in Vancouver.

Finally, a tough fact for those who want to exercise good will toward everyone is the recognition that we are going to irritate each other no matter what we do. We may aim to show everyone good will, but not everyone can return it or, at least, not everyone can stomach me—my laugh, my sense of humor, my interest, my manners. We need to recognize the many differences without regarding them as cause for anger or shock. The difficulties we experience in achieving complete happiness, even in our best relationships, plus the fact that a relationship with us does not appeal at all to many people—all testify to a sort of built-in cross in human existence. Finally, besides humor, sympathy, and understanding, we're left with the constant need to forgive and to be forgiven.

December 8

While we may properly see prayer as a refuge, a moment that can refresh and strengthen us for life, others may see it as a hiding place, an escape from responsibility to the world. For Christians there is no question about the necessity of prayer; the only question is when and how we will make that clear in our lives. But does it echo in our active life, in the kitchen, the office, the school, the cocktail hour, the supermarket, on the baseball diamond, at the board meeting? Our prayer has to be tested by what we are and how we act outside the actual time of prayer.

Mahatma Gandhi wrote somewhere that all prayer is political, that when we pray we have some ideals we want realized, and if they are realized they affect the world and those around us. Further, these ideals are not simply something we pray about and for, but they drive us to act in a certain way and to support certain positions in our world. We are for the preservation of nature's beauty and variety; we are against violence to anyone, any place.

Prayer is no substitute for plans, decisions, intelligence, prudence, care, work. We cannot take it to mean don't study, pray; don't see the doctor, pray; don't look for a job, pray. Or that we can pray for the sick and never take the trouble to visit them. Or that we can simply pray for peace and pass up appropriate opportunities to work for it and against war. Nor does it mean that we simply pray that the Jeannie or John of our dreams will appear whether we try to attract him or her by risking a greeting or demonstrating our downright lovableness and unselfishness.

Genuine prayer must be accompanied by the willingness to do what we can even though the prayer itself may be the very source of our action. When all is said and done, prayer is no substitute for our action, and action itself doesn't replace prayer. There are limitations to what any one of us can do for the world's or our neighbor's woes. In terms of time, talent, place, other responsibilities, we are not all able to fly to the help of Cambodian refugees or the homeless people in an American ghetto. Honest concern must, at times, eventually entrust them and their needs to God as well as to what we humans can do. Concerned prayer, when it does not attempt to simply replace action, is also a form of love.

December 9

What do marriage and the Holy Spirit have in common? Once you start thinking in such bizarre ways, there are a number of similarities. For example, they both have to do with love. But what has struck me recently is how both change us. We ask and expect the Holy Spirit in the liturgy and Christian tradition to come into us, light a fire and change us. (I am not going to compare the Holy Spirit to Jim Morrison!) And marriage certainly has great potential for changing people. In a moving novel about African Americans (Zora Neale Hurston, *Their Eyes Were Watching God*, p. 171), the heroine, against the advice of friends, is about to marry one Tea Cake. One of her close friends tries to dissuade her and tells her she is taking an awful chance. Janie replies that it's no more than anyone takes when they get married; and, marriage, she says, always changes people.

Despite our extraordinarily strong tendency to want to stay put, to have everything settled once and for all, much of our happiness depends on trying to cooperate with the forces that change us. Certainly, there are changes in several directions, but we have good reasons to trust in the power of love to change us for the better. We should broaden all this and realize that it's not simply married love than can do this but any genuine love. That list in 1 Corinthians 13 of what love does could probably be understood of what potential love has for any of us. It can make us patient, kind, free of envy and boasting, conceit and rudeness, unselfish, not hypersensitive, slow to remember wrongs, happy with the truth, able to believe, hope, endure.

Looking at the loves in our life, let's ask ourselves what each has to teach us or how it works to change us. Our cooperation, being open to what love wants to do, how it wants to change us, is really receptivity to the Holy Spirit, from whom all true love comes.

December 10

A good conscience, peace within, peace with God, self, and others, integrity, excellence—all are terms for qualities of personality and character that most probably consider desirable, even essential. And all are distinct from success. The way our world works, excellence and success do not necessarily coincide, though there seems to exist a great desire that they should. One who has integrity and inner peace is not guaranteed success, and vice versa. Look at the greatest example, Jesus Christ. Perfect relation with God and unswerving fidelity to conscience—but dead at thirty-three, on a cross.

Success may be linked to hard work and therefore seem to be deserved, seem right. It may also be linked to chance, fad, fashion, arbitrary factors, to "luck in the gene lottery" that has provided us with some quality much in demand this particular season. And, of course, it may be linked to simple fraud, robbery, unscrupulousness. Too, it is fickle: It easily moves on to other heads, crowns other people. It even gave Jesus the nod for a few minutes on that Palm Sunday. Things looked pretty good for a while.

But we need to realize very deeply that the two are not necessarily identical, success and excellence or goodness. Excellence or a kind of satisfying wholeness is something within, the result of energies and powers being given to the service of what is good. No one can take it away from us, and without it we do not even respect ourselves.

Success can never promise to be there in "sickness and in health . . . till death do us part." But the God-given and hard-earned qualities of a good spirit will endure even when the crowd has altered its tastes. Neither time nor fashion nor the market can take it away.

December 11

That *Mad* character, Alfred E. Newman, is always quoted as saying "What? Me worry?" Judging from the look on his face we can suppose that he is free from worry because of an empty mind incapable of imagining any reasons to worry. Optimism can come from such emptiness or just from being awfully healthy or young or as the result of a great breakfast, an exhilarating jog, or a few beers. There's nothing wrong with this kind of positive attitude toward life and the world. In fact, we shouldn't overlook the necessity of some effort at good health, recreation, and so on, using what nature and life provide to keep us in a courageous frame of mind.

But all this isn't the same as hope. Hope expects better things because of a belief in the God of Jesus Christ, who is both able to and concerned to bring God's world and people to fulfillment. That can be there when we're lying on a sickbed or crying over a disappointment or facing grim news from the doctor.

There's hope when we expect to come across honest politicians and civil servants; when we believe the Church can be better at following Christ; when we do not accept poverty and war as routine; when we expect the new and the better after high school, after the wedding, after retirement; when we take it for granted that there will be some new ideas and practices in our life even after twenty-five; when we expect our children, our parents, the pope, the Church, to change.

Hope expects something from prayer and from our cooperation with grace. Hope is present when we are open to new solutions for nagging, fighting, illness, drug and alcohol abuse, misunderstanding. Hope tells us that we haven't seen anything yet and that God is not limited by what we can imagine. Listening to the golden oldies may be perfectly harmless; in real life we need to live now, of course, but with great expectations for the future. "But my trust is in you, O Lord; I say, 'You are my God. In your hands is my destiny'" (Ps 31:15-16).

December 12

The crosses and medals that may hang today from Madonna or George Michael are a sort of parody of what used to be the situation of many Catholics. Besieged by vendors of all sorts of religious devotions, scapulars of every size and color, devotions to the appearances of Mary at a variety of geographical spots, the responsive (sometimes unthinking) Catholic could end up weighed down by a load of medals and religious hardware. Some of that may persist.

But more frequently today Catholics and other Christians are besieged by a crowd of good causes and movements all asking our time and energy and sometimes promising guilt (as did the old devotions) if we don't pick up the particular cause. The Christian attentive to God and God's will certainly must be open to the challenges put before them: the cause of the grape-pickers, abused children, abortion, famine-stricken countries, civil rights, whales, volunteering for school lunches or something else at the local parish, visiting shut-ins, a renewal program in the parish, ozone depletion, a prayer group. And all this besides the care of one's own family, business commitments, one's aging parents or sick friends, one's health, the need to keep up with one's field, to take a course, a seminar, to update—and one is left with some questions, pulled in a variety of directions. The choices are not the famous and dramatic ones between good and evil, but between a number of good possibilities.

As in the case of the devotions of another day, it was or should have been up to the conscience of the individual to make the choice about what he or she can do or take on. The too pliant among us may need to be reinforced in that conviction, that it is *my* right to decide what I can do, my conscience that must make the choice.

And that doesn't mean simply some individualistic, self-centered stance, but you and I must on the basis of principles relevant to our response to God decide what should be done, where our energies and time are to go. For example, it is definitely a matter of our circumstances, our time, our prior and natural obligations (to family, neighborhood, work), our resources. Not everything that is good and appealing is equally important or available to me. Another basic determining factor is my inclination, my abilities. Allowing, of course, for the exceptional person who may feel obliged to leave family and duties in Oak Park to learn Swahili in order to work in Uganda, Tanzania, or Zaire, most of us have a set of givens that cannot easily be shaken for purely romantic or idealistic reasons.

As we face each day and its requirements, we need to lovingly, without all kinds of regrets that we aren't missionaries in Borneo, accept what lies before us. Ultimately, no one else can be our conscience or tell us how to decide priorities among many different attractions and demands.

December 13

"When all this begins to happen [signs in the sea, stars, etc.], stand upright and hold your heads high, because your liberation is near" (Luke 21:28). "Be on the alert, praying at all times for strength to pass safely through all these imminent troubles and to stand in the presence of the Son of Man" (21:36). Stand upright, hold your heads high, be alert. This is what Jesus says should be the response of his followers to all the talk about the shaking of the powers of heaven and earth. These awesome signs have been taken over by people who apparently wanted to produce horror movies or compete with Stephen King but somehow didn't make it and have turned to "religion," who find it profitable to use these texts to scare the living daylights out of those who listen to or read them. These "terrorists" have almost succeeded in taking over these texts for their negative purposes.

But a closer look at any of them shows us that Jesus is calling us to hope and trust, no matter what may happen to the world around us. That the last word will be his, a word of salvation. Stand up, hold your heads high, be alert—such words certainly do not suggest the stance of those who have been cowed and bullied into fear and terror but, rather, of hope and expectancy. The Lord will come, the Lord will help.

Luther had the right idea when he took the words of Psalm 46 and made them into the great hymn "A Mighty Fortress Is Our God." There, faced with the same shaking of the powers of heaven and earth, is the response we, too, should have.

> God is our refuge and our strength,
> an ever-present help in distress.

Therefore we fear not, though the earth be shaken,
> and mountains plunge into the depths of the sea;
Though its waters rage and foam
> and the mountains quake at its surging.
The Lord of hosts is with us;
> our stronghold is the God of Jacob.

Stand up, heads up, alert; the Lord is nigh, the Lord will come, the Lord is with us.

December 14

Loneliness comes in all sizes, ages, and locations. A successful businessman in his late twenties, the apparently abandoned elderly people in nursing homes or apartments, the boy or girl who feels out of step with peers in school, the man or woman in a marriage where dialogue is limited to argument, the highly placed man or woman with whom no one any longer disagrees—any or all may qualify as lonely. Testimony to the prevalence of loneliness is given to some degree by matchmakers and similar services which seem to be doing well. But, of course, not all the lonely necessarily want a partner, a husband or wife even; they'd just like some satisfying friendship, loving interest from someone else.

Without attempting to compete with dating services, singles' groups or aerobics clubs, I'll suggest a few considerations here about our (it's not just *their*) loneliness, something that seems likely to occur almost anytime or anywhere. We've probably felt it strongly, even at a dance, a wedding reception, or in the midst of a family reunion. Some fundamental loneliness, a recognition that no one can completely respond to everything in me, can plumb my depths, can "understand" me, is an essential part of being realistic about life and about our individual uniqueness. The part of us that is left over when our friendships and loves have done their best, points to our need for, our desire for, a bottomless love, God. Someone has said that there is a heart-shaped vacuum in each of us.

Beyond recognizing this, there may be something you or I can do here and now about it. We can use loneliness to sharpen our desire, our need for God, our openness to God in our lives. This is part of the spirit of Advent, that there are depths in us that are only accessible to God.

We can be spurred by our loneliness to concern ourselves with others and with their needs—probably the greatest way of forgetting our own problems, our own selfishness, and our own loneliness. If we are relatively free of loneliness, we can be more sensitive to those who may be overcome by it or at least touched by it. We can show a sensitive interest in their work, their feelings, even, if appropriate or possible, suggest something that might introduce light or warmth, some excitement, into their lives.

It's odd when we think about it, but it may just be our loneliness or possession of depths not easily opened to others that is what we and they have in common at the deepest level.

December 15

The leper says to Jesus: "Sir, if you will to do so, you can cure me" (Matt 8:2). And Jesus responds: "Be cured." It's all so simple sounding, so crisp in the Gospels. Further, in our day many TV preachers make it sound even more certain, simple, and infallible, especially after our check is received. But we know that it doesn't work that easily. It raises the questions, What should we expect from the Lord in regard to our arthritis, heart trouble, bad back, addicted son or spouse? An immediate and better cure than we've gotten from the doctor? Why do the Gospels tease us with all these stories of cures if they just refer to some person who lived nearly two thousand years ago? Maybe these people were just too gullible or saw miracles in unexplained phenomena.

Many such questions occupy scholars and others. But any fair reading of the Gospels leaves us with the impression that we are to expect something similar from the Lord. Our prayer for help should continue—along with the help of the doctor, the antibiotics, and the Motrin. Christian belief in Jesus Christ as Savior entails the trust that our prayer will have results, is not simply self-hypnosis.

What results? A cure of arthritis, an overnight end to Harry's addiction, remission of the cancer? Possibly, but not necessarily. There are too many examples of prayer not resulting in such dramatic changes. Maybe we are cured or helped on another level. If our depression, discouragement, bitterness, self-pity, impatience, anxiety, is lessened, isn't that a genuine type of healing? The Christian believes even without measurable physical changes. Prayer does cure; prayer does make changes, if not in blood cells, in hearts and wills. We are justified in imitating the leper and so many others in the Gospels who went to the Lord for cures.

December 16

My theory is that when life is going well, when things are satisfying, when we feel happy for whatever reason, why not enjoy it to the full? Why not be as happy as the situation allows? Or carefree and bouncy? When we're young, exuberant and hopeful, confident, why repress that in favor of some conformist propriety? Why be held back by all kinds of conventions of society? Let the happiness expand, grow, be expressed, burst bonds and bounds. In other words, take advantage of happiness and joy, milk them, use them, and spread them.

Another part of the theory, or maybe I should say, a hope involved, is that we should maximize our happiness and joy, take advantage of good spirits and tendencies to burst out into song. Then, when hardship, sickness, failure, pain do hit, we'll—we hope—be so accustomed to being happy with life that we will be able to limit its discouraging aspects. We will be able to persist in some joy, some recognition of all the good that has been given us, a spirit of thankfulness and joy.

Life itself with its harshness will soon enough test us and even wear us down. At least if we start with joy and enthusiasm and remain with them as long as possible we have a sort of cushion against heaviness and fearfulness. Maybe we will be merely sobered rather than crushed by catastrophe and failure. Or at the very least, be able to come back from depression and darkness eventually.

This is not to deny that we may plumb the depths of despair and discouragement but that, with this previous training, somehow we may be able to rebound, to live our lives, to be a help and inspiration to others, to not simply wallow in or resign ourselves to the bad, the awful.

Is this possible? It seems to me that no matter what the answer to that is, it is still the better thing here and now to expand and benefit from joy, happiness. No one loses by our doing this, whereas if we are down in the mouth and for petty causes now, we just add to the burden of pain and suffering that fill so many lives. Help us appreciate, Lord, the happiness you send us.

December 17

If we do any prospecting in the hills of the various religions, we come up again and again with what is often called "The Golden Rule." Many find it the convenient point wherein to find that all religions basically teach the same thing. The Hebrew Scriptures and other religions have something of this nature usually: "Do not treat others in a way you would not have them treat you." In Matthew 7:12, Jesus states it minus the negatives: "Treat others the way you would have them treat you."

The point can be made that the form Jesus uses says more than the other form. The negative form says, do not hurt others if you don't want to be hurt; don't cheat others if you don't like being cheated; don't say unkind things to others if you don't like to hear the same. "Treat others the way you would have them treat you"—Jesus' form of the saying—seems to require more. If we think of what most of us mean by the phrase, "the way you would have them treat you," we realize that most of us don't regard anything as too good for dear old me. How would we have others treat us? With respect, love, sensitivity, kindness, consideration for our comfort and special needs. Jesus is saying: If you want love, respect, comfort, good care and help, peace and joy in your life, then go about providing love, respect, comfort, good care and help, peace and joy for others. Don't just avoid hurting them.

Understood this way, Jesus' statement of the Golden Rule repeats what he has said elsewhere (in the same context, the Sermon on the Mount) about loving others as God does, indiscriminately. God lets love fall on people like the rain and sun, without respect for persons, without distinction. If there is a Golden Rule found in almost any religion, then the rule as Jesus teaches it might better be called the Platinum Rule. It's made of a more precious ore.

December 18

In popular speech people often seem to equate atheists with bad people, as if atheists, once they had gotten rid of God, were out to destroy human life. One could point out that in the past and even today some of the world's greatest terrorists or persecutors act in the name of God.

In fact, genuine atheists deserve some attention and respect from believers because the god they are rejecting is often one that Christians should also reject. They are not so much opposed to the existence of God as to what passes as God or the cartoons of God that even believers support. Any idea we have of God is bound to be inadequate, since God is not another object in the world to which we are so accustomed, the world of trees, tunnels, tornadoes, tomatoes, towers, teeth, and telephones. God is utterly beyond our comprehension, and so we are forced to speak of God in terms taken from our experience, all the while trying to remember that God is more than a father or mother, more than beautiful and strong, more than just dependable. But some of our ideas of God and ways of talking about

God can be seriously wrong, a matter of "defaming" God. These are what many atheists reject.

They say it is impossible, for instance, to believe in a God who is so vengeful that the Son must be put to death to satisfy God's anger; or a God who replaces human effort and know-how, making medicine and safety measures useless; a God who is concerned only that *our* country win a war or that *our* team or race or tribe beat out another; or a God who gives financial rewards to those who believe and makes unbelievers poor; or a God who backs up a bunch of petty rules about what to wear or eat or drink; or a God who reinforces the notion that men are superior to women and should run all serious enterprises, and so on.

Possibly we recognize some of our own distortions in those complaints. If so, we have the God of Jesus Christ to help us correct these images. This God is pictured as loving, sharing our suffering, faithful, patient, like a mother or father in solicitude and unchanging love, one who supports every good done to others. More continual exposure to all the varied pictures the Bible gives us of God can save us from making an idol of any one image. God remains always more than even our favorite picture.

December 19

One summer recently I enjoyed a ride along a beautiful ocean shore with a young couple. They had been married several years and were very happy. Later the same day we had an unforgettable, probably once-in-a-lifetime dinner, prepared by the two of them. The tranquility and happiness of the couple contrasted so strongly with the suffering and hopelessness the young man had experienced earlier.

While in graduate school, he was coming out of a very turbulent love affair where both parties were more deeply involved than they ideally wanted to be. This made for an increase of guilt and worry, real agony on his part. It showed up in letters:

> I am bummed out. I tell myself that she isn't worth crying over but I don't feel that way. . . . I'm still not able to study. I need someone so badly to love, but will I find her? . . . God seems to have cotton in his ears. I remember praying as long ago as five years for someone to love me. . . . I feel like giving up. . . . I really want to do well here for my career but I cannot concentrate. . . . Mass Sunday was especially hard; it was "renewal of vows" Sunday. Why don't I have someone to love and someone who loves me?

That must sound familiar to many of us. Maybe I can be forgiven for allowing a friend to write most of this page—changes made to protect anonymity. Knowing that others have gone through such desolation and despair over love may, I hope, encourage us (1) to regard it as worth the trouble, and (2) to realize there is something better beyond, something rewarding our patience and prayer. With Tennyson, we can all say: "Tis better to have loved and lost [even] than never to have loved at all." In fact, Christ seems to teach: Win or lose, love is always better. And really, in the end, you can't lose. Love led Jesus to the cross and to . . . ?

December 20

Waiting and hoping; we do them in such different ways during our life. We wait with impatience for a bus or for someone who is late for an appointment, or even for the toast or for the water to boil. We wait with excitement and anticipation for a once-in-a-lifetime concert or our wedding. Children wait for Christmas; adults, too, in a slightly different way. We wait for news from the doctor with fear, impatience, resignation. Much of our life seems to be carried along, moved along from one waited-for event or person or happening to the next one. As children or college students, we wait for the end of the school year only to wait, toward the end of August, for the beginning of school and a return to the excitement of life with our friends. Those who are suffering or in great pain wait, sometimes, no longer for a cure or better health, but for death, an end to the misery. We wait for the first snowfall, the first frost (if we have hay fever), for the first signs of spring, for good signs in our crops if we farm.

In Advent we wait for the birth of Jesus, the Lord. The Christian believes that Jesus can be reborn in our lives and actions, that God's grace can make this life in us more profound, more forceful, more all pervading. The ancient Christian prayer of this season is, Come, Lord Jesus, come. Come with your power and life to make us better witnesses of your life. Come with your spirit to make us more patient, hopeful, gentle, forgiving, unselfish, courageous, thoughtful . . . what else? In any case, Come, Lord Jesus, change what is into something better. Give us hope for something better, for a more generous life, for more willingness to begin again each day, to be unburdened by the past.

December 21

A song some years ago spoke of love as a tender trap. I took this to mean the irrational, crazy-seeming, and secondary matters attracting us to someone that serve as a sort of trap. We are led by looks, a capacity for fun, a daredevil attitude, to something more stable and enduring beyond all that—marriage, for instance. All those attractive but often nonessential qualities draw us to something more satisfying and wonderful: mutual sharing, self-giving, deep understanding. Of course, it doesn't have to be marriage; it may be a very rewarding and enduring friendship.

Our gravitation to others often involves some sexual attraction difficult to define but which comes across in what we perceive as the other's warmth or mystery. The result is that we're "trapped" into changes in our life, an expansion of our capacities. We find ourselves polishing the car, tinkering with the motorbike, or sweating through our aerobics. We start finding ways to please him or her, to cement and deepen something so promising. We find ourselves practicing self-giving, sharing, self-forgetfulness, even suspending our favorite pastimes, to be with the other more. Attraction to others, the trap, is something inexplicable in its beginnings, something hardly in our control, which leads us into more genuine communion with another.

As a way of expressing our gratitude to God, why not look today at all the friendships and loves of our life and recall how much tenderness, sympathy, appreciation, gratitude, honesty, they have taught us. Every love leaves some mark, some impression on our development, our selves. Praise the Lord for love, for friends, for Ted, Kath, Ben, Ginny.

December 22

In the opening chapter of his Gospel, John tells us that Jesus is the Word of God. In him, in his life *and* words, God has spoken in a final way to human beings. Insofar as human beings can penetrate the mystery of existence—and we cannot completely—we have in Jesus an opening to it, a privileged, God-given view of it. Jesus, God's Word, confirms that there is a loving Father of us all who intends to bring us to our fulfillment, our salvation. Obviously this revelation does not take away our need to respond, to accept, to surrender in loving gratitude to what has come to us in Jesus the Lord.

But this belief that Jesus is *the* revelation of the Father, that in his life and words we have a rock on which to build our hope and confidence, should help us to evaluate all else that is offered to us. It must mean in practice that we cannot look to someone else, to some other savior, for an improvement on that message or a change in it; not to Shirley MacLaine or some guru or some weekend seminar or some apparent vision or some spiritual leader who claims to have extraordinary detail on it. It does not mean that we can forget the help of human intelligence, talent, and accomplishments. They are all, after all, but expressions of God's power and intelligence, and through them God continues to sustain our life, to improve it.

Our fundamental trust must be in the one who has come, as the same St. John says, to enlighten every one of us. It should mean that we give Scripture and the community that brings that Scripture and Jesus to us a dedication of time and attention that is not superseded by something else. The position of Jesus as the Word of God must make us question continually the place and value we give to other, lesser words and movements. If we expect money, Swami Mahadharma, or Ted ("I can change your life in two weeks for two thousand dollars") Brenner to really save us, aren't we abandoning our true hope, the genuine rock? He, Jesus, is the light that enlightens every one of us, the true light of the world (John 1:4-9).

December 23

Over the past years (and one could take any years almost anytime) Christians have caused traffic jams in order to see the face of Jesus on the side of an oil storage tank, jammed a church where the statue of Mary streamed tears, and crowded Lubbock, Texas, to see appearances of Mary. Evidence for the reality of the latter was offered by one of the visitors: "Maxine of Shreveport, La., was one of dozens who announced that their silver rosary chains had turned to gold" (this and other quotations from November 2, 1988, *Christian Century*).

Theologian and historian Martin Marty comments in painfully appropriate words: "The hungry of Ethiopia do not get fed. The suffering die in Mother Teresa's arms. AIDS spreads. Drought persists. And when God wants to work a miracle to inspire faith, apparitions of Mary turn silver rosary chains to gold." It seems to be another example of how our expectations of what God will do in our world are so theatrical, even recreational. We want shows, circuses, alchemy, anything but what we are taught in chapter 25 of Matthew's Gospel. There Jesus says we meet him and serve him in the hungry and naked, the imprisoned.

In the accounts of the temptations of Jesus in the Gospels, he explicitly refuses to work miracles like turning silver into gold, jumping off tall buildings unharmed, or turning stones into bread (even that would have made more sense than silver into gold!).

Throughout the Gospels Jesus' miracles are those of curing, healing, helping the distressed and sick, the abandoned and rejected. The fact that some appearance of Mary or Jesus would turn silver into gold would be more reason to doubt the appearance than to believe it. It is utterly inconsistent with the picture we have of Jesus in the Gospels, of God's activity among us human beings.

The religion of Jesus, the test for our own religion, for appearances and religious experiences, is put well in James 1:27: "The kind of religion which is without stain or fault in the sight of God our Father is this: to go to the help of orphans and widows in their distress and keep oneself untarnished by the world."

December 24

A little solitude forced on us by illness, waiting, unemployment, tough times, boredom, or a sense of uselessness—any of these can hit us with questions or at least allow time for them to germinate. Why? What's it all about? What should I do? Why am I here? Is there any point to it all? How can the whole thing make sense?

You would suspect that God foresaw this kind of questioning after making us with minds and imaginations. But the answer God has given is not some elegant or, more often, obscure, jargon-filled statement such as one can easily find in theologians or philosophers. It is important that those who think should make the effort to satisfy their minds through serious study and maybe even an obscure vocabulary. But God's answer to us is given in terms much more accessible to any human being: in the person and the life of Jesus Christ.

God's response does not satisfy the human desire for clean-cut laws and order by giving us a set of clear rules that if carried out would answer all our questions. Plenty of Christians over the centuries have tried to do this, and as measured in the checks sent to some preachers, apparently such efforts are much appreciated. Unlike the theological approach, this one simplifies matters: The evangelist or whoever it is somehow is able to tell you exactly what is God's will.

God's response in sending the Son in flesh and blood to live a totally human life is both more human and more demanding. Instead of theories and rigid laws, God pictures love for us in sending Jesus. Further, in that same Jesus, God pictures for us the perfect human response to that love. God's love for us and the ideal human response meet in Jesus Christ. By responding with Jesus to God's love for us, we find or, better, *live* the answers to our questions about the meaning of human life, of our world. We can meet and be energized by this Jesus, our Lord, simply by opening ourselves to him in word and sacraments.

December 25

"I heard the bells on Christmas Day their old familiar carols play, and wild and sweet the words repeat of peace on earth, good will to men." The carol that opens this way, though written over a hundred years ago, is surprisingly in tune with the mood of many as it goes on to say, "I thought how, as the day had come, the belfries of all Christendom had rolled along the unbroken song of peace on earth, good will to men. And in despair I bow'd my head; 'There is no peace on earth,' I said, 'For hate is strong, and mocks the song of peace on earth, good will to men.'" Are fighting and famine, oppression and hatred ever far off? "There is no peace on earth and hate is strong," continues the carol. The temptation to give up on the world is understandable.

The carol goes on: "Then pealed the bells more loud and deep, 'God is not dead, nor doth he sleep; the wrong shall fail, the right prevail, with peace on earth, good will to men.'" Though God may seem dead in many hearts and lives, God is very much alive. If we have the courage to take the birth of Christ seriously, it means that we have evidence that God is far from dead. God is concerned about humans, about us. God loves us, and in fact, has shared our life, its crowns and crosses. "The wrong shall fail, the right prevail"—this is the basic core of Christian belief, of faith in Jesus Christ. Somehow, sometime, very much dependent on our good will and energy as well as on God's power and love, the good will win out. The child whose birth we celebrate brought into our world the energy, the grace it needs to do better, to rebuild. Jesus the Lord endured the world's worst and rose to new life. As we celebrate his birth, we also celebrate the rebirth of hope for our world and ourselves.

December 26

About eight or nine months ago in the Easter season we picked up the refrain from Jesus, "I have risen and am still with you." In the Christmas season we likewise celebrate his presence with us; Matthew tells us a good name for him would be Emmanuel, God is with us (1:23). In a sense, all of the Church's celebrations try to accent something we so easily forget: God is truly with us in everything, everywhere, from debts to death, in jogging and joy, in sorrow and singing, from Rio de Janeiro to River Forest. It seems so obvious, yet many in all ages demand that God show some special signs.

Some years ago there was a crowd that expected the conjunction of the comet Kohoutek and Christmas to somehow signalize something special; anyone who hires Madison Square Garden or the Houston Astrodome can get a crowd in to hear an announcement of some new and splashy arrival of God or return of Jesus. One had the message "The Second Coming is near and America is the landing site."

Some continually complain about the lack of clear signs of God's presence. We perhaps should complain more about the oversupply of those ready to see it only in something shiny and tinsely. The point is that Christ is always present, already at our door. What is lacking is not signs from him but responses from us, clearer eyes, a willingness to change, to see him in unexpected and unpleasant places, persons, and events.

Christ is as close as his word in the Gospels or the Church, as close as the very ordinary-appearing bread and wine that become his body and blood. He is in everyday life, in every hand we shake, every smile we receive or give, every cheek we kiss; in the patience and pain of the suffering, in those who are elderly and alone; in the fast mind of one, another's physical ability, the way one moves a hockey puck or another bakes bread. The poet Francis Thompson tells us that the fish doesn't soar to find the ocean, the eagle plunge to find the air. Neither should we look in strange and exotic places for Christ and find excuses for not seeing him in our midst in everyday life.

December 27

Christmas is for many educated people an impossible sort of event. The feast celebrates the idea that God took on the form and life of a human being and lived among us. For people with a certain kind of education (scientific, but limited), if there is a God, that God must be all-perfect, self-sufficient, unmoved by what goes on down here, certainly not losing sleep over human suffering. In this view we are only so many grains of sand on a fairly unimportant planet spinning around the edge of one of many galaxies, our planet itself also like one grain of sand among many. Depending solely on our reason and using it to judge all, we arrive easily at the belief that God becoming a human child and living a human life is just incredible.

In a way this kind of thinking is close to the truth: that God should go to such lengths, out of love should take on human form, is, if not incredible, at least beyond all that reason could expect. It is not just reasonable; it is more than reasonable. It shows what lengths the love of God will go to. The great point about the Christmas season is that it celebrates the total involvement of God in human affairs. God didn't come here on a three-day junket, sort of slumming, like a politician visiting the war zone. But God became one of us; St. John says, "The Word (Son of God) became flesh" (1:14), lived for thirty-some years a not very easy life, and died very young.

This is one of the places where God in Jesus has revealed something that our minds cannot conceive. We see here a God who did not simply wind up the universe and then go off to play golf, but who has entered into our life, become one of us, to show us how to live this life and to heal and help us in our pains and problems.

Practically, it means we have every reason for calling on God for help, for trusting God's presence and power in the midst of the disappointments, pains, worries of daily life. Without a belief that God did and still does get involved in human life and can do something about our situation, we hardly have a belief in the God shown us in Jesus Christ. But with that belief nothing is too small for us to put before God with hope and trust.

December 28

The ad and promotional material I received in the mail pictured a leather-jacketed man in his late twenties with a head of curly hair surrounded by a sort of halo of light. The man was called Zen Master Ravi or some such. Apart from the technology-given halo, he could have been Earl Riley from Syracuse or Jim Schmitt from Wichita. But no. Inside the brochure, the mystery was heightened in accounts of his appearances at seminars: "No one knows where he comes from. . . . and—who is he? No one knows. . . ." All meant to heighten the consumer's conviction that this vendor of enlightenment is a superior being, come from who knows where. A lot of mystery—or hype—surrounding a fellow who looks like he's ready for a ride on his Honda or Harley.

The Gospels, which bring us the earliest Christians' reports on Jesus, on the contrary, tell us that he was from a couple named Mary and Joseph, born in Bethlehem, lived in Nazareth (two undistinguished little towns), was Jewish. They even offer family trees, all this to emphasize that *this* teacher, this master, had a real history, lived a truly human existence.

On the human side Jesus, like us, had certain givens from his background. We may get our big nose, athletic ability, liking for gardening, from the Swanson side of the family, our weak ankles and low blood pressure from the Kosloskis. Both in the nature we've been given and the nurture we've received from a particular family, there are burdens and blessings.

A great part of our existence, our happiness, is linked with the conditions of our existence, the framework in which we must live our lives. While our surroundings, heritage, neighborhood, and family may have faults and serious deficiencies, a great part of our happiness comes from learning to love and use the good elements we've been given and about which, often, there is little we can do. While there is room for revolt and change, even a move from where we are, we must come to terms with the reality around us and use it for good. We usually know where we come from or, at least, where we are. Let's love and use whatever there is of good given us in what may seem to be a very ordinary background.

December 29

We're sometimes overwhelmed by all the miracles surrounding the birth of Jesus. They seem so unreal to us who are used to having things accomplished in more routine fashion. We don't depend on angels, voices, visions, odd movements of the stars, but more on plodding, perspiration, and patience. We should be encouraged to know that the early Christians rejected a number of other books (that is, did not include them in the Bible) calling themselves gospels. They were loaded with miracles and make the Gospels we have look very sober and restrained by comparison. They made an effort to satisfy curiosity about matters like Jesus' behavior as a child and tried to make a more flashy Jesus, even a more flashy child Jesus. In these gospels, one of which is subtitled appropriately "a book of the miracles of the Lord," people are cured by the bath water of the baby Jesus; Jesus helps Joseph correct errors in carpentry by stretching the piece of lumber at hand. In the crib he gives his mother religious instruction even in somewhat theological language, "I am Jesus, the son of God, the Logos (Word)." Playing in the sandbox and making little clay birds, he claps his hands and the birds take off into the trees, something the other kids can't quite pull off. A neighbor's boy pushes Jesus or runs into him, and Jesus zaps him, as we might say, kills him. Jesus doesn't just amaze the elders in the Temple (as in Luke's Gospel) but instructs them about everything from physics to physiology, everything except computer science.

Thank God and goodness, the early Christians saw Jesus and knew him as a healing and hurting Savior and found these pictures of him to be just silly, inconsistent with his mercy, love. The New Testament may seem to us to be heavy on the miracles, but the marvels we see there reflect the love and care of Jesus. The tendency to think we find God or the Lord in the bizarre and the sensational is still with us today. Our concern should be to see and appreciate the miracles of love and healing still going on in and around us, not to look for miracles of merely entertainment value.

December 30

We idolize youth—one of the charges made very often against us Americans. It may mean that we try to deny reality: Grandpa with his sagging chest and potbelly runs around in a tank top, or matronly mom apes her teenage daughter's ability to wear a pair of close-fitting jeans. If that's what we mean, there may be a lot of truth to it, and it isn't so much deadly serious as maybe slightly pathetic.

But there is a sense in which we are right in idolizing youth, if that's the right term. Possibly it would be better to say—and certainly a better practice—that we value, prize, and appreciate youth. There are a number of elements in this God-given state, youth, to admire and treasure. What we can rightly value in youth (especially if they aren't our own peers or teenage sons and daughters!) is an easy joy in living, quick smiles, an ability to be wholehearted, and lacking in stratagems and plots. And what about the way in which they can be so frank, unafraid, trusting, willing to expose their hearts, exuberant (maybe a bit loud but what the heck), so carefree and hopeful? Certainly, it's related to age, health, and inexperience, but still—couldn't we try to keep some of that, based on our trust and hope in the Lord? Shouldn't Christians by their belief tend to be youthful longer, more joyous, more lighthearted than those without belief and hope? As the vitality and energy of youthful bodies fades, can't some of that be replaced by the energy of the Spirit within us, the Spirit that enables us to hope, love, trust?

I hope it can. Abbot Marmion is credited with saying that "joy is the echo of the life of God in us." That life of God in us should fill us with more reassurance than it often seems to in the face of life's little difficulties and even its real horrors. If God is with us, who in any final effective sense can be against us or overcome us? If eternal youth is one way of picturing eternal life, our faith and hope should here and now help us approach our day, our problems, our worries, a bit more like that brash, bouncy, resilient kid who lives next door or whom we see moving so jauntily down the street. "The victory that defeats the world is our faith, for who is victor over the world but he who believes that Jesus is the Son of God?" (1 John 5:4b-5).

December 31

A slightly jocular letter from the mother of four betrays ever so gently some of the hurt parents go through as their children grow: "Jim plays hockey and the team goes all over the city. Most of the kids drive which saves me time, but when I hear how they roar in and out of the driveway . . . ! Tim's report card and Marge's were not good. . . . We think Tim is president of his class. . . . Marge never tells us anything either. . . . If only they liked each other as much as they like the cat. . . . His teacher is frustrated because Jim's so bright but never hands in any work. . . . All in all, it's been a good year for us." An unmarried and very successful businessman has a shadow cast over his life because he cannot meet the right woman. Another, slightly younger and at his first job, writes:

"As you know, I'm not happy here; there is no challenge to me or my education." Another couple, happy that their son chose Dad's college, are crushed when he is expelled for a prank.

Whether we're married or single, elderly or young, some of that must sound familiar. It speaks of the frustration and difficulty inherent in any life. From a Christian perspective, it all confirms for us that the cross is always present in no matter how mild a form. Our knowledge of the cross of Christ should tell us that there is more to the story: resurrection. In baptism we were introduced into a life of constant dying and rising with Christ. In the ideal form of baptism one walks down into a pool, is submerged momentarily in it, and rises on the other side. A picture of what human life is like: dying and rising.

Leaving aside the more dramatic ways in which we share in the dying, there are hundreds of smaller ways in which we go through frustrations, suffering, little deaths, daily. Following Jesus and sharing his risen life, we should be able to glimpse, at least occasionally, where all this is leading. We should be able to sympathize with the crosses, sufferings, pains, disappointments of those around us. If we die with him we shall rise with him (Rom 6:8). With the writer of that first letter quoted above we may be able to say also: All in all it's been a good day, a good year.